A PLACE TO
LIVE IN PEACE

A PLACE TO LIVE IN PEACE

*Free People of Color in
West Feliciana Parish, Louisiana*

Evelyn L. Wilson

University Press of Mississippi / Jackson

The University Press of Mississippi is the scholarly publishing agency of
the Mississippi Institutions of Higher Learning: Alcorn State University,
Delta State University, Jackson State University, Mississippi State University,
Mississippi University for Women, Mississippi Valley State University,
University of Mississippi, and University of Southern Mississippi.

www.upress.state.ms.us

Any discriminatory or derogatory language or hate speech regarding race,
ethnicity, religion, sex, gender, class, national origin, age, or disability that has
been retained or appears in elided form is in no way an endorsement of the use
of such language outside a scholarly context.

The University Press of Mississippi is a member
of the Association of University Presses.

Copyright © 2024 by University Press of Mississippi
All rights reserved
Manufactured in the United States of America
∞

Library of Congress Cataloging-in-Publication Data

Names: Wilson, Evelyn L., author.
Title: A place to live in peace : free people of color in West Feliciana
Parish, Louisiana / Evelyn L. Wilson.
Other titles: Free people of color in West Feliciana Parish, Louisiana
Description: Jackson : University Press of Mississippi, [2024] | Includes
bibliographical references and index.
Identifiers: LCCN 2024002730 (print) | LCCN 2024002731 (ebook) | ISBN
9781496852168 (hardback) | ISBN 9781496852175 (trade paperback) | ISBN
9781496852182 (epub) | ISBN 9781496852199 (epub) | ISBN 9781496852205
(pdf) | ISBN 9781496852212 (pdf)
Subjects: LCSH: Free Black people—Louisiana—West Feliciana
Parish—History—19th century. | African Americans—Louisiana—West
Feliciana Parish—Social life and customs—19th century. | African
Americans—Race identity—Louisiana—West Feliciana Parish. | Plantation
life—Louisiana—West Feliciana Parish—History—19th century. | West
Feliciana Parish (La.)—History. | Louisiana—Race
relations—History—19th century. | BISAC: HISTORY / African American &
Black | SOCIAL SCIENCE / Race & Ethnic Relations
Classification: LCC F377.W5 W557 2024 (print) | LCC F377.W5 (ebook) | DDC
946.3/0500496073—dc23/eng/20240216
LC record available at https://lccn.loc.gov/2024002730
LC ebook record available at https://lccn.loc.gov/2024002731

British Library Cataloging-in-Publication Data available

CONTENTS

vii   Acknowledgments

3   Introduction

11   Chapter 1. West Feliciana Parish, Louisiana

29   Chapter 2. Free People of Color in West Feliciana Parish

51   Chapter 3. Land Sales, Loans, and Litigation

69   Chapter 4. Earning a Living

107   Chapter 5. Black-White Personal Relationships

127   Chapter 6. And Then the War Came

143   Epilogue

147   Notes

185   Bibliography

193   Index

ACKNOWLEDGMENTS

In 1946, Charles Hatfield Jr., a graduating senior at Xavier University in New Orleans, requested an application from the Louisiana State University and Agricultural and Mechanical School, Louisiana's premiere public university, to apply to its law school. The dean of the law school wrote to Hatfield: "Louisiana State University does not admit colored students."[1] Hatfield filed a lawsuit against the university demanding that he be admitted. When Hatfield was asked what motivated and sustained him in his quest to desegregate the law school, he spoke about his family. Hatfield's family had lived and worked in West Feliciana Parish, Louisiana, since the early 1800s. Hatfield believed that his family's long-term residence in the state and their contributions to it had earned for him the right to attend the state's only public law school.[2]

The rural community where Hatfield's grandparents were raised was heavily invested in slavery for its cotton and sugar production. In 1840, the population of enslaved people was five times the population of free people there. Census records, conveyance records, succession records, and litigation records document that free people of color were an integral part of this community. I thank Hatfield for making me aware of this rural population of free people of color.

Many people contributed to the completion of this work. Helen Williams, then museum director of West Feliciana Historical Society, encouraged me and assisted while I accessed Elisabeth K. Dart's research on people of color in pre–Civil War West Feliciana Parish. Felicia Ann Hendl, then clerk of court of West Feliciana Parish, allowed me complete access to the well-kept records in her office, and her staff aided me in using those records. Staff members at various other archives and libraries gave me access to the materials available in their respective collections and assisted me in using them. I thank them all.

I also thank all those who read and listened to my research for their comments and suggestions, especially Gaines M. Foster, and I thank Emily Bandy, acquisitions editor at the University Press of Mississippi, and her editorial board for finding my work worthy of publication. More than anyone else, I thank my family and friends, who allowed me the space to work on this book and who insisted that I finish it.

A PLACE TO LIVE IN PEACE

INTRODUCTION

Courses on American history tend to suggest that, prior to the Civil War, all the people in the United States with any discernable African descent were illiterate, unskilled, and enslaved. While some Americans are aware that free people of color were present in the northern states or in coastal cities, north and south, few know that free people of color also lived and thrived in small, rural, southern communities.

Initially, the Africans brought to the North American colonies against their will served as indentured servants alongside Europeans who had agreed to serve in exchange for passage to the colonies. Once their period of indenture was completed, usually after four to seven years, African and European indentured servants were free to seek other employment or to otherwise seek their fortunes. Free people of color populated the continent, as did others who came or were brought to the colonies. Free people of color lived throughout the United States.

The area that now comprises the state of Louisiana enjoyed a rich history of government by France and Spain. That history has influenced and continues to influence its laws and its culture. The state is divided into political subdivisions comparable to counties in other states of the United States. Beginning in 1790, West Feliciana Parish housed an important port on the Mississippi River as cotton and sugar cane production in the parish increased. That cane and cotton production was highly dependent upon slavery. Persons who appeared to be of African descent were presumed to be perpetually enslaved and bore the burden to prove otherwise. In 1810, the Superior Court of the Territory of Orleans, in *Adelle v. Beauregard*, called this premise "the presumption arising from colour."[1] To distinguish those persons of African descent who were enslaved from those who were not, and when promulgating rules that applied to people of color and not to people raced white, colonial governments adopted the practice of indicating the free status of persons of discernable African descent in their governmental records. Whether a colony of France or of Spain, or a territory or state of the United States, the public records and in the laws governing the area comprising West Feliciana Parish used the term "free people of color" and the gender-indicating terms "free man of color" and "free woman of color" to identify people so designated.

For the French, free people of African descent were called *gens de couleur libres*. The Spanish called the population *gente de color*. An 1830 statute in Louisiana referred to "free negroes, mulattoes, or other free persons of colour" as one category, to "white" people as another category, and to "slaves" as the third category of people when describing the populace of the state.[2] The category of free people of color included more than only people of African descent. The court, in *Adelle v. Beauregard*, recognized: "Persons of colour may have descended from Indians on both sides."[3]

Military and sales records often contained more detailed information about skin color, as did the required registrations of free people of color after 1830. The 1850 and 1860 census records asked if a person was "white," "black," or "mulatto," but most public records and public laws of the time distinguished people of color from white people and free people from people held in slavery without further delineations.

In telling the stories of West Feliciana's free people of color, I follow the public records in determining who is a person of color and who is not. I use terms such as "mulatto," "Negro," or "colored" as they were used in the sources. When a person's public records did not indicate that the person had the status of a free person of color or the status of an enslaved person, I presume the person was categorized as white.

Historians have endeavored to educate readers of American history about the prewar presence of free people of color in the country. In 1943, John Hope Franklin analyzed the economic and social conditions of free people of color in North Carolina. Franklin considered North Carolina a lenient slave state because it was slower than other southern states in deciding to restrict the freedom of free people of color and did not vigorously enforce the laws it did have. Free people of color served in the state militia until 1812 and could vote in North Carolina until 1835. Franklin attributed this treatment to the state's rural character. Franklin rooted the urban opposition to free people of color in the competition for employment opportunities: "Free Negro mechanics were especially irritating to the white artisans . . . white mechanics began a concerted action to prevent the use of free Negroes. Printed petitions were circulated, signed, and sent by citizens . . . to the Legislature."[4] African descent became an important basis for discrimination in North Carolina only when it threatened the economic advantage those raced white could enjoy.

Franklin noted that North Carolina enacted increasingly stringent restrictions on its free people of color as the nation marched toward a war over slavery, as did other southern states. After 1838, masters were no longer obligated to teach their free-people-of-color apprentices to read and write, although white apprentices continued to be entitled to that education. Franklin characterized this as "a clear effort on the part of legislators to prevent free Negroes from rising out of the low intellectual attainments which characterized the group."[5] Many states, including North Carolina and Louisiana, enacted statutes that criminalized teaching enslaved people to read or write. Once free, a previously enslaved person would have to overcome this enforced illiteracy.

In 1974, Ira Berlin completed a study of free people of color living in the southern region of the United States. In *Slaves without Masters*, Berlin considered data from the colonial period through the Civil War. Berlin wrote that, in Lower South states, such as Louisiana, where free people of color were numerous, white people allowed the three-caste system of the West Indies to develop. He found that free people of color in these communities held an elevated status compared to enslaved people. White people were not threatened by this population because many free people of color shared similar cultural values and attitudes toward slavery.[6] Free people of color were not oppressed or denigrated because they distanced themselves from people who were enslaved. Many of them were slaveholders themselves. Loren Schweninger, writing in 1989, described prosperous free people of color living in small, tightly knit communities, in the same neighborhoods or on nearby plantations, whose children intermarried. This group kept to themselves, separated from other people of color and from white people.[7] Both Berlin and Schweninger found wealthy free people of color who benefitted from the elevated status afforded them in a three-caste system. Less wealthy free people of color were not included in their studies, and their status in their communities was not considered.

In contrast, in his 1981 book, *The Free Black in Urban America, 1800–1850*, Leonard P. Curry found universal approbation of free people of color and impediments to equality with white people in both northern and southern cities. In the fifteen cities across the United States that he studied, Curry found free people of color were prohibited from entering the jurisdiction, prohibited from certain occupations, required to register, and were given different punishments for the same crimes. Curry's review of the legislation in effect in those cities failed to consider the extent to which those rules were enforced. As Franklin pointed out in his study of North Carolina, enacted laws are often ignored in day-to-day interactions.

Curry explained that he stopped his study in 1850 because the last ten years before the war were different from earlier years. Support for the antislavery movement in the North led to greater repression of free people of color in the South. In the North, the widespread construction of multifamily homes increased residential density and eliminated the intermixture of housing for white people and free people of color.[8] The end of the war against Mexico and the addition of the large land mass to the south and west of the already-settled states renewed the question of the expansion of slavery and threatened the political balance of free and slave states. The antislavery movement threatened the institution from outside, and southerners saw free people of color as internal threats.

Recently, Warren Eugene Milteer Jr. examined the place of free people of color in the southern states. He contended that free people of color were woven into the colonial world's social fabric and, for more than a century, lived as neighbors, worked together, prayed together, and fought together with people raced white. The earliest Africans brought to the colonies, who worked alongside Europeans and Native Americans as indentured servants, often chose to intermarry with their coworkers after their periods of indenture were complete. The children of these relationships formed a category of people distinct from those considered white and distinct from those of solely African ancestry.[9] Africans released from their indentures, their descendants, and the descendants of Europeans and Africans, were initially accepted into their communities without stigma.

Milteer argued that people he labeled "proslavery radicals and white supremacists" worked to circumscribe the freedoms of free people of color and that free people of color worked with white allies to fight against those restraints.[10] Eventually, proslavery radicals gained the upper hand, and states began to reshape the social landscape. The advocates of white supremacy created spaces inaccessible to people of color and privileged white people through segregation, although some communities were slow to accept these new laws. Milteer warned that ascribing to a simplified analysis of southern life prevents a full appreciation of the diversity experienced by southerners before 1865.[11] No one description or depiction can capture that diversity. Free people of color lived lives as varied from one another as from any nonfree person of color. Any generalizations are both inaccurate and incomplete.

Stories based in New Orleans of "quadroon balls" and *plaçage* have drawn attention to Louisiana and its population of free people of color.[12] Free people of color were present in New Orleans since early in its settlement. Alice Dunbar-Nelson, in her 1916 and 1917 *Journal of Negro History* articles, reported the presence of free people of color in the early 1700s. The 1724 Code Noir provided a legal channel for the emancipation of people held in slavery. Enslaved people could purchase their freedom using money they earned in the marketplace or could earn their freedom in exchange for their military service.[13] Slaveholders were permitted to grant freedom when they wished. The Spanish, like the French, offered freedom in exchange for military service and allowed similar channels for emancipation. According to Dunbar-Nelson, black officers commanded Spanish troops in 1735.[14]

Dunbar-Nelson attributed a large portion of New Orleans's population of free people of color to miscegenation. Few white women were present in the colony. Spanish and French troops and other settlers freely intermingled with enslaved Africans and Native Americans, marrying them when that was permitted and living with them in committed relationships when it was not. A similar shortage of white women would have existed at military outposts outside of New Orleans. Free people of color were found in larger numbers in St. Landry and Natchitoches Parishes where the Spanish or French military were present.[15] After 1812, noted Dunbar-Nelson, a steady stream of free people of color who had been living in other states moved into Louisiana as a haven.[16] Because a large number of free people of color were already there, free people of color may have believed they would be treated with more kindness in Louisiana than elsewhere.

In 1820, Louisiana's population included 10,476 free people of color; in 1830, it included 16,710. Most of them lived in New Orleans or surrounding parishes or near the former French and Spanish military outposts. In 1830, only ninety-four of those free people of color lived in West Feliciana Parish. This study of this small population of free people of color in this rural community of sugar cane and cotton plantations examines how they came to be in the parish, where they lived, how they earned a living, and how they related to people raced white in the parish. It looks at how the Civil War impacted their lives and their relationships. The parish, which belonged to Spain until 1810, maintained its attitude toward free people of color after Spanish occupation ended. Free people of color lived and worked in the parish without the stigma that would characterize the lives of people of color in the twentieth century. Discrimination on the basis of perceived African descent, the "presumption arising from colour" recognized by the court in *Adelle v. Beauregard*, developed as the population grew with migrants from other states. Politicians in Louisiana, influenced by these migrants, began to perceive free people of color as a threat to the institution of slavery and, therefore, undesirable.

Scholars have studied the legacy of Spanish rule in the Americas. Historian Frank Tannenbaum, in his *Slave & Citizen: The Negro in the Americas*, contrasted the laws and customs pertaining to slavery under Spanish and Portuguese rule with the laws and customs typical under English and American rule. Influenced by the Catholic Church's tenet that all men were equal in the sight of God, the Spanish and Portuguese policymakers saw slavery as a temporary status, the result of misfortune, and they often facilitated manumission. Enslaved people were easily freed, and freed people could quickly become respected members of their communities. Conversely, under English and American rule, a person of color was identified with slavery and a free person of color was an anomaly. Justifying slavery by characterizing the enslaved as unworthy of freedom was incompatible with permitting an enslaved person to be free. The English and American demeaning of enslaved people engendered animosity toward any person of color not enslaved. American and English rulers limited the opportunities for manumission and sought to excise free people of color from their jurisdictions.[17] A competition between the French/Spanish viewpoint and the English/American point of view as described by Tannenbaum would play out in Louisiana and in West Feliciana Parish, and the treatment of free people of color would be more severe as the English/American viewpoint became dominant in the parish.

Historian H. E. Sterkx agreed with Tannenbaum. He believed that Louisiana's history as a former possession of France and Spain influenced its treatment of free people of color.[18] According to Sterkx, French and Spanish settlers and free people of color intermingled freely. Consequentially, free people of color in Louisiana, under French and Spanish rule and initially under American rule, were allowed a "quasi-citizenship" status. They could not vote, but they could petition the government for redress and could testify in court cases, even against the interests of those who were raced white. They could serve in the military and could travel freely. When legislators introduced state laws to expel free people of color from the state or to limit their right to testify in court, these laws failed to pass. Many legislators believed that the people of color who had been freed in Louisiana had been manumitted because they were faithful to the state's interests. They considered these faithful servants and their descendants to be peaceful, industrious, educated, and honest, and believed they were entitled to their "quasi-citizenship" status.[19] Louisiana's French and Spanish heritage served as a beacon to free people of color looking for a place to settle in peace. However, as more Americans moved into Louisiana, the influence of French and Spanish customs waned, and the Louisiana Legislature increasingly imposed restrictions on the freedom of free people of color.

In studies of Orleans, St. Landry, and Natchitoches Parishes, where Spanish authorities had located their military and trading posts, Ira Berlin's three-caste analysis held true. Gary B. Mills, in *The Forgotten People: Cane River's Creoles of Color*, wrote about the Metoyer family of the Cane River neighborhood of

Natchitoches Parish whose freedom had begun under the government of Spain. Mills reported that Spanish and French attitudes toward free people of color allowed this family to occupy an intermediate position between white people and enslaved people. The Metoyer family, large landowners who had enjoyed their freedom for a long period of time, were regarded by their neighbors with respect.[20] They were slaveholders themselves and, due to their wealth, enjoyed an elevated status in their community.

In *Creoles of Color in the Bayou Country*, Carl A. Brasseaux, Keith P. Fontenot, and Claude F. Oubre described the land holdings and marriage relationships of wealthy free people of color in St. Landry Parish. Free people of color there called themselves by the French term, *gens de couleur libre*, and distanced themselves from the slave population with the objective of melding into the white population. These *gens de couleur libre* were very protective of their social position and cultural heritage and, except for a period immediately following the Civil War, continued to distance themselves from freed people up until the 1950s.[21] Likewise, James H. Dorman, in *Creoles of Color of the Gulf South*, commented on the persistent determination of New Orleans Creoles, the product of white and black ancestry, to self-isolate and intermarry.[22] In these three areas, Berlin's three-caste system properly categorized at least some of the free people of color living there. Mills, Brasseaux, Fontenot, Oubre, and Dorman did not discuss the free people of color in their parishes who were not wealthy landowners. The three-caste system was not a social reality for all the free people of color in those parishes and was not a social reality in other parts of the state.

The three-caste system was not a social reality in West Feliciana Parish. This study of West Feliciana Parish reveals a community heavily invested in slavery where free people of color lived harmoniously with white people. The free people of color who inhabited West Feliciana Parish were a very mixed group of people. Some had entered the parish already free, others had purchased their freedom, while others had been freed by slaveholders for differing reasons. Some were the product of white and black fore parents, but others were not. This was not a settled population of people with a common background or a long history of freedom. They did not self-isolate or form a distinct social group or a third caste in a structured caste system. They were, instead, distinct individuals who happened to live in this sparsely inhabited, cotton-producing parish at around the same time.

They were not segregated because of their African or other heritage in home ownership, business relationships, or friendships but were integrated into the larger community and, at times, interacted with people enslaved in the community. They bought and sold homes in whatever part of the parish suited them and were often surrounded by white neighbors. They bought and sold goods and services from and to free white people, loaned and borrowed money from and to free white people, and sued and were sued by free white people. They found themselves in a community that valued their talents and skills, and they contributed to their community, providing needed services and owning successful businesses. Their varied life experiences reflected their individual interests, abilities, opportunities, challenges, and responses to those challenges. As Emily Clark wrote: "Free black lives unfolded in patterns that confound simple generalizations."[23] The lives of free people of color in West Feliciana Parish did not fit any particular configuration but reflected the freedom they enjoyed as a part of this community.

In his 1899 study of people of color in Philadelphia, *The Philadelphia Negro: A Social Study*, W. E. B. Du Bois described how discrimination because of perceived African heritage severely limited the social and economic choices of the people of color living there. Every obstacle was put in their path to discourage their presence and to frustrate their advancement. Half of the black skilled tradespeople in the city were forced to abandon their trades because they could not find employment. Segregation forced people of color to pay abnormally high rents for the poorest accommodations. Du Bois lamented the "unrelenting prejudice" on the part of white people that led to the social and economic exclusion of people of color from white society. He beseeched white people to, at a minimum, extend "little decencies of daily intercourse" to people of color.[24] Du Bois painted a dismal picture of the life many people of color experienced in 1899 Philadelphia.

Life in 1829 West Feliciana Parish was not like life in 1899 Philadelphia. The "unrelenting prejudice" Du Bois found in 1899 Philadelphia had not yet settled on 1829 West Feliciana Parish. Free people of color in the parish were an integral part of their community, and white people extended to them those "little decencies of daily intercourse" absent in Du Bois's Philadelphia. The acceptance of free people of color in this parish reflect its French/Spanish heritage, its position as an important river port, and its frontier nature. The lives and experiences of the free people of color in West Feliciana Parish demonstrate that segregation by perceived African heritage was not always a characteristic of southern life.

CHAPTER 1

West Feliciana Parish, Louisiana

West Feliciana Parish sits in a curve of the Mississippi River that puts the river on its western and southern boundaries. The state of Mississippi lies directly to its north. East Feliciana Parish is to its east. The Houma were the first known settlers of this heavily forested area, but the Tunica, who had traded with Europeans since the 1600s, drove them out. Around 1729, the French claimed the land and built a small fort in the area that they named Ste. Reyne aux Tonicas. They soon abandoned the fort. In 1762, in the Treaty of Fontainebleau that followed the French and Indian War, Spain lost all the land it had claimed east of the Mississippi River to Great Britain. To compensate Spain, an ally of France in the war, France gave all the territory it claimed on the west side of the Mississippi River to Spain. The Mississippi River became a boundary between British ownership to the east and Spanish ownership to the west. Despite British occupancy, Spanish Capuchin monks crossed the river to bury their dead on the high eastern ridge in what would become West Feliciana Parish. During the Revolutionary War, Spain retook control of the area east of the Mississippi River, and after the Treaty of Paris, the governor of Spanish Louisiana continued to welcome British settlers into the region with Spanish land grants.

Two towns developed in the parish. Around 1785, the Capuchin monks built a monastery next to their cemetery and named the resulting nearby settlement after their patron saint, St. Francis. St. Francisville housed Spain's governmental offices: the courthouse, the prison, the post office, and the printing office. The town had a theater, homes, and businesses, and some of its earliest residents were free people of color.[1] In 1790, Virginian John Mills moved down river from Natchez, where he had been living, and partnered with Christopher Strong Steward to establish a trading post and cotton port below the bluffs near the mouth of Bayou Sara Creek.[2] This natural port became invaluable for the large cotton, indigo, and sugar cane plantations that came to dominate the parish from the 1790s until well after the Civil War. Mills and Steward, two white men, named the river town after the creek that met the river at that port, Bayou Sara. At various times, Bayou Sara has been called New Valencia, Town under the Hill, or Bayou Sarah, with an *h*. In 1793, only 237 people lived in fifty-seven residences in Spanish Feliciana.[3]

The rich black soil in the parish, crisscrossed by numerous streams, proved to be very productive. Author Lee Malone described West Feliciana Parish as the "most verdantly beautiful parish in Louisiana." He explained that the soil had been "enriched for centuries by fine-grained, fertile loam deposited by transcontinental winds from glacial deposits" and noted the vast, productive plantations established along the banks of waterways.[4] The land supported the agricultural pursuits of its inhabitants.

In 1800, Spain transferred the land west of the Mississippi River to France. West Feliciana Parish, located on the east side of the river, was not transferred to France in 1800 or to the United States in the 1803 Louisiana Purchase. It continued to belong to Spain until 1810 when residents of the parish seized the Spanish barracks in Baton Rouge and declared themselves independent of Spain. They called their country the Republic of West Florida and named St. Francisville its capital. After a short period of independence and many petitions to the US government, the United States took possession of the Republic of West Florida on October 27, 1810.[5] The area became a part of the Mississippi Territory. In 1812, Louisiana became a state and included Feliciana Parish within its borders. John Mills, one of the founders of Bayou Sara, died that same year.

When the American authorities arrived in the Mississippi Territory, they found substantial numbers of free people of color living there. Free people of color were not unknown to American authorities. In the early 1800s, free people of color lived in every state and territory of the Union.[6] The fervor of the colonies' revolt against the purported tyranny of Great Britain led many individuals to release people they had held in slavery. Because cries of "Liberty and Freedom!" seemed hypocritical alongside the practice of keeping people in perpetual bondage, the fight for freedom from Great Britain triggered a desire, among some slaveholders, to free people held enslaved in the newly created nation. In the northern parts of the United States, hundreds of individual slaveholders acted on their own to free thousands of enslaved people, and states adopted immediate or gradual emancipation statutes. Historian Ira Berlin called this emancipation fervor "egalitarian enthusiasm" and credited it with generating large numbers of free blacks, especially in the mid-Atlantic states.[7]

In 1790, the US census counted 59,557 free people of color, 1.5 percent of the US population, most of whom lived in Virginia (12,866), Maryland (8,043), Pennsylvania (6,531), or North Carolina (5,041). By 1830, the number of free people of color had reached 319,529, and their percentage of the population was at 2.5 percent.[8] Wherever they settled, they raised the question of how they fit into the American republic. Different jurisdictions answered that question in different ways, with a variety of laws and customs, most of which changed over time. The rules that governed the rights and opportunities open to free people of color reflected what policymakers believed ought to be their proper place in society, and these beliefs changed with the shifting priorities of decisionmakers.

Louisiana, however, could not attribute its large population of free people of color to America's revolutionary ideas. It was not a part of the country until decades after the Revolution. Instead, Louisiana's French and Spanish occupiers provided the early population of Louisiana's free people of color. The ease of manumission under French and Spanish rule resulted in the presence of free people of color who were welcomed into that frontier community. The French and Spanish military forces located on the American continent more readily fathered children with the Indian and African women found there than did the British. These fathers often freed their children and sometimes freed the mothers of their children. In addition, in 1809, refugees from Saint-Domingue who had fled to Cuba after the Haitian Revolution and were now forced to leave Cuba on short notice added significant numbers of free people of color to Louisiana's count. More than 3,102 free people of color took refuge in New Orleans.[9] Few of these came to Spanish-held West Feliciana Parish, but they did add to the state's count of free people of color. Nearby states had far fewer residents who were free people of color. In 1820, Louisiana had 10,476 free people of color living in the state, while Alabama had only 571, Mississippi had 458, and Arkansas had fifty-nine.[10]

In Louisiana, large-scale emancipation was uncommon. Emancipation was an act of paternalism, a kindness rendered to a particular individual, or an option available to someone personally known to the slaveholder. A slaveholder might free a few faithful servants or might permit selected individuals to generate and accumulate sufficient funds to purchase their freedom. An enslaved person might be allowed to keep some of the money earned from working for someone other than their enslaver or by selling crops or animals they raised. The opportunity to earn money was not available to everyone. Emancipation in Louisiana was a personal act, the result of a relationship between individuals, not a political act. The emancipation of individuals by individual Louisiana slaveholders was not a renouncement of slavery.

Quite the opposite was true. Slaveholders asserted their right to hold slaves as an inalienable property right, which predated and, therefore, overrode any newly declared personal right to self-government. They were convinced that free or quasi-free laborers were dangerous. Slaveholders believed that the rising expectations of free laborers often led them to rebel when they were faced with the limited opportunities available for their advancement. Persons under complete control had no choice but to accept the limits on their prospects and, through coercion, could be made to be more productive. Increased productivity meant greater profits. Aspiring to achieve a lifestyle akin to that of the British elite, Louisiana slaveholders grasped more tightly to their human bondsmen. Historian V. Elaine Thompson explained that the ownership of enslaved people allowed residents to both accumulate wealth and demonstrate their wealth. Enslaved laborers served as symbols of the status of their enslavers.[11] Alexis de Tocqueville wrote: "In the South, labor itself is stigmatized as degrading."[12] In West Feliciana Parish, those with the means avoided that stigma by purchasing others to labor for them. Wealth and community standing grew out of the use of unpaid laborers and took priority over republicanism and its celebration of liberty.

As arguments opposing slavery resonated more forcefully across the nation, slaveholders' efforts to enshrine their property rights and to justify a continuation of slavery accelerated. Protecting slavery became the paramount agenda in Louisiana. In 1824, the general assembly of the state of Ohio proposed a plan to end slavery in the United States. It resolved "that the consideration of a system providing for the gradual emancipation of the people of colour, held in servitude in the United States, be recommended to the legislatures of the several states of the American Union and to the Congress of the United States."[13] The plan called for freeing each bound child born after the adoption of the plan once the child reached age twenty-one but only if the person accepting freedom agreed to be transported to a place of colonization. In 1826, when the Louisiana Legislature next met, it responded to that resolution by vehemently opposing the idea.[14] The protection of slavery was important for the state's economy. Its legislators could not approve of even the gradual emancipation of its laborers. Individual emancipation did not threaten the institution. Individuals could be emancipated so long as other individuals remained enslaved.

As a frontier agricultural region in a slave state, West Feliciana Parish had a full complement of enslaved people. In 1820, the US census counted 12,733 people in Feliciana Parish, 7,164 of whom were held in slavery. In 1824, the parish was divided along Thompson's Creek, creating East Feliciana and West

Feliciana Parishes. The 1830 population of West Feliciana Parish included 6,245 people in slavery, 2,290 free white people, and ninety-four free people of color. By 1835, most of the best land in the parish had been claimed.[15] Enslaved workers, using whatever rudimentary tools were available to them, had done most of the labor-intensive work required to develop this virgin land into a wealthy agricultural community. They cut the trees and prepared the land for crops. They cultivated and harvested the indigo. They planted and picked the cotton. They laid and cut the sugar cane. They built the roads and bridges and constructed the homes and other buildings to house the parish's growing population.

By 1840, the count of enslaved people reached 10,910. Enslaved workers gathered more than 16 million pounds of cotton, almost one-tenth of the entire cotton production for the state. Only St. Landry, Rapides, and Concordia Parishes produced more cotton that year.[16] Most of the agricultural, skilled, domestic, and unskilled labor for the region was provided by people held in slavery. The enslaved population increased in size by 75 percent in the ten years between 1830 and 1840, while the population of free people decreased slightly. In 1840, only 2,065 free white people and ninety-one free people of color lived and worked in the parish.[17]

In 1850, 10,666 of the 13,245 residents in West Feliciana Parish were enslaved, and 84 percent of households in the parish included at least one slave.[18] Only in three parishes—Orleans, Rapides, and St. Landry—were more people held in slavery than in West Feliciana Parish. Historian Wattine Frazier identified thirty-eight planters in 1850 West Feliciana Parish who enslaved more than one hundred people; five of those enslaved between two hundred and five hundred people, and two enslaved more than five hundred people. In addition, 106 free people of color lived and worked in the parish.[19] According to the tax rolls of 1853, 10,298 enslaved people, 2,231 free white people, and seventy free people of color produced 2,873 hogsheads of sugar, 4,318 barrels of molasses, 334,000 bushels of corn, and 23,860 bales of cotton. The total population of the parish had begun to fall. The 1860 census report showed only 9,571 enslaved people, 2,036 white people, and sixty-four free people of color—a decrease in all three population groups.[20] Yellow fever in the parish had a devastating impact during that decade.

The parish's decline in population was not duplicated statewide. Louisiana's population of enslaved people escalated from 168,452 in 1840 to 244,809 in 1850 and to 331,726 in 1860. Its population of free people, both free people of color and white people, similarly grew from 352,411 in 1840 to 517,762 in 1850 and 708,002 in 1860. Its free-people-of-color population, however, did not show the same growth pattern. In 1840, the statewide population of free people of color was 25,502. By 1850, it dropped to 17,462. In 1860, it was up only slightly to

18,647. Whereas West Feliciana Parish experienced a population decline from 1850 to 1860 in all population groups, the rest of the state did not.[21]

The distribution of free people of color was uneven throughout the country and within Louisiana. In 1850, 434,495 people, just over 2 percent of the United States' free population of 19,987,563, were free people of color. In Louisiana, where 17,462 free people of color constituted 6.4 percent of the free population, more than half of them—9,961—lived in Orleans Parish and represented 9.8 percent of the free population there. Natchitoches Parish, which included the Cane River area where the Metoyer family lived, had the highest concentration of free people of color at 881 or 13.9 percent of the free population. St. Landry Parish, in Bayou country, had 1,242 free people of color, second in number only to New Orleans and constituting a greater percentage of the free population in the parish at 10.9 percent. In 1850, West Feliciana Parish had only 106 free people of color, 4.3 percent of the free population.[22]

Across Louisiana, in 1850, five of Louisiana's forty-seven parishes had no free people of color, and eighteen had fewer than thirty. Thirteen parishes, including West Feliciana, had between forty and two hundred free people of color, and five parishes had between two hundred and five hundred free people of color. Four had between five hundred and one thousand. Only two—Orleans and St. Landry—had more than one thousand. Far fewer free people of color lived in the northern part of Louisiana than in the southern part. Far fewer people lived in the northern part of Louisiana than in the southern part. West Feliciana Parish, near its center, had more free people of color than twenty-seven parishes, fewer than sixteen parishes, and about the same as three other parishes. East Feliciana Parish, to the east of West Feliciana Parish, had only twenty-four free people of color in 1850 despite having a population of 13,598, just slightly more than that of West Feliciana Parish at 13,345.[23] West Feliciana Parish's total population was larger than that of forty parishes, smaller than only five parishes, and about equal to the populations of two other parishes. Although now it is considered a small rural parish, West Feliciana Parish was a major cotton- and cane-producing region with an important port on the Mississippi River. Its large population consisted primarily of people held in slavery. Nevertheless, a small population of free people of color flourished there.

Immigrants and Americans coming into the state were faced with a fait accompli. Free people of color were already present in large numbers in Louisiana before 1812. The new arrivals struggled both to adjust to and to change the relationships that had developed between white people and free people of color. Their plans for protecting slavery shaped their treatment of free people of color, and white supremacy became their primary tool. American colonists had enslaved American Indians and used the differences in their language and culture to discriminate against the Indians and to form an identity as Americans. Similarly, Americans emphasized the physical and cultural differences between black and white Americans to facilitate white solidarity. Historian Edmund S. Morgan explained that Virginians, shaken by Bacon's Rebellion during which poor people found common cause irrespective of ancestral heritage, used racism to separate black people from white people to reduce the likelihood of a subsequent insurrection. Virginians encouraged their white indentured servants to identify with their masters rather than with their peers by transforming superficial physical or cultural differences into distain, thereby engendering white people's contempt for people of color as they had done for American Indians. Any discontent with upper-class leadership was channeled into animosity toward people who were not of European heritage.[24] Over time, Louisiana's legislators used an identical tactic to foster white solidarity in support of slavery. Louisiana's legislators passed laws to demean people of color and to set them apart as undesirables. West Feliciana was a part of Louisiana, and its citizens were subject to its laws.

Slavery provided a floor beneath which even the most unworthy white person would not fall, but free people of color, by their existence, defied the moral justification for slavery: innate inferiority. Slavery could not be the preordained destination for people of color if not all people of color were held in slavery. Self-sufficient free people of color rebutted arguments that people of color were chronically dependent. Successful free people of color, by virtue of their success, offered a direct affront to claims of white supremacy. Free people of color threatened white racial unity by demonstrating that white skin was often irrelevant to social or financial success.

Louisiana's legislators prohibited free people of color from settling in the state and required from them obsequiousness toward free white people. These rules belittled free people of color and promised white people a social position higher than that of any person of color. Defining people of color as immutably inferior to all white people protected the self-esteem of lower-class white people unable to move into the social circles of more wealthy Americans. It permitted poorer white people to believe that their interests were aligned with those of wealthier white people. Aware that degraded conditions produced degraded people, legislators put obstacles in the path of free people of color with the intent that what was said about them would eventually become true.[25] Free people of color became targets for the legislators because they undermined arguments in support of white supremacy.

In addition, for some legislators, free people of color raised fears of insurrection. Some white slaveholders feared that free people of color would undermine their control over their enslaved population. They told de Tocqueville that free people of color would agitate the minds of enslaved people.[26] Their independence would inspire enslaved people to rebel against their enslavers. Even worse, free people of color might act as abolition agents, intentionally operating to destroy slavery by law, or they might assist enslaved people to organize rebellions.[27] Ignoring the fact that many free people of color were slaveholders themselves, legislators limited the permissible interactions between free people of color and enslaved people to protect their enslaved population from these envisioned unnerving influences.

Legislative action to protect slavery and support white racial identity in Louisiana began early. In October 1804, the governor and judges of the Indiana Territory, the political body authorized to make laws for the District of Louisiana, required all free people of color to carry a copy of their emancipation papers with them and empowered any justice of the peace to imprison any emancipated person caught traveling without these papers.[28] Legislators wanted anyone who had escaped from slavery to be returned to their place of servitude. Beginning with the premise that most people of color were enslaved, emancipation papers allowed officials to distinguish people of color whose freedom could be documented from those whose freedom could not. Free people of color lived under the constant threat of being mistaken for a person subject to perpetual and hereditary slavery. Any white person could stop any person of color and demand to see proof of either their free status or their permission from their enslaver to be away from their enslaver's land.

Additional 1804 statutes made other distinctions between the rights and obligations of white people and people of color. White residents could own as many guns as they liked, but lawmakers restricted gun ownership for free people of color. A homeowner of color could keep only one gun, although someone living at a frontier plantation could request a license from a justice of the peace to keep additional offensive and defensive guns and other weapons. The governing authorities did not want a stockpile of weapons in the hands of free people of color where they could be made available to assist enslaved people in a revolt. To further discourage rebellion, legislators imposed a penalty of up to thirty lashes "if any negro or mulatto, bond or free, shall lift his hand in opposition to any person not being a negro or mulatto" unless in defense. The legislature imposed a penalty of death without the benefit of clergy for plotting to rebel.[29] No penalty was prescribed should a person raced white lift his hand in opposition to a person of color or if a person of color struck another person of color. This legislation provided no recourse to law for people of color who might become the victims of violence. It was designed to give people raced white an advantage. They could physically attack a person of color, and that person of color would earn thirty lashes if he or she acted in his or her own defense.

In May 1806, the first session of the first legislature of the Territory of Orleans sought to establish the subordination of free people of color already within the territory. It declared: "Free people of color ought never to insult or strike white people, nor presume to conceive themselves equal to the white; but on the contrary that they ought to yield to them in every occasion, and never speak or answer to them but with respect, under penalty of imprisonment according to the nature of the offense."[30] This law required free people of color to speak to white people only with respect; white people did not have to show the same level of respect to free people of color. No matter their economic or educational status or their physical or intellectual abilities, white people could, by law, be assured that people with a darker skin color would show them respect even when people with a lighter skin color did not. Reverend H. Cowles Atwater, visiting from Massachusetts, observed that poor white people in the South felt the scorn of the upper-class white people. Their only consolation was to have a class below them.[31] In 1928, historian Ulrich B. Phillips agreed that slavery was defended as a guarantor of white supremacy and civilization.[32] This law required free people of color to act as if they were inferior when they were not. It supported white racial unity by mitigating the scorn more wealthy whites felt for those without wealth.

In 1806, aware of the revolution in Saint-Domingue that ended slavery there, the legislature of the Territory of Orleans enacted "an Act to prevent the introduction of Free People of Color from Hispaniola, and other French Islands of America, into the territory."[33] The act exempted free women of color and young people under age fifteen; men aged fifteen and older who arrived had to leave the state within three months. The Louisiana Legislature did not want advocates of slavery's abolition to enter the state. In April 1807, the legislative council of the Territory of Orleans prohibited all free people of color from settling in the territory. It imposed a penalty of twenty dollars per week if the person stayed more than two weeks. Whoever failed to pay the fine could be sold for a term to cover the costs of the fine or could be employed on public works.[34] This statute made clear that free people of color were not welcome in the territory.

Despite its enactment, in 1809, Louisiana welcomed approximately 3,102 free people of color into New Orleans. More than nine thousand French-speaking refugees originally from Saint-Domingue were expelled from the Spanish colony of Cuba on short notice and made their way to New Orleans. These refugees had left Saint-Domingue for Cuba in 1803 after Napoleon Bonaparte's French forces failed to reestablish slavery in the colony. When Napoleon invaded Spain, these French refugees were deemed potential enemies of Spain and were expelled by the Spanish governor of Cuba. Because much of the Gulf Coast was still claimed by Spain, New Orleans, a US territory with a French-speaking population, became the logical place to which to flee. Convoys of ships arrived at New Orleans carrying these refugees. Most accounts record that 3,102 free people of color arrived from Cuba that summer with 2,731 people classified as white and 3,226 people considered enslaved. Free men of color more than fifteen years old were asked to give security warranting that they would leave the state within two weeks.

The governor of the Mississippi Territory welcomed the refugees and urged Congress to allow them and the people they claimed to hold in slavery to enter the country. In 1807, the US Congress had banned the importation of enslaved people into the United States after January 1, 1808. When they arrived in New Orleans, any people said to be enslaved were not permitted to leave the ships. William Charles Cole Claiborne, governor at the time, described the plight of the refugees in a May 17, 1809, private letter to Thomas Jefferson at Monticello, Virginia: "These unfortunate People, are for the most part destitute of pecuniary resources, and for the means of present support must depend upon the Bounty of this Society."[35] In a May 28, 1809, letter to Julian Poydras of Pointe Coupee Parish, Claiborne sympathized with the "poor people from Cuba" who could not bring people they held as slaves into the United States. For one father of a family, "two or three faithful slaves constitute[d] his only means of support."[36] A lady solicited his pity because her infant's nurse was not permitted to leave the vessel.

Historian Rebecca J. Scott argued that the people these refugees claimed to hold as slaves were not, in fact, enslaved. Slavery had been abolished in Saint-Domingue in 1793. The French National Convention had ratified that decree in 1794. These refugees did not leave Haiti to travel to Cuba until 1803. The servants they carried with them were no longer legally enslaved. Ignoring this history well known to US authorities, in June 1809, after entreaties from politicians and planters in the Mississippi Territory, Congress allowed the refugees from Cuba to retain ownership of those persons they claimed to hold in slavery without facing the penalties prescribed in the 1807 law.[37] Many of these refugees then sold the people they had claimed to own to generate the capital they needed to start over in their new home.

As to the free people of color coming into New Orleans from Cuba, on July 18, 1809, James Mather, mayor of New Orleans, reported to Claiborne: "These very men possess property, and have useful trades to live upon. . . . [T]here has not been one single complaint that I know of, against any of them concerning their conduct since their coming to this place."[38] As if he had not read the letter from Mather, on August 9, 1809, Claiborne wrote to Mather:

As regards the people of Colour, who have arrived hence from Cuba, the Women and Children have been received;—But the males above the age of fifteen, have in pursuance to a Territorial Law been ordered to depart.—I must request you Sir, to make known this circumstance, and also to discourage free people of Colour of every description from emigrating to the Territory of Orleans;—We have already a much greater proportion of the population, than comports with the general Interest.[39]

On August 7, 1809, Mather informed Claiborne:

I have caused all free men of color above 15 years, who have come within my reach to give security for their departure from this Territory, as the law directs. . . . I have further to observe . . . that many men of color . . . having been granted some delay to show proof of their freedom . . . have not returned and could not be found since.[40]

The mayor of New Orleans, reflecting local attitudes toward the free people of color, saw no problem resulting from their presence. He had experience living side by side with free people of color and was not concerned that the men over age fifteen had disappeared into the population. Claiborne, reflecting a more "American" point of view, decided that the territory already had enough free people of color in it.

The territorial council emphasized that free people of color were different from white people. In 1808, the council imposed a one-hundred-dollar fine for any notary who failed to note when a free person of color was party to a notarial act.[41] All sales had to include a notation identifying any seller or buyer who was a free person of color. All wills had to indicate when a testator or a legatee was a free person of color. All judicial proceedings added a label to the names of any free people of color who were litigants. This statute reinforced the notion that the difference between being considered "white" and being considered "of color" was significant. If he or she cared to, any buyer considering a purchase could search the property records to learn whether a free person of color had ever owned the property. The buyer could attach whatever significance to that information the buyer wanted. Few buyers in prewar West Feliciana Parish ever cared. They bought and sold property without concern for the skin color of any prior owners. This labeling stigmatized being "of color," but to the benefit of free people of color, it created another public record of their freedom. Records of their free status served to protect free people of color who might at any moment be asked to prove they were free. This stigmatization in the Louisiana public records paled in comparison to a 1793 North Carolina statute that required free people of color to wear a shoulder patch that said "FREE" to distinguish free people of color from people who were enslaved.[42] Free people of color in Louisiana did not have to wear a patch; they did, however, have to keep records of their free status.

Louisiana drew yet another line in its treatment of free people of color and white people. In 1812, when the state authorized the governor to organize a military corps of free men of color, it insisted that its commanding officer be a white man.[43] This requirement rejected merit and gave white men an opportunity unavailable to black men. Other state statutes would continue to disadvantage free people of color to the advantage of white people. For example, in 1830, legislation in Louisiana required all people who wanted a license to sell spirituous liquors to first give the parish judge a bond of five hundred dollars. Free people of color, however, had to get the consent of the parish police jury, the governing body of the parish, before giving their bond and obtaining their license.[44]

Antislavery sentiments frightened Louisiana's legislators. In 1829, abolitionist David Walker wrote a tract to promote the end of slavery. Walker's *Appeal, in Four Articles; Together with a Preamble, to the Colored Citizens of the World, but In Particular, and Very Expressly, to Those of the United States of America* was distributed throughout the country.[45] On March 8, 1830, Robert Smith, a merchant in New Orleans, was arrested for possessing and circulating a copy of the tract.[46] Finding Walker's *Appeal* in the hands of a free man of color in the state exacerbated fears that free people of color would act as abolitionist agents. A month later, Louisiana's legislators determined that they needed a stronger deterrence against free people of color coming in from outside of Louisiana. They authorized the arrest and expulsion "of any free negro, mulatto, or other free person of colour . . . [who has] come into this state [in violation of the 1807 act] since the first day of January 1, 1825."[47] A person convicted of entering after January 1, 1825, had sixty days to leave or would be imprisoned at hard labor for a year. Apparently, the free people of color who entered the state between 1807 and 1825 in violation of the 1807 act would be forgiven and allowed to remain in the state. Their investment in and contributions to the state would not be lost. Only those who entered after 1824 would be asked to leave.

To distinguish new arrivals from free people of color already in the state, the 1830 act required all free people of color in the state to enroll with a judge of the parish where they lived. Each person would declare their name, birth state, age, and occupation. The cost to enroll was fifty cents. The fine for failing to enroll was fifty dollars, and the punishment was a month in jail.[48] The law placed the burden of proving residence in the state prior to 1825 squarely on the free person of color. It provided, "the presumption shall always be, that they have actually come into the same in violation of this act."[49] By creating a census of free people of color, this act protected the institution of slavery by providing a place to check should any enslaved person claim to be free. Authorities could readily identify free people of color who entered the state after 1830 and could identify those people of color who escaped from slavery and sought to blend into the free population. The emancipation papers free people of color were required to carry could be forged. A registration in the public records of the parish was more difficult to counterfeit. Registration provided irrefutable evidence of free status; the absence of registration suggested an unfree status.

Section 7 of the 1830 statute forbade a free person of color who left the United States from returning to Louisiana, although the statute was amended the next year to exempt permanent residents who were property owners or who exercised a useful trade, so long as they did not travel to the West Indian islands. Section 8 imposed a fine of one thousand dollars, payable to the victim, if any person, white or of color, brought a "free negro" into the state as a slave.[50] The legislature was aware that free people of color were being kidnapped and sold into slavery and aware that wealthy free people of color sent their children to be educated abroad. It feared those outside influences. A kidnapped free person, who had known freedom but had not known the tyranny of the middle passage or been broken in the West Indies, was less likely to passively submit to enslavement. A person educated outside of the United States might recoil at its system of perpetual slavery based on skin color and might fight to destroy the practice. This 1830 statute hoped to protect against these dangers. Landowning permanent residents were as likely as not to be slaveholders themselves and posed no threat to slavery.

Section 9 of the 1830 statute expressly prohibited the publication of abolitionist documents with disparate consequences for white people and people of color. White people who authored, printed, or published "literature to diminish the respect free people of color have for whites" could be fined an amount between three hundred and one thousand dollars and could be jailed for six months to three years.[51] Free people of color who committed any of those acts would be fined one thousand dollars and could be jailed for three to five years. In addition, after serving their sentence, free people of color convicted of this crime would be banished from the state. The legislature wanted to prevent documents like Walker's *Appeal* from being circulated in the state.

That same year—1830—in a different statute, the legislature forbade the writing, publication, or distribution of "any thing having a tendency to produce discontent among the free coloured population of this state, or insubordination among the slaves therein." This crime was punishable by hard labor for life or by death at the discretion of the court. The statute forbade the use of language "from the bar, the bench, the stage, the pulpit, or in any place whatsoever ... in private discourses or conversations ... having a tendency to produce discontent among the free coloured population of this state, or to excite insubordination among the slaves therein, or whosoever shall knowingly be instrumental in bringing into this state, any paper, pamphlet or book, having such tendency."[52] The penalty was three to twenty-one years of hard labor or death at the discretion of the court. The legislators made no distinction in the punishment for these crimes between people of color and people raced white. Not only writing but also speech was restricted. Worried legislators wanted the free people of color in the state to act as if they were content or, at least, to hide their discontent even as these same legislators enacted laws that discriminated against and disadvantaged them. They wanted their state to be free of any discussions that might undermine slavery.

A threat to slavery could come from within the enslaved community as well as from without it. In case the prohibition on the dissemination of incendiary literature or language was ineffective, section 3 of this 1830 act made it a crime to teach enslaved persons to read or write. Any teacher would be imprisoned for one to twelve months.[53] This precautionary statute was designed to protect against enslaved persons gaining any information or encouragement that might be of assistance in planning an escape or in fomenting a rebellion. If free people of color or others successfully smuggled Walker's *Appeal* or other similar literature into the state, the enslaved population would be rendered unable to read it. Policing ideas that might lead to rebellion against slavery was important to Louisiana's legislators. It was less important in West Feliciana Parish. It is unlikely that many slaveholders in West Feliciana Parish made any effort to educate their laborers. Many of the slaveholders themselves could not read or write. Louisiana did not yet have public schools for its citizens.

In 1835, a resolution of the state legislature asked the state's attorney general to investigate the distribution of the "report of the committee to whom was referred the subject of the religious instruction of the colored population" and the "Annual Report of the Missionary to the Negroes" to determine if those reports provoked discontent, excited insubordination, or disclosed that enslaved people had been taught to read.[54] Ministers of the Gospel would need to use care in what they said, and people reporting on the activities of ministers of the gospel would need to use care in their reports. As voices increasingly were raised in opposition to slavery, Louisiana's legislators acted to prevent them from being heard in Louisiana.

Locally, residents of West Feliciana Parish readily accepted free people of color into their community, but they also wanted to protect slavery. In 1835, parish residents formed the Committee of Vigilance with twenty-one people to protect the interests of the parish from the designs of abolitionists. The committee thanked the postmasters in New York, St. Francisville, Charleston, and New Orleans who refused to send incendiary materials through the mail. It passed a resolution in favor of planting a colony of free blacks in Texas to which Louisiana could send its free people of color and sought a federal appropriation to pay for it.[55] Louisiana's legislators demonstrated an increasing antagonism to free people of color, but parish residents shared that antagonism only in the context of a threat to slavery.

In 1841, the West Feliciana Parish–diarist Bennet H. Barrow recorded his displeasure with his local district attorney, who failed to expel free people of color from the parish: "Our District Attorney (W. D. Boyle) made a beginning toward enforcing the Law, in removing free negroes from the Parish, came to old Greys [sic] family, saw the Law in a different Light, no doubt bribed."[56] White planter Josias Gray lived openly with Ann Maria, a woman he had held in slavery. He legally and publicly acknowledged his children born to her and traveled throughout the community in their company.[57] Barrow seemed to believe that Gray convinced Boyle to forego expelling free people of color from the parish. Gray's family, however, was not subject to the law as they had not moved into Louisiana as free people of color. Ann Maria had been born in Maryland and entered the state enslaved; her children were born in the state. Gray had no need to bribe Boyle to protect Gray's family. The law did not apply to them. Barrow may have been correct when complaining that Boyle did not expel free people of color from the parish. West Feliciana Parish authorities were not interested in removing free people of color from the parish. The number of free people of color in the community was small, and to Barrow's chagrin, their individual contributions were valued. Free people of color provided substantial services to their community and were welcome there.

Louisiana's legislature continued in its efforts to subordinate free people of color to white people. The 1806 statute that required free people of color to yield to white people on every occasion apparently did not have the desired effect.[58] In 1843, legislators felt the need for a statute that threatened disrespectful free people of color with expulsion from the state. It provided that the right to remain in the state could "be forfeited by any violation of the laws regulating the duties of the free persons of color towards the whites."[59] The state was struggling to create a subclass based on skin color but seemed to have difficulty convincing free people of color to accept their subordinate status in the proposed hierarchy and seemed to lack the cooperation of whites to enforce the subordination. The state legislature wanted to privilege whiteness, to give Atwater's poor white people a class below them, but free people of color were not responding with sufficient deference. Free people of color continued to live in the state, continued to find ways to support themselves, and continued to contribute to their communities.

Legislators sought other ways to enhance the value of white skin and thereby cultivate white unity and support for slavery. In 1846, when the legislature contemplated starting public schools, it ordered the assessors in each parish to create a list of white children aged five to fifteen. It made no plans to educate free children of color, and in 1847, it authorized funds for educating white children aged six to sixteen.[60] Free people of color, taxpayers or not, would not receive support from the state to educate their children. In 1848, the legislature offered both black and white veterans of the War of 1812 a pension of eight dollars per month for two years. The money to pay the pensions of white veterans was appropriated by the legislature; the money to pay the black veterans was to come out of funds not otherwise appropriated. That is, they were only compensated if money was available after other state expenses had been paid.[61] These variants in treatment by the state gave weight to the difference between being classified "of color" and classified "white" and allowed white people to feel more important simply because they were white. As Warren Milteer Jr. explained: "Politicians . . . adopted attacks on free people of color as an indirect defense of an economy propelled by slave labor."[62] Supporting slavery was a paramount objective. If it meant stripping free people of color of their dignity, so be it.

In 1850, the legislature became more aggressive in nudging free people of color to leave the state by further restricting their freedoms. It forbade free people of color from incorporating for religious purposes or for creating any secret associations, and it revoked the corporate status of any existing organizations of free people of color.[63] Abolitionist voices had become increasingly loud, and the supporters of slavery feared that any meetings of people of color could facilitate plans for abolishing slavery.[64] This statute outlawing associations had little effect in West Feliciana Parish as there is no record of any organizations of free people of color formed there before 1850. Yet, free people of color in New Orleans had established many religious, fraternal, and occupation-based organizations that would have been impacted by this legislation had it been fully enforced.

In 1852, the legislature took a different tack to further restrict the freedom of people of color. It threatened white people with a fine of one hundred to one thousand dollars and with imprisonment for one month to a year for "gambling or betting with free negroes, mulattoes, or slaves."[65] This law would punish white people for interacting with people of color as equals. It protected white people from the indignity of losing in games of chance to people of color by prohibiting the games. It consequently robbed people of color of the opportunity to gloat about gambling victories over white people and of the opportunity to acquire money from gambling successes. It was not until 1855 that free people of color were prohibited from gambling with an enslaved person. The fine and the threat of imprisonment for free people of color gambling with enslaved people were the same as established in 1852 for white people gambling with free people of color.[66] This new statute thwarted one source of money that enslaved people might have used to purchase their freedom and protected against possible abolitionist activity under the guise of gambling.

In 1859, Louisiana's legislature bowed to a different economic interest and enacted a new statute that limited commercial opportunities for free people of color. No free person of color could get a license to "keep a coffee-house, billiard table, or retail store, where spiritous liquors are sold."[67] This statute, however, did not shutter restaurants or boarding houses owned by free people of color, only coffeehouses, billiard tables, and retail stores. It probably targeted a specific source of competition for liquor sales. Historian John Hope Franklin reported significantly increased hostility from white people in North Carolina when free people of color were economic competitors. Historians Michael Johnson and James Roark reported the same phenomena in Charleston, South Carolina. Craftsmen in both communities demanded laws that restricted free people of color from engaging in certain skilled occupations where white people wanted those opportunities for themselves. Unlike the statutes in North and South Carolina, Louisiana's statute targeted economic competition from competing liquor sales and not competition from skilled craftsmen.[68]

Notably, these statutes did not impose segregated housing or segregated shopping or segregation in employment. They emphasized that free people of color were unwelcome in the state and sought to create a caste system where free people of color should not presume to be equal to white people, but they did not physically separate white people from black people or prohibit them from interacting with one another when not gambling. The state was concerned about protecting slavery, and its legislators enacted statutes to address those areas where they felt slavery was under assault. These statutes privileged whiteness and provided a balm to white people who did not share in the wealth of the state. They did not severely handicap free people of color in their daily pursuits. Historian David C. Rankin correctly concluded that most people in Louisiana ignored many of the provisions of these laws.[69]

West Feliciana Parish had been under Spanish control, and free people of color had been readily accepted as a part of their community. American control of the area led to legislation intended to protect slavery by restricting the freedom of free people of color and by appealing to a notion of white supremacy that would garner support for the institution of slavery from nonslaveholders. In response to increasing threats to slavery, legislators added additional restraints on free people of color to discourage their settlement in Louisiana and to protect the enslaved population from their influence. Despite statutes that privileged white people and sought to establish a caste system to the disadvantage of free people of color, free people of color continued to move into the parish, and people newly emancipated stayed. The reality the state legislature sought to establish by enacting laws prejudicing free people of color, whether creating a three-caste system or completely separating white people from people of color, did not take effect in the parish. Free people of color became a part of their community. They acquired property, worked, owned businesses, attended church, and interacted with other free people in the community, both black and white. They established business and personal relationships with their neighbors and were treated fairly by the courts. In West Feliciana Parish, free people of color were well integrated into their community; they were a part of it and not separate from it.

CHAPTER 2

Free People of Color in West Feliciana Parish

The free people of color in West Feliciana arrived there through many different pathways. Some were already free when they moved into the parish from other states or other parishes in Louisiana. Other free people of color were brought to the parish while enslaved and became free after arriving. Still other free people of color were born free, the children of women of color who were themselves free. The number of free people of color in West Feliciana Parish increased from sixty-nine in 1820 to ninety-four in 1830. It decreased to ninety-one in 1840 but rebounded to 106 in 1850. By 1860, the number had fallen to sixty-four.

More than 10 percent of the free people of color in the parish were already free when they arrived. They traveled alone, with their families, or with free white people moving to the parish. They joined other Americans and people from other countries answering the siren call of advertisements that promised wealth to all who would move to Louisiana. In 1806, the *Alexandria Daily Advertiser* published in Virginia contained a newspaper article about Louisiana entitled "Riches of Louisiana." It promised: "Those who have attempted the cultivation of the Sugar Cane there are making immense fortunes . . . the cultivation of Indigo, Rice, and Cotton, . . . within a very few years ha[s] increased the riches of the inhabitants of the Mississippi territory and Louisiana generally, in a proportion that would not be believed, except by those who have seen the change."[1] Free people of color moved to Louisiana, as did other people, to benefit from the opportunities it offered.

The conveyance records, which recorded the registrations of free people of color, documented that, between 1816 and 1844, at least twenty free people of color moved into the parish. They came from Massachusetts, New York, Pennsylvania, Maryland, North Carolina, South Carolina, Indiana, Ohio, Kentucky, and other Louisiana parishes. Approximately thirty other free people of color may have come into the parish already free, may have been born free in the parish, or may have been freed once in the parish. The conveyance records are not clear as to when or where they first knew freedom.

Drury Louis Mitchell, born in 1793 of free parents in the Abbeville District of South Carolina, moved to West Feliciana Parish in 1816. When he registered as a free person of color in 1830, six-foot-tall Mitchell described himself as "well known in this parish as a reputable and useful man, and a carpenter by his profession and trade."[2] Matthew Edwards Jr., who was white, declared that he knew Mitchell's mother, a free woman living in South Carolina, and remembered going to school with Mitchell when they were boys.[3]

Julia Ann Cornish arrived before May 1820 from Chatham County, North Carolina, and brought with her proof of her registration as a free person of color in Maryland.[4] Cornish's record began in Maryland, where she was fined thirty dollars for failing to register. She paid a total of $54.25, the thirty-dollar fine, a twenty-dollar registration tax, $1.25 for her jail fee, and one dollar each for registering, for an affidavit of freedom, and for the cost of her arrest.[5] After paying her Maryland fine and costs on May 20, 1818, she carried her receipt with her as proof of her free status while she traveled to North Carolina and then to Louisiana. Once she arrived in West Feliciana Parish, Cornish created a local record of her free status by recording her receipt in the parish conveyance records.

In obedience to the 1830 statute that required free people of color to register with the parish judge, in 1831, Cornish appeared with James H. Coulter, a white man, to register. Coulter swore that Cornish was a free woman he had known for twenty years and that she resided all that time in Louisiana.[6] His affidavit was clearly inaccurate. According to the receipt Cornish had placed in the West Feliciana Parish conveyance records in 1820, Cornish had been in Maryland in 1818, thirteen years earlier. Regardless of its inaccuracy, the affidavit was sufficient to satisfy Cornish's 1830 registration requirement.

Jesse Wilson moved from Floyd, Indiana. In August 1821, he purchased a claim to land fronting on the Mississippi River for six hundred dollars.[7] From December 1821 through November 1822, he bought another five hundred acres on the Mississippi River, five miles above the mouth of the Red River, from the heirs of Samuel Jones, who was white.[8] The heirs of Samuel Jones signed using an *x*; Wilson wrote his name. In 1824, Wilson sold four hundred of these five hundred acres to Thomas N. Hosea, also a white man, for 250 cords of good, merchantable ash wood delivered to a steamboat on the bank of the Mississippi River.[9] In that act of sale, Wilson described himself as a resident of Feliciana Parish.

Elsey Scott moved to West Feliciana Parish from New Orleans. In 1823, one of her St. Francisville neighbors "vilified her character." She contacted some of the officers of the US Army stationed in New Orleans for whom she had worked as a laundress. They declared they had known her for "upward of Twenty-One Years" and agreed: "her character then and ever since has been that of a frugal industrious honest woman."[10] M. Nicholson, a white officer, wrote:

> I have known Elsey Scott since the year 1808. She has been my washerwoman ever since, acted twice as my nurse when sick. I have never known of any accusation derogatory to her character during that period. On the contrary she was highly recommended to me in the first instance and I have no hesitation in saying that she has maintained the same good character. New Orleans 15 Aug 1823.[11]

Despite the insult to her character, Scott stayed in West Feliciana Parish until shortly before her death. In 1842, she died in New Orleans and left her West Feliciana Parish property to a niece who lived in New Orleans.[12]

In 1831, George Douse, born in 1790 in Philadelphia, Pennsylvania, filed his declaration of free status. He and his wife, Eliza, settled in St. Francisville around 1824 with their two Philadelphia-born sons, John Francis Douse, born 1818, and George P. Douse, born 1819.[13] In West Feliciana Parish, Douse and his wife became the parents of three more sons and a daughter.[14] Douse worked as a steward on the steamer *Brilliant*, a passenger boat that traveled weekly between Bayou Sara Landing and New Orleans. He later opened a house of entertainment popular with plantation owners in the parish. In 1840, Douse appeared before a parish judge to say that he knew William Jones to be a free man of color who had been born in New York of free parents. Douse asserted that Jones had lived with Douse since 1821 and had two aunts living free in New York City.[15]

Free people of color came to the parish from different places with different skills and talents. A variety of opportunities awaited them, and each individual was motivated by his or her own circumstances. When they registered their free status, they declared their professions but did not explain what prompted them to make the journey or why they chose this parish in which to exercise their freedom. They moved to the parish and felt entitled to make it their home.

Not all declarations of free status were readily accepted. When Grandison Williams moved to West Feliciana Parish, Dr. Samuel A. Jones, a white parish resident, challenged Williams's claim to his free status. Jones wrote to Jacob Kirby of Highland County, Ohio, to verify Williams's claim. Kirby obtained statements from three men personally well acquainted with Williams and replied to Jones's inquiry: "Your favor in relation to the colored man Grandison Williams . . . I have procured the proper evidence in favor of his freedom. I am well acquainted with the fact he is a free man." Kirby noted that Williams's mother, Nancy Williams, was free and added, "His mother wishes you to say to him that she wishes him to return immediately home."[16] Williams was the child of a free mother but was not free to travel into Louisiana without addressing the challenge from Jones. The "proper evidence in favor of his freedom" was necessary for him to retain his freedom.

Free people of color were wise to register their freedom as it provided local proof of their status in case an ambitious district attorney decided to enforce the law prohibiting their entry into the state. Julia Ann Cornish, who had traveled to Louisiana from Chatham County, North Carolina, and created a local record of her free status in 1820, was prosecuted for moving into West Feliciana Parish. District Attorney Thomas G. Morgan arrested and charged Cornish on February 23, 1827, "for emigrating to and settling in the Parish of West Feliciana, contrary to the form of the Statutes of the State of Louisiana in such case made and provided and against the peace and dignity of the Same."[17] From February 23 until May 26, 1827, when the charges against Julia Cornish were dismissed, Cornish's freedom was in jeopardy.

Along with Cornish, Morgan prosecuted thirteen other free people of color for entering Louisiana after 1807. Bass, Prussia, Sophia, Nathan, Lucy, Abby, Nathaniel Harding, Eliza, Claridon, Elijah, Margaret, Peter, and Albert Prince were each arrested and jailed.[18] By May 28, 1827, the district attorney had dropped the charges against all of them.[19] The law that forbid the entry of free people of color into the state after 1807 was not generally enforced. Its primary usefulness was to allow a district attorney to inspect the status of people who claimed to be free. The free people of color Morgan arrested were able to prove their free status and were released from custody. His prosecution and dismissal of the charges created a record of the defendants' free status that might prove useful to them should that status be challenged in the future. It also reminded other free people of color that their freedom was precariousness. Free people of color unable to prove their free status could be sold into slavery.

Martin Barker, who came into West Feliciana Parish in 1827, had an experience in Illinois very much like that of Cornish and her thirteen codefendants. Barker had traveled through Randolph County, Illinois, before arriving in West Feliciana Parish. He was stopped and jailed in Illinois because he was not carrying his free papers with him and was presumed to be a runaway. He explained that his papers had been forcibly taken from him at Rock King Cavern on the Ohio River. Barker was kept in jail in Illinois until he could prove his free status. On January 22, 1827, Barker presented a certificate of his freedom from Dearborn County, Indiana, that had been certified by the Court of Common Pleas in Hamilton County, Ohio. The Illinois court released him and allowed him to continue his journey. Barker carried the certificate with him to Gallatin County, Illinois, where he filed it in the court records there and, in November 1827, carried it to West Feliciana Parish where he filed it in the conveyance records there.[20] Barker hoped that all of these records, in Indiana, Ohio, Illinois, and Louisiana, would protect him from being jailed or, at least, would aid him in getting out of jail should he again be presumed to be a runaway.

Traveling without one's certificate of freedom could have even more serious consequences than a jail term while waiting for papers to arrive. In 1837, Bennet H. Barrow, a white West Feliciana Parish planter who kept a diary in the 1830s and 1840s, demonstrated the vulnerability of free people of color to the whims of white people. He called out to a person of color on horseback to stop. The person did not respond and did not stop, so Barrow's riding companion put a load of small shot in the rider's leg.[21] Traveling without proof of one's free status could have dire consequences for free people of color. Free people of color risked injury or death for failing to obey a white person's instructions to stop and show emancipation papers or other evidence of their free status.

The indignity of having to answer to a stranger must have been galling for free people of color, and the fear of having their proof of free status destroyed by that stranger caused free people of color to be cautious in their travels, to record multiple public records of their free status, and to remember where those records were filed. As Barrow reported in his diary, white people felt entitled to challenge any person of color they saw and felt free to shoot on sight any person they chose to believe was a runaway.[22] Although their free status was challenged, free people of color who could document their free status were allowed to present their evidence in court and received decisions in their favor. People in West Feliciana Parish were committed to slavery but were willing to allow people of color who were free to remain free.

Sometimes a person who did not consider himself a person of color created a public record of that fact and of their free status. In 1842, Robert Baron filed an affidavit from some of his acquaintances asserting:

> We have known Robert Baron for several years and entertain no doubt that he is and has been from his birth a free man—never questioned. Said Baron is not, as has been generally supposed, of Negro or African Blood, but is the offspring of an Indian woman and a West Indian Spaniard, born on the island of St. Croix

in the year 1815. He first came in the Packet Ship DeWitt Clinton as a cabin boy and made his home in New Orleans. He now works as a steward or servant to gentlemen on a steamship.... He has on every proper occasion shown the most decided hostility to the designs of fanatical abolitionists."[23]

For Baron's affiants, his hostility toward abolition was a guarantor of his position on the white side of any black-white line. It was generally believed that free black seamen brought abolitionist literature with them when they traveled into the slave states and that they enticed enslaved people to escape aboard their ships when they left.[24] A seaman's hostility to abolitionists would help to protect his freedom by assuring the protectors of slavery that he posed no threat. Free people of color and others who might be mistaken for free people of color needed records of their free status.

Even after the 1830 legislation forbade their entry and required them to enroll with the parish judge, free people of color continued to come into the parish. Ellen Campbell, born of free parents in Pennsylvania, came to Louisiana in 1837. Once there, she married George Britton, a free man of color.[25] Thomas Phelps, a shoemaker born in Annapolis, Maryland, registered in the parish in 1844.[26] Jordan Ritchie, from Woodford County, Kentucky, may have planned to only visit when he came to the parish in 1831. Being "sick and weak of body," he wrote his will in St. Francisville shortly before his death.[27]

Although most of the free people of color who moved into West Feliciana Parish came alone, a few traveled to Louisiana as part of the households of white people. Bennett J. Barrow, a white plantation owner and enslaver in the parish, swore that he was acquainted with Lucinda Wilkins and with her mother and knew that they were free. Wilkins's mother had been a free woman when Barrow's father brought her with him to Louisiana.[28] Lucinda Wilkins, her daughter, was born free. Julia Gardner, born a free native of Salem, Massachusetts, was taught to read and write before she left there. In a November 1840 statement written in Cincinnati, Ohio, Joseph Pierce, who was white, declared that Gardner had been "placed under my protection in 1810 and emigrated with the author and his family to the Western country in 1821."[29] Gardner brought her literacy skills with her when she traveled to Louisiana. Capt. A. L. Walsh, a white plantation owner in West Feliciana Parish, brought two free men of color into the parish with him. Both Aaron and Caesar had been his indentured servants. When their terms of service expired, they stayed in the parish.[30]

Free people of color came to West Feliciana Parish to find a better life, to engage in their professions, and to live their lives in peace. West Feliciana Parish offered an environment acceptable enough to attract them and to allow them to remain. Whether drawn to the parish by happenstance, word of mouth, newspaper articles, or travel companions, free people of color chose to move into the parish and chose to remain there.

Most of the parish's free people of color had been enslaved. Sixteen of them were able to earn the money needed to purchase their freedom. Under both French and Spanish law, an enslaved person could purchase themselves by paying a price negotiated with their slaveholder. Louisiana's 1825 Civil Code continued to allow self-purchase. It declared that an enslaved person had no capacity to enter into any kind of contract except a contract related to his or her own emancipation. Once negotiated, a contract between an enslaved person and his or her enslaver could be enforced. An enslaved person could not require an enslaver to agree to a sale, as was possible under Spanish law, but once an enslaver consented to a certain price, the enslaver was bound to the sale when the price demanded was paid.[31] The problem came in getting the money to make the purchase.

Article 175 of the 1825 Civil Code created difficulties for the accumulation of money: "All that a slave possesses, belongs to his master; he possesses nothing of his own, except his *peculium*, that is to say, the sum of money, or moveable estate, which his master chooses he should possess."[32] Only a limited number of opportunities existed for an enslaved person to acquire money, and an enslaved person could only keep whatever sum of money the enslaver allowed him or her to keep. A slaveholder might allow enslaved people to hire themselves out and keep a portion of their earnings. This opportunity was more readily available to enslaved people living in cities or to those with skills in high demand, but others, in other places, sometimes were granted this limited liberty. Other enslaved people might be allowed to raise crops or to keep animals they could sell.

In 1832, when Henry Flowers, who was white, manumitted Abel, Flowers noted that Abel had been allowed to labor for himself. He wrote, "Abel ... has resided since 1823 in the neighborhood, has labored for himself, his conduct for sobriety and industry have been exemplary."[33] Abel had been allowed to work for someone other than his enslaver and had been allowed to keep enough money to purchase his freedom. Sometimes, an enslaved person was allowed to keep a garden or care for chickens or pigs. Generally, as an incentive, the enslaved person was allowed to keep some portion of the proceeds from the sale of the produce or of the animals.[34] In 1850, when Hardy Perry, a white plantation owner, died, his estate paid $76.97 to people he had held in slavery for corn belonging to them that was sold on their behalf.[35]

West Feliciana Parish appeared to offer enough self-hire opportunities that enslaved people from outside of the parish came to work there. Samuel Nesmith, a white man living in Amite County, Mississippi, gave Nitty, who he claimed to own, permission to go to Bayou Sara to hire herself out "to whomever she pleases to work for or whomever pleases to hire her and liberty to pass and repass from my place in Amite County Mississippi to Bayou Sarah unmolested for the year."[36] Chauncey Pettibone, a white resident of Wilkinson County, Mississippi, sent his servant Silvia to the town of St. Francisville to earn the rest of the seven hundred dollars she needed to pay for her freedom. She had already paid $441.45 and was expected to send him fifteen dollars per month until she paid the balance. She made her last payment on January 3, 1838, and was freed.[37] When allowed to earn money and to keep a portion of their earnings, enslaved people could save their peculium to purchase their freedom.

In 1820, Amos Hoe listened to others bidding for him at the probate sale of his deceased enslaver's property. The last and highest bidder had offered twelve hundred dollars for Hoe. Hoe paid the twelve hundred dollars for his freedom.[38] Similarly, Phil paid $450 to the heirs of Stewart for his freedom.[39] In 1856, Titus paid six hundred dollars for his freedom,[40] and in May 1863, forty-two-year-old Daniel Davis paid fifteen hundred dollars for his freedom.[41] These men and women took advantage of the opportunities given to them to earn money they could use to pay their purchase price. They were not born free but became free through their labor and their discipline.

Two enslaved men agreed with their slaveholders to purchase their freedom on payment plans. William Chew made irregular partial payments toward his $350 purchase price from January to October 1827.[42] Reuben Adams contracted with Jesse Boyd, a white enslaver, to pay fifteen hundred dollars plus 8 percent interest from January 1, 1855, until paid, plus expenses for his freedom. In February 1857, Boyd recorded that Adams had already paid $635. Adams paid the remaining nine hundred dollars in December 1857.[43] These transactions reflected the personal relationships that existed between slaveholders and the enslaved persons who bought their freedom. Those enslaved people allowed to accumulate sufficient funds to purchase themselves were personally known to their enslavers. They were favored with opportunities not available to everyone who was enslaved.

Some enslavers negotiated sales where an enslaved person would pay the agreed upon purchase price in full but not be freed immediately. In 1857, that same Jesse Boyd who accepted partial payments from Reuben Adams took five hundred dollars from fifty-five-year-old Caroline Boyd but required her to stay and remain enslaved to him until his death and required her to pay all the expenses incurred in obtaining her freedom papers after his death.[44] There is no way to know if Caroline Boyd actually paid the five hundred dollars. It may be that Jesse Boyd planned to emancipate Caroline Boyd at his death but characterized his manumission of Caroline as a sale to protect Caroline from his creditors. Because the conveyance records recorded Caroline's emancipation as a sale, Jesse's creditors would be bound by that record. Caroline would not be free until Jesse's death, but Jesse's creditors could not sell Caroline to pay Jesse's debts. Similarly, in a sort of plan to pay now, get free later, Phoebe paid three hundred dollars cash in 1831 but had to wait nine years for her freedom.[45] In 1832, Peter Ambrose paid $530 to Henry Burroughs, who was white, but would not be free until four years later.[46] According to the parish conveyance records, a total of sixteen adults purchased themselves. Two mothers included their children in their self-purchases.[47]

Other free people of color used the money they earned to purchase their family members. From 1837 until 1850, twenty-seven people, primarily family members, were owned and then freed by free people of color. After William Chew purchased his freedom in October 1827, he saved to buy his wife, Mariah, for $225. By 1839, he had bought four of his children, George (aged thirty), Harriet (twenty-seven), Mary (thirteen), and Arie Ann (twenty-two), and had bought Harriet's daughter, three-year-old May Lilly. In that year, he emancipated them.[48] After searching, Chew found another son, Wilson, in West Baton Rouge Parish. Chew purchased Wilson in 1845, then set him free.[49] In 1837, William Marbury applied to the police jury to free John Hill.[50] Their relationship was not indicated in the act of emancipation. That same year, Eliza Wilkins, who had purchased her father, Caesar, emancipated him and gave him his absolute freedom. As her reason, she wrote, "In consideration of [the] love and friendship and gratitude she owes to her father."[51]

In 1840, Nelly Wooten purchased her granddaughter Margaret and Margaret's son, Augustine, from Mrs. Mary Stirling, the widow of white plantation owner Henry Stirling, who had once held Wooten in slavery.[52] In April 1842, when Priscilla Davis dictated her will, she expressed in it a desire to free her sister, Rose Ann Davis, and her niece, Cassy Ann Davis, at her death and to leave her entire estate to them to be held in common during their lives. She included a clause to free Elizabeth, who was then thirteen years old, but only on condition that Elizabeth continue to live with Rose Ann Davis and Cassy Ann Davis for the remainder of their lives. Elizabeth and her children would inherit the estate if both Rose Ann and Cassy Ann Davis died before Priscilla Davis or if Rose Ann and Cassy Ann Davis died without having other children. In 1842, Davis changed her mind, and instead of waiting until her death, Davis freed her sister and niece during her lifetime. Their deeds of emancipation were recorded in the West Feliciana Parish conveyance records.[53]

In 1848, when Celia Guibert wanted to purchase her twenty-five-year-old daughter, Louise, she had only $604.59.[54] She had to mortgage her daughter for the remaining $249.41 needed to pay her purchase price. Louise would be free but could be re-enslaved if her mother failed to pay the remainder due on her purchase price. Henry Oconnor, who had been free since his childhood, chose as his mate a woman who was enslaved. On June 3, 1847, Oconnor purchased his wife and five children. In 1850, after another child had been born, Oconnor received permission from the parish police jury to free "his slave Ann and her six children."[55] He had selected an enslaved woman as his wife, and consequently, his children were born enslaved. He worked to purchase them so they too could be free from slavery. Maria Wicker had purchased her own freedom and that of three of her children in 1842. In 1855, she located and purchased two of her sons who had been sold away from her.[56] These free people of color used their earnings to pay for what was important to them: protecting their loved ones from slavery. Family was a priority for free people of color, and they wanted to share with their family the freedom they enjoyed.

Other enslaved people were freed by white slaveholders. Some white fathers of enslaved children freed their children and, sometimes, the children's mothers. For other people of color enslaved in the parish, freedom came as a gift or came as a reward for good conduct. Freedom might have come during the lifetime of a slaveholder or might have come through a slaveholder's will. Slaveholders often cited "faithful services" as the reason for the emancipation. West Feliciana experienced no mass emancipations. Each of the enslaved people freed was personally known to their enslaver.

Approximately 15 percent of the free people of color in the parish were freed after a white slaveholder's death. Louisiana's laws expressly permitted manumission by will. Testators were free to dispose of their property however they chose, so long as all their creditors were paid and so long as the portion required by law to be left to their children, if the testator had children, or to living parents in the absence of children, was given to the children or to the living parents of the testator.[57] Although a testator may have intended to free a person by means of a will, that person could be deprived of their freedom if the testator's estate could not afford to free them. Creditors would be paid before enslaved people were freed. Children or parents would get their portion before an enslaved person would be freed. Despite the slaveholder's intent that an enslaved person would be freed after the slaveholder's death, an enslaved person could be sold to pay a decedent's debts or to pay the portion due to the testator's children or parents and would continue in bondage.[58] When estates could otherwise meet their financial obligations, estate administrators generally followed the wishes of the testator, but not all estate administrators were compliant. Enslaved people who were aware that a will provided for their freedom might be forced to sue a noncompliant administrator to be freed. Those unaware would remain enslaved.

Historian Clayton E. Cramer observed that, with testamentary emancipations, slaveholders could relieve their consciences without impacting their pocketbooks.[59] During their life, slaveholders benefitted from the free labor provided by enslaved people. After their death, they could go to eternal rest believing they had done something good by their dying. A slaveholder who released an enslaved person from slavery during his or her life could be sure that the intended beneficiary would indeed be freed. Priscilla Davis wanted that assurance and decided to free her sister during her lifetime instead of through her will. An enslaver who planned to release a person after his or her death might have their plans frustrated by subsequent events.

Moses Kirkland, a white resident of West Feliciana Parish, instructed that, at his death, Peter should be freed. The heirs of Kirkland refused to release Peter despite the language in Kirkland's will expressly directing them to do so. Peter sued the executors of Kirkland's estate to secure his freedom. As early as 1807, the legislature of the Territory of Louisiana allowed "any person held in slavery to petition the general court . . . stating the grounds on which the claim to freedom is founded."[60] When Peter sued, the court saw no reason why Peter should not be freed as Kirkland had intended because no creditors or heirs would be deprived of their entitlements.[61] The law allowing emancipations by will left the power to emancipate in the hands of the testator. Only creditors and heirs could frustrate the testator's intent and only when the amounts due them could not otherwise be paid. Persons intended to be emancipated, however, had to know about the will in order to enforce it.

Testamentary emancipations demonstrated the very personal nature of emancipation in West Feliciana Parish. The enslaved people who were freed by will were known to their enslavers and were being treated differently from other people enslaved by those same slaveholders. Some service or relationship distinguished people scheduled for freedom from others who were not. Some slaveholders made an extra effort to care for underage children or to give the newly emancipated person some initial support in their new life. Others did not. At their deaths, none of the slaveholders in West Feliciana Parish emancipated more than a handful of slaves.

Some testamentary emancipations by white slaveholders were simple. James Doherty directed that Mary be emancipated from all his heirs. John Norris directed that Sall should have her freedom immediately after his death.[62] Others were more complex. In his 1807 will, Joseph Lejeune set Fortune and his wife, Louisa, free and at full liberty to provide for themselves after his death. He also set free Celia's son named Joe, but he required his wife to cloth and nourish Joe until Joe was twenty years old, "but only if he behaves well."[63] In 1830, Lejeune's widow, Constance Beauvais, published the appropriate application, and Joseph Lejeune became a free man.⁶⁴ In 1832, at her death, Beauvais asked that Celia Lejeune, Joseph Lejeune's mother, be freed, but only if Celia wanted her emancipation. Celia would have to weigh the responsibility of providing for herself against the yoke of continuing under the control of someone else. She would consider her age, her skill level, her health, and whether her son could care for her before deciding whether she wanted her freedom. In 1836, Joseph Lejeune bought a lot in St. Francisville, probably to provide a home for himself and his mother, but neither Joseph nor Celia Lejeune appears in the 1840 census of the parish.⁶⁵

In his May 30, 1816, will, William Weeks acknowledged his relationship to a woman he had held in slavery. He had recently freed "the mulatto woman, Ann Maria Curtis, now living with me as house-keeper," and wrote:

> It is known to my legal and forced heirs . . . that the children of said Ann Maria, viz: Edmund or Edward Wilson, Mary-Ann or Mary Anna, and William, still slaves, I acknowledge to be my illegitimate children, and that it is my desire that they be enfranchised as soon as it can be done by law—and it is further known to my heirs aforesaid, that the youngest child of said Ann Maria named Wellington Curtis, born free, I also acknowledge to be my illegitimate child.⁶⁶

Weeks had two legitimate children, David and Pamela Weeks, born of his 1768 marriage to Rachel Hopkins, who died in 1790. David and Pamela Weeks received four-fifths of his estate. Weeks's younger children were considered illegitimate because Weeks was not and could not be married to their mother. The four illegitimate children shared the remaining one-fifth of his estate with their mother. Weeks's bequest to them began, "Now to do by these my illegitimate children and Ann Maria aforesaid, their mother, the part that becomes a man and a Christian, I give and bequeath. . . ." Ann Maria Curtis received one twenty-fifth of his estate. Wellington, the child born free, received one twenty-fifth. The remaining three twenty-fifths also went to Ann Maria Curtis with the intent that the three children still enslaved would acquire its ownership once they were freed. Weeks instructed his estate executors, his son David Weeks, a successful sugar cane planter in southern Louisiana, and his grandson that if the three children still held in slavery could not be freed within three years, they were to take the children to Pennsylvania at the expense of his estate and to free them there.

Weeks gave his son sixteen thousand dollars for the benefit of the children. The interest from the money was to pay the costs of caring for and educating the four children, and each child was scheduled to receive four thousand dollars from the principal as that child became an adult.⁶⁷ In addition, Weeks instructed his son to give to Ann Maria Curtis 195.5 acres of land on the west side of Bayou Sara and to give her an enslaved ten-year-old girl named Hannah. On July 17, 1816, Curtis personally appeared to accept these donations.[68] She held onto the land until 1825, when she sold it to a white buyer, and she died in 1826.[69] Weeks waited until he was near death to decide to free his children and their mother, but he discussed their welfare with his son and daughter and left money, property, and instructions for their benefit.

In 1841, Moses Horn used his will to set free his house woman Ann Higdon.[70] He directed that his executors give Higdon five hundred dollars cash and that his "negro man" named Guy also should be free. He added that his "colored boy," probably his child with an enslaved woman, should remain with Drury Mitchell, a free man of color and master carpenter, until March 1845 and then be free.[71] In 1850, John C. Morris gave his servant Betsey her freedom, fifty dollars cash, and all her furniture.[72] Just as Horn had given Higdon some cash along with her freedom, Morris gave Betsey a bit of a head start as she began her life as a free woman. With fifty dollars, she could rent a place to live while she looked for work. These testators died instructing but not ensuring that, after their deaths, individuals particularly known to them would be released from bondage immediately. Other testators contemplated a delayed freedom.

Ann Chew asked that Jerry, then ill from disease, be required to serve his new master for three years before he should be freed.[73] John Bettis left Hannah to his brother but asked that Hannah be freed after one year and six months.[74] Samuel Kemper bequeathed Betsey Kemper and her two children, Nancy and Alexander, to his sister Betsey Fishback but arranged for Betsey and Alexander to be freed. When Betsey Kemper could pay $150, she should be freed. Alex was to be freed when he turned twenty-one on November 15, 1833. If Samuel's sister died before then, Alex was to be bound as an apprentice to a house carpenter or a house joiner for the three years just before he came of age "to enable him to make a living due to the defects in his eyes."[75] Betsey Kemper paid Betsey Fishback $150 on August 28, 1815, and was freed.[76] Alex's freedom would come later. Nancy remained enslaved to Fishback.

Other white slaveholders created even more complicated arrangements. In 1833, Henry Collins sold Mary Anne Jane to Hardy Perry on condition that Jane would stay with Collins until Collins died. Perry would then become Jane's guardian. In the agreement, Perry promised to allow Jane to labor for herself and promised to arrange for her freedom should Jane outlive Perry.[77] Jane would not be freed when Collins died, but she could be freed if she outlived Perry and if Perry, before his death, fulfilled his promise to arrange for her freedom. Perry lived until 1854. Jane's freedom depended on her outliving him and on his actions to free her.

Similarly, John George Shrim held onto Clorressy until his death. Shrim owned 640 acres between the east and west prongs of Thompson's Creek. He sold 440 acres to Solomon M. Brian outright for one thousand dollars.[78] In exchange for buying the remaining two hundred acres and for Shrim's cattle, hogs, household and kitchen furniture, and three enslaved persons, Brian agreed to give Shrim fifty dollars on January 1 of each year, attend to Shrim's business, and furnish Shrim with a workforce for the rest of Shrim's life. At Shrim's death, Brian was instructed to free Clorressy at Brian's expense. Brian was to keep Clorressy under his care and protection after she was emancipated and to give her three cows and calves and "sufficient household and kitchen furniture to enable her to go to housekeeping."[79] Clorressy would not be free until after Shrim's death, but, once free, she would not be set adrift in her old age. She would be cared for and given furnishings to establish her household. Although the terms of the will delayed Clorressy's freedom, it provided for her support in a way that revealed the personal connection between Clorressy and Shrim, just as Collins's will revealed his closeness and concern for Jane despite prolonging her servitude.

Even when a will did not expressly call for an emancipation, family members of a deceased former slaveholder might decide on their own to emancipate a person. Heirs of a deceased person might satisfy a dying request of the decedent. When Joseph Johnson freed Jim, about fifty years old, from slavery, he stated that he was obeying a wish expressed to him by his father, Isaac Johnson.[80] The heirs of Thomas Ambrose freed his faithful servant Peter and acknowledged the intent of Ambrose to free Peter: "Thomas was prevented from this act by his sudden and unexpected death." They requested that the administrators of Ambrose's estate perform whatever further acts were necessary to complete the emancipation.[81] With the consent of the heirs of Mary Ratliff, Adam Bingaman, the administrator of Ratliff's estate, emancipated Sandy, aged fifty, who, Bingaman said, had been of great service to Mary Ratliff and her family. Bingaman concluded: "He merits his freedom."[82] Some of these white heirs satisfied a dying request; other heirs decided that granting freedom to a faithful servant was the right thing to do. In all these cases, the relationship between the decedent and the enslaved person who gained their freedom was personal.

John J. Collins, a white resident of Mississippi, appointed Norman Davis, a free man of color, as his attorney in fact to carry Catherine Childress, a black woman about twenty-seven years old, and her children, Dulcinia, about seven, Christopher, about three and a half, and William, about two, into one of the states of Illinois, Indiana, or Ohio to free them. In the 1840 act emancipating Childress and her children, Collins wrote that he was the only brother of William Collins, Childress's enslaver until his death, and that Collins had no children or parents or wife who could make a claim to his estate. Aware of Childress's "meritorious services and . . . faithful, honest + discreet conduct," John Collins carried out the intentions of his brother to free Childress and her children at his death.[83] Childress's act of emancipation particularly noted that William Collins left no creditors, children, or parents who would be deprived of any property due them by this emancipation. John Collins, who had inherited Childress and her children free of any other person's claim, could emancipate them if he wished to do so. He wished to do so, and he did. One white heir, Ezekial Haynie of Somerset County, Maryland, was simply reluctant to hold a man in slavery. Without any prompting by his progenitor, Haynie emancipated Peter, "a man who fell into my hands on the division of my mother's estate."[84] Rather than sell Peter for financial gain, Haynie set him free.

While an attempted emancipation by will could be frustrated by an insolvent estate or ignored by estate administrators, an emancipation during the life of a slaveholder usually resulted in freedom for the intended beneficiary. The enslaver was alive to ensure that the emancipation took place. Actions that complied with the laws regulating who could be emancipated and what process and language to use to accomplish the emancipation usually produced the desired result. Those laws and procedures would change over time and became increasingly costly and challenging for the potential emancipator.

Consistent with Spanish legal tradition, the legislators for the District of Louisiana were initially liberal in permitting enslavers to offer freedom during the lifetime of the enslaver. The slaveholder needed only to sign an act of emancipation before two witnesses and a notary. An 1804 statute even required the freeing slaveholder to support and maintain any freed person who was not of sound mind and body, any person who was above age forty-five, and any person who was still a minor. If male, one was considered a minor if under the age of twenty-one; if female, under the age of eighteen. Each person freed would be given a copy of the papers evidencing their emancipation.[85]

Very quickly, though, those legislating for Louisiana began to implement restrictions on lifetime emancipation. In 1807, the legislature for the Territory of Louisiana passed a law so that only enslaved people over age thirty and of good character for the prior four years could be set free. However, age did not matter when the freedom was a reward for saving the life of their enslaver or their enslaver's wife or child.[86] The slaveholder wanting to emancipate a person would publish a notice of an intent to emancipate in a local newspaper. If no opposition to the emancipation was filed with the court, a parish judge could issue the emancipation papers.[87] To emancipate someone who was not yet thirty, the slaveholder had to petition the state legislature for permission.[88] West Feliciana Parish was subject to Spanish laws until 1810 when its residents declared themselves independent from Spain. When the United States took possession of West Florida in 1810, West Feliciana Parish became subject to the laws of the Territory of Louisiana. White slaveholders seeking to emancipate those they held enslaved were aware of these laws and often worded their acts of emancipation to conform to these legal requirements.

In 1819, when David Weeks, a white plantation owner in the parish, emancipated and "forever set free and at liberty" Leah Savage, he needed to state that she was over age thirty and had good character. Weeks stated that Savage was thirty-two years old and was freed "for a very good cause and consideration, to wit [her] honesty, probity and good conduct."[89] In 1824, when Mary Lane, a white small landowner in the parish, emancipated Old Dinah, she characterized Old Dinah as a faithful servant who always conducted herself to the satisfaction of her owners. Lane wrote, "if she errs hereafter it will be through ignorance."[90] In June 1825, white plantation owner Josias Gray wanted to free Ann Maria, the mother of his children, and wanted to free their two children. He stated in her act of emancipation that she was thirty years old.[91] He had to seek authorization from the state legislature to free their children, four-year-old Thomas Hardy Gray and two-year-old Josephine Gray, because they were under age thirty.[92]

In 1827, the legislature further limited who could be manumitted. This new statute made no distinction between people over or under age thirty. An enslaver who wanted to free an enslaved person would file a petition with the parish judge that included the reason for the emancipation. If the judge approved of the emancipation, he was to present the petition to the parish police jury, which was authorized to decide on the emancipation. Freedom was not easily obtained. It was only available to people who had been born in Louisiana, and it required a favorable vote from three-fourths of the members of the police jury in addition to the concurrence from the parish judge.[93] Perhaps a million enslaved people had walked or been transported from Upper South states to Deep South states in the early nineteenth century. This law foreclosed freedom for these victims of the domestic slave trade who had been brought into Louisiana for sale. Under the new law, they could not be emancipated in Louisiana. It also foreclosed freedom for enslaved people imported into the United States legally before 1808, for those imported illegally after 1808, and for those brought in with the 1809 refugees from Cuba. Louisiana's legislators did not want people unfamiliar with the state's mores and priorities to be free to introduce discord. People born in the state could be presumed complicit in the state's intent to protect slavery. The 1841 petition of John Collins to free Catherine Childress and her three children reported that they were native to Louisiana.[94]

Louisiana's free-people-of-color population stood at 10,476 in 1820 and at 16,710 in 1830. In response to this growth, Louisiana's legislature enacted a series of complex statutes that sought to limit the number of free people of color in the state by adding to the cost of emancipations. As abolitionist attacks intensified, fears of rebellion kept pace.[95] Increasingly, Louisiana's legislators considered free people of color a destabilizing force. To protect the investments of those whose livelihoods were amplified by slavery, 1830 legislation required emancipated people to leave the state within a month after their emancipation and demanded a bond of one thousand dollars to ensure their departure. Exceptions were made for people who were emancipated for meritorious service, such as saving the life of a slaveholder or a family member of a slaveholder. Exceptions were also made for people who were given permission by their enslavers to travel to a state where slavery was prohibited to obtain their freedom. Enslaved people who were freed outside of Louisiana could return and remain in Louisiana as free people of color as could those freed for meritorious services. That statute was amended in 1831 to add an additional exception. Enslaved people who were freed for "long, faithful or important services" could remain in the state.[96] People who purchased their own freedom had to leave.

When the legislature required newly freed people to leave the state, it demonstrated an animosity toward free people of color that was not shared by slaveholders in West Feliciana Parish.[97] These slaveholders exploited the exceptions in that statute. Slaveholders who wanted to release a person from slavery but wanted that person to continue to live with them in Louisiana often sent that person to another state to become free. The concept was not new. Since the early 1800s, white male slaveholders in West Feliciana Parish had been sending people to Pennsylvania and Ohio to become free. These free states were easily accessible by water either up the Mississippi River or along the Atlantic Coast. Sometimes the newly freed person would return to Louisiana to live.

In 1816, William Weeks instructed his son and grandson, who were free and white, to take his enslaved children to Pennsylvania at the expense of his estate and to free them there if the three children could not be freed in Louisiana within three years.[98] In 1817, twelve-year-old Eliza Gorham was sent by her father to Philadelphia to become free.[99] She returned to Louisiana in 1820. In 1819, Richard Ratliff's will left all his property, except two mulatto girls, Fanny and Sarah, to his two white sons. He instructed that Fanny and Sarah be taken to Ohio and legally emancipated at the expense of his estate.[100] On April 30, 1827, William Hendrick took Fanny and her children to Cincinnati and, for one dollar paid, released them from slavery.[101] Fanny and her children returned to Louisiana. Louisiana's 1830 law that allowed people who were freed outside of the state to return and remain as free people in the state codified a practice already in place.

In 1832, Indiana was added to the list of states where white male slaveholders in the parish sent enslaved people to acquire their freedom. Barthelemi Bettelany emancipated Lucy, aged thirty-four, and her children, Sarah, about fifteen, and Charles, about nine, there.[102] In 1837, Abisha Davis emancipated Charlotte and two mulatto children there, Alexander and Ferdinand, about three years old, "from motives of benevolence and humanity."[103]

In July 1842, Hardy Perry allowed Caroline, who he described as a "mulattress" about thirty-three years old, "to go to the City of Cincinnati in the State of Ohio, for the purpose of residing there + enjoying the benefit of the law of the said State of Ohio, which confers freedom on all slaves who are allowed by their owners to live in said State, and to return to the State of Louisiana after effecting her emancipation, if she thinks fit."[104] The "if she thinks fit" language in the declaration suggested that Perry did not travel with Caroline and that Perry was not sure Caroline would want to return to Louisiana. Caroline did return, and Perry recorded her Ohio certificate of emancipation in Louisiana six weeks later.[105]

Thomas R. Purnell "declared his intent to permit his slaves to go to Cincinnati to get free and return to Louisiana" although he had already freed his family in 1829.[106] Later in 1842, Purnell recorded in the West Feliciana Parish conveyance records a certificate of the emancipation of Mary and her seven children that had been filed in the Negro Records of the Hamilton County clerk of court.[107] The trip to Cincinnati was unnecessary for Purnell's family, but it provided additional documentation of the free status of his children and their mother. Purnell was aware of the continuing stream of state legislation intended to prevent free people of color from entering or remaining in the state and was justified in his concern that this legislation jeopardized the freedom of free people of color already in the state. He was anxious to protect his family. When free woman of color Priscilla Davis sought to free her sister and her niece, Rose Ann Davis and Cassy Ann Davis, she sent her sister and niece with Purnell's family and with Caroline Perry to Cincinnati, Ohio, to be freed.[108]

Once a person was freed from slavery and could document that freedom, courts in West Feliciana Parish respected their rights. In 1835, Frank Irvin asked the district court judge in West Feliciana Parish to acknowledge his free status. Irvin had been born in 1809 in Pittsburg, Pennsylvania, and was scheduled to become free at age twenty-one. His enslaver moved with him to Kentucky before he turned twenty-one but allowed Irvin to live and work in Cincinnati, Ohio, where slavery had been abolished in 1802. While in Ohio, Irvin was kidnapped and delivered to someone named Harris. Harris carried Irvin back to Kentucky where he was cruelly treated. Thomas Powell, a trader in enslaved people, then brought Irvin to West Feliciana Parish and offered him for sale. These white men—Irvin's kidnapper, Harris, and Powell—acted to frustrate Irvin's right to be free. Louisiana's court system, however, was open to hear Irvin's claim to freedom.

Once he arrived in the parish, Irvin sued Powell for his freedom. In his pleading, Irvin asked to be held in jail so that Powell could not sell him before the court reached a decision on his suit. Thomas Gibbs Morgan, judge for the Third District Court in West Feliciana Parish, found Irvin's allegations to be true. Irvin had been owned by a white man named Taylor in Kentucky who had allowed Irvin to live and work in Ohio. Because Irvin had lived in a free state with the consent of his enslaver, Irvin had become free. Morgan ruled, "The plaintiff has fully established his claim to freedom."[109] Irvin was allowed to return to Ohio.

This 1830 law that codified a practice already in place was not unique to Louisiana. In 1772, James Somerset was purchased in Boston and taken to England. Once there, he was freed by an English court because slavery was considered contrary to natural law and had not been affirmatively established by law on English soil. Courts in the colonies followed suit. Enslaved persons taken by their enslavers into states where slavery was not authorized by law could claim their freedom and would not be re-enslaved if they traveled to a place that allowed slavery. The *Somerset* ruling and Louisiana's 1830 statute supported Judge Morgan's decision that Irvin was entitled to his freedom.

The 1831 amendment that allowed a person who was emancipated as a reward for long, faithful, or important services to remain in the state appears to backtrack on prior efforts to rid the state of free people of color.[110] Saving a life or traveling to a free state were no longer necessary. Faithful service was enough. This legislation demonstrated the very personal nature of each emancipation. A slaveholder who proclaimed the faithful service of the newly freed person had to know that person well. The freeing slaveholder attested to the character of that person and assured all listeners that the newly freed person was not a threat to the institution of slavery. Free people of color believed to share a proslavery viewpoint could be trusted to remain in the state.

Even before the 1831 statute allowed this category of newly freed people to remain in the state, white slaveholders in West Feliciana Parish often cited faithful service as the reason for emancipation. In 1826, Hardy Alston emancipated Lucy "for and in consideration of [her] faithful, honest, and devoted services."[111] In 1827, James Doyle set free Lidy, about forty years of age, who had resided in Louisiana for about ten years but was already "residing by my consent at Cincinnati Ohio" in consideration of her faithful services.[112] In 1828, H. A. Carstens emancipated Rebecca and her son Isaac, about seven years of age, for "faithful and honest and devoted services and the general good character of this woman."[113] In 1830, Mary L. Mills emancipated Priscilla "for services and good conduct for several years."[114] After the 1831 statute, slaveholders continued to cite "faithful services" as the reason for the emancipation. In 1848, Jane was freed "after long and faithful services."[115]

Despite the hurdles impeding emancipations, from 1819 until 1848, white slaveholders freed fifty-two people in the parish during their lifetime, about one-third of the total number of free people of color in the parish. Of the fifty-two people freed, probably eighteen were mulatto children and five were their mothers. Fathers who wanted their children to be free generally freed them during their lifetimes. However, not all fathers in West Feliciana Parish were concerned with the freedom of their children. The 1860 census of West Feliciana Parish reported that of the 9,571 people held in slavery, 1,208 were mulattos.

Occasionally, white parish slaveholders ignored the legislative requirements governing emancipations. In 1835, Phillip Piper emancipated nineteen-month-old Ruffin, whose mother was enslaved, and placed Ruffin with Drury Mitchell as an apprentice. That same year, William Norvell emancipated three children whose mother had died, and like Piper, Norvell placed them as apprentices.[116] Neither Piper nor Norvell sought permission from the legislature for the children to remain in the state. Neither appears to have asked the parish police jury or the state legislature for permission to free these children, all of whom were under age thirty. These slaveholders simply filed their emancipation documents, and the children became apprentices.

Free people of color who wanted to free their family members were more inclined to follow the steps mandated by these laws. By 1839, William Chew had paid for his own freedom and purchased his wife, four of his children, and one grandchild. He wanted them free, but he also wanted to keep them near him in West Feliciana Parish. He could not claim that they had provided long and faithful services to him because he had only recently purchased them. Nor could he claim that they had saved his life. He probably did not want to expend the money necessary for them to travel to a free state so they could become free there and return to Louisiana to live. Instead, in 1839, he petitioned the state legislature for special legislation that granted his children permission to stay in the state after they became free. The parish police jury allowed him to free his children a few months later.[117] His wife had died in 1837.

In 1846, the state legislature, evidencing a greater hostility to the presence of free people of color in the state, abolished emancipation by travel to a free state: "No slave shall be entitled to his or her freedom, under the pretense that he or she has been with or without the consent of his or her owner, in a country where slavery does not exist, or in any of the States where slavery is prohibited."[118] This new statute reversed Louisiana's long-standing law and its well-established legal principal that conformed to England's *Somerset* decision. Emancipation for faithful services was still available and would allow a newly freed person to remain in the state, and the state legislature could still grant permission for a newly freed person to stay. Trips to Philadelphia or to Ohio, though, would now be fruitless.

While the number of free people of color in the state reached 25,502 by 1840, the number fell to 17,462 by 1850 and increased only to 18,647 by 1860. In West Feliciana Parish, the number peaked in 1850 at 106. The legislation directed at limiting the number of free people of color in the state had effect statewide but had only begun to have effect in West Feliciana Parish after 1850. The parish would lose 40 percent of its free people of color in the decade 1850 to 1860. Some parish residents moved south to New Orleans while others moved north to states like Michigan and Ohio. In 1852, new legislation required newly freed people to leave the state within twelve months of their emancipation on penalty of re-enslavement for noncompliance. The police jury granting the emancipation was to collect $150 from the emancipating slaveholder to apply to the cost of passage to Africa should the newly freed person choose to travel there.[119] Only the state legislature could grant permission for a recently freed person to remain in the state; faithful service was no longer enough.

An 1855 statute added further costs to emancipations. Now, a slaveholder had to file a suit against the state to effect an emancipation. The local district attorney was expected to raise any legal objections and to ensure that proper procedures were followed. The emancipating slaveholder would have to advertise the proposed emancipation for thirty days. To allow the newly emancipated person to remain in the state, the emancipating slaveholder would have to post a bond of one thousand dollars while waiting for the legislature to respond to a petition requesting that permission to remain. These statutes severely undercut the motivation to emancipate family members. Slaveholders had to choose between keeping a family member enslaved or risk having to send the family member out of the state.

In 1842, Maria Wicker purchased her freedom and that of three of her children. She supported them by operating a boarding house and restaurant in Bayou Sara. In 1855, she located and purchased two of her older sons who then became her property. No doubt she wanted to free her newly purchased sons, but she also wanted to keep them nearby after having been separated from them for so long. After paying $1,669 to purchase them, she may not have had the money to bring the suit against the state and petition the state legislature for them to stay in the state. Or she may not have wanted to risk the possibility that the legislature would not allow her to keep her sons nearby. Instead, she gave her sons permission to hire themselves out to whomever they wished and to keep their own wages.[120] In this way, they could remain near her and would be free to make their own choices. Wicker's sons were still enslaved but could act as if they were free people of color.

In 1857, emancipation was prohibited altogether: "From and after passage of this Act no slave shall be emancipated in the State."[121] Then governor Robert C. Wickliffe, a white resident of West Feliciana Parish, argued that the statute would protect slavery. He believed that free people of color had a pernicious effect on the population of enslaved people, and he did not want an increase in the number of free people of color in the state. In 1858, Louisiana's legislature joined other states that allowed free people of color to enslave themselves.[122] This option would allow freed family members to remain in the state close to other family members who could not be freed. It also would allow impoverished free people of color to find shelter in someone else's home. No one in West Feliciana Parish took advantage of this opportunity. Only thirteen free people of color in the entire state of Louisiana opted for re-enslavement.[123]

One other stream is responsible for the increase in the number of free people of color in the parish. Under Louisiana's Civil Code, a person born to a free mother was free from birth.[124] As more free people of color came into the parish and as more enslaved people of color acquired their freedom, more and more children of color were born free, further enlarging the population of free people of color in West Feliciana Parish. Julia Cornish was free when she moved into Louisiana, so Mary Ann Cornish, her daughter, was born free.[125] Because Leah Savage was freed in 1819, her daughter, Sarah Jackson, born in 1824, was born free.[126] Ann Maria Gray was freed in June 1825.[127] Her subsequent children, William Hargis, born in December 1825, and Virginia, born in September 1828, were born free.[128] Slightly more than 10 percent of the free people of color in the parish were born of free mothers and were free at their birth.[129] Free people of color born free in the parish tended to remain there.

West Feliciana Parish did not experience any large emancipations. The free people of color there became free one by one. The population of free people of color in West Feliciana Parish included people who had moved to the parish of their own accord and people who had been brought there under duress. It included people who had been freed by their own efforts and those freed by the benevolence of their enslaver. Whether they moved into West Feliciana Parish already free, were freed in the parish, or were born of free mothers in the parish, free people of color tended to stay in the parish until around 1850. The laws written to discourage the presence of free people of color in the state had little impact on them until then. Free people of color had found a place where they were accepted as people. They could support themselves, raise their families, and live companionably with their neighbors. West Feliciana Parish offered a space where their freedom could be exercised, where free people of color could live in peace.

CHAPTER 3

Land Sales, Loans, and Litigation

In early nineteenth-century West Feliciana Parish, free people of color and white people participated in the same economy, bought and sold land, people, and other property to one another, borrowed and lent money to one another, and sued one another when their debts were not paid. Their property transactions were recorded in the conveyance records, their purchases on credit were recorded in merchant account books, and their court cases were recorded in judicial records. Free people of color were an integral part of the parish's neighborhoods and of its economy.

In both the towns and the rural areas of the parish, free people of color and white people lived side by side. Free people of color who wanted to buy property chose from whatever was available and purchased on the same terms as white people. They paid the same interest rate over the same number of years. When they were ready to sell, white purchasers were ready to buy at market, not discounted, prices. When the West Feliciana railroad was under construction, Drury L. Mitchell, a master carpenter and farmer, sold the railroad a strip of land through his property. He, consequently, and quite literally, owned land on both sides of the tracks. The physical separation characteristic of early twentieth-century housing did not exist in the parish. White people and free people of color lived in West Feliciana Parish without segregation by skin color, perceived African heritage, or previous condition of servitude. They lived as neighbors and, sometimes, in the same households.

The town of St. Francisville, on the bluffs overlooking the Mississippi River, was laid out in twenty-eight squares, each containing twelve lots measuring sixty feet by 120 feet. Squares numbered one through four ran along the bluff facing the river, while squares numbered five through eight were on the next row over, inland. Ferdinand Street ran through the middle of St. Francisville and was the main thoroughfare into Bayou Sara. Bayou Sara was laid out in thirty-nine squares with squares one through five along the Mississippi River and squares six through eleven one block inland. Most squares were divided into twelve lots.

In 1820, five free women of color were heads of their households in the town of St. Francisville. These five households accounted for five children and nineteen adults over age fourteen who were free people of color. Betsey Kemper, Dina and Clarinda, and Sally O'Connor headed households with only free people of color living in them: a total of three children under age fourteen and sixteen adults aged fourteen or older. Judique Lacour lived with one enslaved person and seven white males aged eighteen to twenty-five years old in a house she purchased on December 12, 1816.[1] She paid three hundred dollars in cash for lot three in square nine in St. Francisville. She had earned the money to buy the house by washing for people and by caring for people when they were ill and probably used her home as a boarding house for seamen.[2] That would account for the seven young white males in her household. In 1822, Lacour sold her property to Mary Higgins, a white woman, for twelve hundred dollars, a sizeable increase in price, and moved to Alexandria in Rapides Parish, Louisiana.[3] Lacour's purchase had not caused white flight out of the town of St. Francisville. Higgins did not refuse to purchase the property because the house had been owned by a person of color.

Molly Sears, the head of the fifth household in St. Francisville, was more than forty-five years old and lived with two children and one adult male who were free people of color. Two enslaved people and one white male between ten and fifteen years old also lived with her.[4] The white child may have been an orphan Sears had been asked to care for or may have been a light-skinned free person of color who the census taker believed was white. Classifications based on perceived African ancestry, imprecise at best, could be confounded by hereditary mixture with people from other continents. After 1820, Molly Sears disappeared from the public records along with any information about the people who lived in her household.

The presence of enslaved people in these households may be explained in one of two ways. Free people of color did buy, sell, and exploit the labor of enslaved people in the parish just as other parish residents did. Judique Lacour would have wanted help caring for her boarders and the standard source of help in the parish was enslaved laborers. However, some free people of color also purchased their relatives or friends with the intent to free them. It is not clear why Molly Sears held two people in slavery in her household. The 1820 census provided no occupation or place of birth, nor did it include the names of the people in the household other than the head of the household.

In Bayou Sara, Nelly Wooten, who became free in 1818, lived with one child under age fourteen. She operated a tavern at the mouth of Bayou Sara Creek on the lot next door to where she lived. The two other free people of color living in Bayou Sara were not heads of their households; they lived in the homes of white people.

Three free people of color who were heads of their households in 1820 owned land outside of the two towns in the parish. Household heads Ned and Bob lived in the Mississippi census subdistrict with one female child and three other adult free females of color. Ann Maria Curtis and Leah Savage each headed their households in the Big Bayou Sarah census subdistrict.[5] In 1816, Curtis had purchased about thirty-six acres of land. Later that year, David Weeks donated 195.5 acres of land and an enslaved woman named Hannah to Curtis. The 1820 census showed Curtis living with two children and one free man of color over age forty-five.[6] In 1819, David Weeks freed Leah Savage.[7] Savage lived near Curtis with one free male of color over age forty-five and with six free children of color. The families of Ned and Bob, Curtis, and Savage accounted for nine free children of color and for ten free people of color over age fourteen.

The 1820 census taker counted a total of sixty-four free people of color in the parish, twenty-one children and forty-three people over age fourteen. Fifteen children and thirty adults lived in the nine households headed by free people of color. The remainder of the free people of color in the parish in 1820, six children and thirteen adults, lived in households headed by white people. There was no great divide separating where white people lived and where free people of color lived.

There also was no divide in the economic life of white people and free people of color. On October 16, 1820, after the census was taken, Amos Hoe purchased lot one in square fourteen on Fidelity Street in St. Francisville for one thousand dollars.[8] He would not be free until two months later, so, technically, when he paid for his lot, he was still enslaved and forbidden by law to own immovable property. Nevertheless, the act of sale filed in the conveyance records labeled Hoe a free man of color. Hoe purchased his lot, and no one challenged his right to do so. Two months later, in December 1820, Hoe purchased himself at the probate sale of his deceased owner's estate.[9] It is likely that Hoe had been a buyer and seller of horses during his enslavement. Once he was free, he sold horses and showed a high level of sophistication in his business transactions.

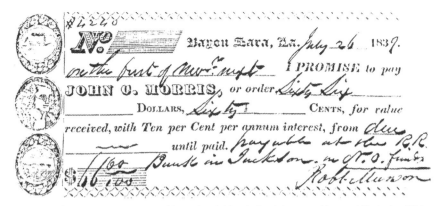

Preprinted promissory note used by John C. Morris. Louisiana and Lower Mississippi Valley Collection, Louisiana State University.

In 1822, with Hoe not yet two years out of slavery, his white neighbor, Jacob Potter, asked Hoe to sign a promissory note as surety for Potter. Hoe, as surety, lent his good name and creditworthiness to Potter to induce James Calvin, who also was white, to make the loan to Potter. Hoe promised to pay the debt to Calvin if Potter did not. When Potter failed to pay the note, Calvin sued Potter and Hoe. Hoe successfully urged the court to have Potter's property seized and sold to generate money to pay toward the debt. After the value of Potter's property was exhausted, Hoe paid only the remaining balance due on the note.[10] A week after Hoe was sued on Potter's note, Hoe brought his own suit against Henry Sterling, another white resident in the parish. Sterling had issued a promissory note to C. Woodroof, also white, on May 21, 1823, for one hundred dollars. The note had been "regularly transferred and endorsed" to Hoe but had not been paid. Sterling did not file an answer to the suit, so Hoe was awarded the full one hundred dollars due on the note plus interest at 10 percent.[11]

Because banks were not readily available to make loans, parish residents regularly issued promissory notes to one another when making purchases or borrowing money. These notes were then passed from hand to hand in lieu of cash. Promissory notes were often a simple "I owe you" written on a scrap of paper. However, the practice was so prevalent that one white merchant of luxury goods, John C. Morris, ordered a supply of preprinted notes naming him as the payee. These preprinted notes allowed customers to fill in the sale date, the due date, and the amount owed and to sign their names.[12] The note became evidence of the indebtedness and, should Morris need to file a lawsuit to collect on the debt, he could easily produce the promissory note in court rather than carry his account books from his store. Also, the note could be transferred from one person to another person as readily as cash. The local courts would enforce the collection of the notes, and the same rules applied to both white people and free people of color who were litigants. Potter and Hoe were made to pay the note to Calvin, and Sterling was made to pay the note to Hoe.

In 1824, Hoe successfully sued the parish sheriff. Hoe had sold two horses to William Kennedy, a white man who had died before paying for the horses. After Kennedy's death, the sheriff seized and sold the horses to pay Kennedy's other debts. Hoe convinced the court that the horses belonged to him because Kennedy had not paid for them. The court ordered the sheriff to pay to Hoe the amount the sheriff had received from the sale of the horses. Hoe then sued Kennedy's heirs for the remainder of the price Kennedy had agreed to pay.[13] In Louisiana, free people of color could testify in court in civil matters, and the court system in West Feliciana Parish did not appear to favor white litigants over black litigants. Historian Kimberly M. Welch argued that the southern legal system was organized around protecting property rights. White southerners considered denying claims based on skin color in support of white supremacy to be less important than upholding a system that protected their property rights regarding enslaved people.[14] Whether plaintiffs or defendants, the cases in which free people of color were involved were decided on their merits and not according to the litigants' skin color. Hoe raised his claims in these parish courts, and the judges ruled in his favor.

Hoe's transition from enslaved person to property owner to surety to successful litigant in just four years suggests that West Feliciana Parish provided an environment that was not hostile to free people of color. Newly freed Hoe was readily accepted as a member of his community, and people in the parish included him in their economic activity. They purchased from him and borrowed using his reputation. They sued him and were sued by him. Hoe even became a slaveholder himself. In 1825, Hoe placed an ad for a runaway, Aaron, in a local newspaper.[15] In 1831, when Hoe was ready to leave West Feliciana Parish, Hoe sold his lot to Sophia Slaughter, a white widow, and moved to New Orleans.[16] Free people of color were completely integrated into the parish economy and were treated fairly by its courts[17]

Not only were white people comfortable buying horses and land from free people of color, they were also comfortable buying personal items that had belonged to free people of color. When Jeremiah Shelton died in 1822, an inventory of his belongings included a paper desk and apparel. At the sale of this property, John Ketchum, a white man, purchased the paper desk, a vest, a beaver hat, and a razor. Other white people purchased pantaloons, a cloth coat, shirts, boots, and shoes.[18] These white purchasers showed no reticence in acquiring property that had once belonged to a free person of color. There was no stigma attached to the property. Nor was there condemnation of the white people who purchased it. The services and property of free people of color were as much in demand as anyone else's. The twentieth-century distain for people of color and for everything they touched was not a part of the parish's ethos. The value of property mattered, not the skin color of its prior owner. White people looking to acquire property were not dissuaded from purchasing it because its prior owner had been a person of color.

After George and Jane Clark died in November 1826, the March 9, 1827, inventory of their estate listed a $5.25 jar, twelve head of cattle, four horses, cash, sundries, a promissory note for hay, and sixty bundles of cane, all valued at $436.50.[19] Three contestants argued for ownership of the property. Their son, also named George Clark, was still enslaved at that time. Clark moved into his parents' house and took possession of their property, probably presuming the property belonged to him. He may have been unaware of the legal barrier to his inheriting it. By law, enslaved people could not inherit, even from their parents.[20] Emily Bridges, the white woman who held the younger Clark in slavery, argued that a Louisiana law made her the rightful owner of the property. That law read in part: "All that a slave possesses, belongs to his master; he possesses nothing of his own." Bridges argued that this law made her the owner of whatever Clark inherited from his parents. Her argument conveniently ignored the law that precluded Clark from inheriting the property in the first place.[21] If Clark had never inherited the property, Bridges could not claim it as his enslaver.

The third contestant, Charles McMicken, a wealthy, white land speculator, argued that George and Jane Clark had not been free at the time of their deaths. According to McMicken, Nathan Lythe, a white plantation owner, held George and Jane Clark in slavery before Lythe's death. When Lythe died, he left a house and some property under their charge. McMicken asserted that Jane and George Clark were caring for the property but were not the owners of the property. According to McMicken, the property belonged to Lythe's estate. Because McMicken had been a creditor of Lythe, McMicken claimed that he should get the property to satisfy Lythe's debt.[22] McMicken spent money for his court filings trying to acquire property that he argued had been in the custody of an enslaved couple. No one was bothered by the fact that black hands had touched the property.

The court that heard the dispute accepted that George and Jane Clark had been free people of color at the time of their deaths and that the property inventoried as their estate had in fact belonged to them. McMicken did not get the property. George Clark, their principal potential heir, was enslaved and could not accept ownership. Neither Clark nor Bridges got the property. Because no one was entitled to the property, the state took possession. The state, however, did not retain possession of the property. The records do not report what machinations took place behind the scenes, but on December 7, 1829, Emily Bridges set George Clark free "from the bonds of slavery forever and forever."[23] She gave no reason for his emancipation. Once he was free, Clark petitioned the legislature to allow him to take ownership of his parents' property. On March 6, 1830, the Louisiana Legislature passed special legislation that allowed Clark to inherit his parents' property even though he had not been free at the time of their deaths and even though the laws in place otherwise did not permit him to take ownership of the property.[24]

When handling the litigation, the court followed the law and rejected the arguments of all three claimants to the property. No litigant was favored over another. The legislature, however, had discretion to address individual requests. It opted to enact a special statute that would allow Clark to inherit his parents' property. The legislature had a legitimate opportunity to legally deprive Clark of his parents' property but chose not to do so. When addressing the petition of Clark, the individual, the legislature acted to his advantage. The very next day, March 7, 1830, the same legislators who awarded the property to Clark passed a law banning free people of color from entering Louisiana and requiring those already in the state to register with their parish judge.[25] The legislators apparently saw no incongruity between the personal act of giving Clark his parents' property, although he had been enslaved at the time of their death, and the political act of imposing additional restrictions on free people of color, including on Clark.

The legislature's 1830 act may have influenced the 1830 census taker in West Feliciana Parish, who failed to record any free people of color as heads of households in the parish.[26] There were nine free people of color who were heads of households in the 1820 census and sixteen in the 1840 census, but none were listed in the 1830 census. Parish conveyance records, however, document home ownership by free people of color in 1830. Homeowners, more likely than not, were heads of their households. Amos Hoe still owned his property in the town of St. Francisville. Nelly Wooter still lived in the same house she had occupied in 1820 and still operated her tavern in Bayou Sara. Judique Lacour had moved, and Ann Maria Curtis had died, but the other free people of color who were heads of their households in 1820 should have appeared as such on the 1830 census. In addition, in 1821, Jesse Wilson of Floyd, Indiana, purchased about five hundred acres of land fronting on the Mississippi River.[27] In 1828, William Marbury bought a fraction of a lot on Ferdinand Street in St. Francisville.[28] The census taker did record that eighty free people of color lived in the parish in 1830, but all were listed as living in the households of white people. According to his records, thirty-six households headed by white people contained one or more free person of color.[29]

Map showing lots purchased by free people of color in St. Francisville, 1830 to 1839.

After 1830, free people of color continued to purchase property in the parish. Free people of color did abide by the law that required them to register with the parish judge, but that law did not discourage them from participating in the economic life of the parish. Free people of color purchased noncontiguous lots in the two parish towns and purchased acreage outside of those towns. As before, those land purchases did not create a distinct community of color. Most free people of color had white neighbors on all sides of their property. In St. Francisville in the 1830s, free people of color purchased lots in squares twenty-seven, seventeen, nine, ten, two, and one.[30] Practically all the other lots in those squares were owned by white people. In Bayou Sara, they purchased lots in squares ten, eleven, eight, thirteen, nine, thirty-seven, one, twenty-four, twenty-seven, and four.[31] These lots were also intermingled with properties owned predominately by white people.

The only cluster of land ownership by free people of color in West Feliciana Parish was on Woodville Road, north of St. Francisville, then the main north-south thoroughfare between Baton Rouge and Natchez. Woodville Road is now a portion of US Highway 61, which runs from New Orleans in Louisiana

Land Sales, Loans, and Litigation   59

Map showing lots purchased by free people of color in Bayou Sara, 1830 to 1839.

to Wyoming, Minnesota. George Douse, Elsey Scott, and Drury L. Mitchell bought contiguous acreage there in the 1830s.

George Douse had purchased land on Woodville Road about three and a half miles north of St. Francisville before 1831. In 1831, he purchased an adjoining two and a half acres. He added about four acres of land in 1835 and another twenty-two and a half acres in 1837.[32] In 1833, Elsey Scott purchased five acres of land that abutted Douse's land. The next week, Drury L. Mitchell bought seventeen acres just north of Elsey Scott and then bought another six acres so that his land also touched Douse's land.[33] All three had entered the parish already free. All three could have purchased land anywhere in the parish. The lands of these free people of color were adjacent to one another by choice or coincidence, not because of discrimination based on skin color.

In 1840, the West Feliciana Rail Road Banking Company wanted to put railroad tracks through the property owned by Drury Mitchell and Elsey Scott. Mitchell held onto his property and sold the railroad the twenty-five-foot-wide servitude it needed, a 9,518-square-foot strip, for $33.57. Scott sold her entire five acres. She had already purchased three improved lots in St. Francisville, and she moved to live there. In 1833, Scott had purchased the unimproved rural property on Woodville Road for six hundred dollars. She sold the land to the railroad company with its improvements for $2,500. The railroad company held onto the land until 1849 when it sold those five acres for seven hundred dollars to Josephine Gray, the daughter of white plantation owner Josias Gray and Ann Maria Gray. In the sale to Gray, the railroad company reserved for itself a twenty-five-foot-wide servitude.[34] When purchasing or selling land, the railroad company did not discriminate against free people of color.

Other free people of color bought acreage in other rural areas of the parish. In 1836, Kesiah Middleton and white Jonathan Ellsworth together purchased about eight acres on Cat Island near Bayou Sara. In 1837, Betsey Givins bought four acres of land and its improvements on Woodville Road closer to St. Francisville than the Douse, Scott, and Mitchell properties. In January 1839, Norman Davis purchased a little less than eleven acres along the Mississippi River, far away from Woodville Road.[35] Free people of color bought whatever available land they desired and could afford on the same terms as those offered to white purchasers. Usually, a purchase required a down payment of one-third or one-fourth of the purchase price. The remainder of the cost would be paid in annual installments over the next two or three years.

In the 1840 census, ninety-one free people of color were counted. Sixteen appeared as heads of their households.[36] Only Nelly Wooten appeared in both the 1820 and 1840 censuses as the head of her household. By 1840, some of the other 1820 heads of households had died, and others had left the parish. According to the 1840 census, forty-one free people of color lived in the town of St. Francisville, and nine of them headed their households. However, from 1840 until after the Civil War, only William Chew purchased property in the town. From 1831 to 1843, Chew purchased a total of eleven lots in St. Francisville.[37]

William Chew was born in Maryland around 1778. He was moved from Maryland to Kentucky where he met Mariah and where their three older children,

Map showing lots purchased by William Chew in St. Francisville, 1831–1843.

George, Arie Ann, and Wilson were born.[38] Chew and his family then joined so many other enslaved people who were taken from Upper South states to the Lower South states and to places to the west that were not yet states. Chew was fortunate in that his wife and children moved together with him to Louisiana. Many families of enslaved people were torn apart by enslavers and traders.

Once in Louisiana, Chew's family probably stayed together until 1826, when his last child was born. The separation of his family may have prompted Chew to negotiate for his freedom with his owner, John H. Mills, the white son of the founder of Bayou Sara. In early 1827, Chew and Mills agreed upon a purchase price of $350. Chew made irregular partial payments from January to October in 1827. His initial payment of $29.62 and one-half cent was followed by payments of twenty-two dollars and thirty-seven dollars in March, twenty-seven dollars in June, and twenty dollars in July. Mills freed Chew in July, before he had completed his payments, trusting him to follow through. Mills described Chew as about forty-five years old and five feet six inches tall. He declared that he emancipated Chew "for and in consideration of the faithful and honest devoted services and the general good character of his mulatto man."[39] He did not mention Chew's purchase price, but he did attach the tally of Chew's payments to the public record evidencing Chew's emancipation. Mills undoubtedly allowed Chew to work for himself while Chew was enslaved and allowed Chew to keep a portion of his earnings. Mills trusted Chew to complete his payments because Mills was personally acquainted with Chew and knew his character. After he became free, Chew made additional payments of $19.75 and $17.50 in August and a final payment of $27.12 and one-half cent on October 16, 1827, totaling three hundred dollars. The receipt for his payments indicated that Mills "contributed gratuitously" the sum of fifty dollars, thus satisfying the agreed upon purchase price of $350.[40]

William Chew was a drayman. He moved things from one place to another. He also worked as the sexton for the Grace Episcopal Church in St. Francisville and was often called upon to retrieve the bodies of the dead for burial. In 1833, he was paid five dollars for hauling a coffin out for the body of a white woman, Mary Constance Beauvais, and returning with the corpse to Bayou Sara Landing. In 1834, when Michael Ditto, the white owner of a dry goods store, died, his estate owed Chew $1.50 for the plank Chew provided. In 1845, Chew charged $9.50 for digging a grave for William Marbury and for hauling Marbury's things to the courthouse for sale. Chew performed other jobs in the parish. In 1841, the parish police jury agreed to pay Chew $250 to furnish wood and water to the courthouse.[41] Chew was well known in his community and provided important services to it.

On March 8, 1831, three and a half years after he purchased himself, Chew purchased Mariah from Mary Shouler, a white resident of West Feliciana Parish. Chew paid $225 for Mariah and, a week later, bought a lot on Fidelity Street in St. Francisville to provide a home for her. For the lot, Chew paid sixty dollars cash down and owed sixty dollars, due by January 1, 1832. Chew and his wife then worked to unite and free the rest of their family. His children had been sold to different enslavers, and the Chews set out to locate and purchase them one by one. Unfortunately, Mariah died September 10, 1837, and did not live to see her children freed. R. H. Ranney, rector at the Grace Episcopal Church in St. Francisville, officiated at her funeral services.[42] In 1838, Chew traveled to Hinds County, Mississippi, to purchase his daughter Harriet and his granddaughter May Lilly. Charles Mead, who was white, sold Harriet for five hundred dollars and sold May Lilly "for the great regard I have for the Said William as a member of the church of Christ and for the sum of one dollar to me paid."[43] By 1839, Chew had located three more of his children, George (age thirty), Arie Ann (age twenty-two), and Mary (age thirteen).

Chew petitioned the state legislature for the freedom of his children and his grandchild and for permission for them to stay in Louisiana. In March 1839, an act of the Louisiana Legislature authorized the police jury of West Feliciana

Parish to emancipate the children and to allow them to remain in the state.⁴⁴ On June 3, 1839, the police jury freed the children and grandchild of William Chew. Chew posted a one-thousand-dollar bond on June 7, 1839. The act of emancipation granted his descendants "perfect and entire freedom in all and every respect whatsoever."⁴⁵ Three-year-old May Lilly would grow up free. George Chew, William Chew's oldest son, would get married.

On July 9, 1840, George Chew, who had been born in 1809 in Kentucky, married Sylvia Green, who had been born in 1810 in Virginia. In February of the next year, his father, William Chew, purchased three lots in St. Francisville next door to the law office of Cyrus Ratliff.⁴⁶ On April 13, 1841, Chew purchased an additional six lots that were across Prosperity Street from the lots he already owned.⁴⁷ He was now the owner of seven lots in square eleven, comprising two sides of the square and three corner lots, and the owner of three lots across the street. He had plenty of space for his reunited family to live close to one another.

The following week, Chew donated a portion of his land to his recently married thirty-two-year-old son, George Chew. A few years later, in 1843, Chew purchased another corner lot across the street from his property.⁴⁸ Chew had reunited his family as best he could and had provided for them a place where they could live together.

In April 1845, Chew located and purchased his son Wilson in West Baton Rouge Parish. Wilson was then twenty-eight years old. The West Feliciana Parish police jury allowed Chew to emancipate Wilson in June 1845.⁴⁹ Like Chew, his two sons, Wilson Chew and George Chew, were draymen. The 1850 census showed William Chew living with his children, Wilson, Arie Ann, and Mary, and with a grandchild, Susannah. Harriet had married Isaac Williams and moved with him and May Lilly to Wayne County, Michigan. Chew's son George lived next door with his wife, Sylvia, and their daughter, Mary.⁵⁰

Chew's name appears once more in the parish conveyance records. Sarah Jackson asked William Chew and Clary Simms, a midwife, to declare that Jackson was the daughter of Leah Savage, a free woman of color. Their joint declaration stated that Jackson had been born in West Feliciana Parish subsequent to her mother's emancipation.⁵¹ Simms, the midwife, was probably present at Jackson's birth and could give a first-hand account; Chew's name was respected in the community and gave weight to the declaration.

On November 1, 1853, William Chew died at age eighty of yellow fever.⁵² Chew's headstone in the cemetery of Our Lady of Mount Carmel Catholic Church in St. Francisville reads, "Loved, honored and respected by all who knew him."⁵³ The church record included the inscription "Blessed are the pure in heart For they shall see God."⁵⁴ Chew did not leave a written will, but before he died, he told his children which of them should get which pieces of property.

Arie Ann had predeceased him. On May 18, 1857, his remaining children recorded an amicable partition to ratify and confirm his verbal partitioning. The children then sold most of the lots. In March 1856, Wilson Chew sold two lots to the "Rector, Wardens, and Vestrymen of Grace Episcopal Church," and George Chew and the church exchanged one lot for a different one.[55] In May 1857, Wilson and Mary Chew sold the other lots they had inherited, and in 1859, Harriet sold the land that had been left to her.[56] All their sales were to the Episcopal Church or to white purchasers. Only George Chew, William Chew's eldest son, remained in West Feliciana Parish as a landowner. He held onto the land his father had given him in April 1841. By June 1860, two of George Chew's siblings, Wilson and Mary, were living in Oberlin, Ohio, where Wilson was a laborer.[57]

William Chew had been brought to the parish with his family while enslaved. As he watched his family members being sold away from him, he resolved to reunite his family and doggedly went about locating and redeeming his children from their owners. He was able to earn enough money to purchase his freedom, and given a chance to use his labor for his own benefit, he put his family first. He served his community as a drayman and served his church as a sexton. He spent his earnings to reconnect with his wife and children and to provide a place for them to live. He never had a large amount of money, but he felt committed to provide a home for his family and purchased contiguous lots so they would be near to one another. He worked hard to bring his family together, and after his death, his family chose to disperse. When they left, they did so as free people, and they each chose their own destinations.

In Bayou Sara, four free people of color were heads of their households in 1840. From 1840 until 1850, free people of color bought lots in squares eight, twenty-five, twenty-seven, four, and one.[58] The economic downturn of 1837 that led to many bankruptcies in the parish may have accounted for the relatively low number of land purchases by free people of color during that decade. Or it may be that most of the free people of color in the parish already owned their homes and had no need to buy another.

The 1840 census reported that three free people of color were heads of households in the rural areas of the parish, and four free people of color purchased land there after 1840. In 1846, Ann Maria Gray bought Drury L. Mitchell's seventeen acres on Woodville Road. In 1849, Josephine Gray, her daughter, purchased the five acres Elsey Scott had sold to the West Feliciana Rail Road Banking Company, adjacent to her mother's property. In 1842, Nelly Wooten purchased a 220-acre tract near Bayou Sara, where she raised cotton and corn and kept cattle. In that transaction, Wooten used a promissory note issued by one white man and made payable to another. The second man endorsed the

Land Sales, Loans, and Litigation

Map showing lots purchased by free people of color in Bayou Sara, 1840 to 1850.

note to Wooten, and she passed it along in partial payment for her property. She gave her own promissory note for the balance of the sales price left unpaid.[59] Like Amos Hoe and other people in the parish, Wooten used promissory notes as cash. Free people of color were not excluded from the credit economy of the parish.

Henry Oconnor also made use of promissory notes in his land transactions. On May 12, 1849, Henry Oconnor recorded three transactions in the West

Feliciana Parish conveyance records. In the first transaction, he purchased approximately six acres from the West Feliciana Rail Road Company for five hundred dollars. In the second, he sold the land, with two horses and two cows, to Angus McRay, a white purchaser, for fifteen hundred dollars payable in three annual installments due May 12, 1850, 1851, and 1852. He received promissory notes for the three annual payments. In the third transaction, Oconnor leased the same land from McRay for five years at a cost of one hundred dollars per year. It was unusual that Oconnor accepted promissory notes for the total sales price of the land and did not require a down payment for this property sale. The sale may have been a ruse to provide Oconnor with promissory notes. It is likely that McRay agreed to loan Oconnor the fifteen hundred dollars he needed to purchase supplies and equipment for his farm.[60] He may have required Oconnor to file the act of sale in the conveyance records in case Oconnor did not repay the loan. Oconnor could use McRay's promissory notes as cash to make his purchases. At some point McRay reconveyed ownership of the land to Oconnor because, in 1853, Oconnor sold the land to Isaac N. Maynard and his wife, Mary E. Baines, a white couple, for four hundred dollars.[61]

In 1835, Oconnor had been a seventeen-year-old carpenter apprentice to Drury Mitchell.[62] On May 12, 1838, he was married by the rector of Grace Episcopal Church to Ann Griggs who was still being held in slavery. Their marriage was recorded in the marriage record book of the Grace Episcopal Church with no notation that Ann Griggs was enslaved. Nine years would pass before Oconnor purchased his wife and five children on June 3, 1847.[63] The 1850 census showed Henry Oconnor, age thirty-six, living with his wife, Ann, six children, and two unrelated men, Benjamin W. Greenwood, a white gardener who had been born in England, and Andrew Jackson, a black carpenter who had been born in Louisiana.[64] When Oconnor recorded the 1853 sale of his six acres of land to McRay, he did not intend to divest himself of the land. He had planned to raise his family on it.

Other free people of color who sold their land in West Feliciana Parish in the 1850s did intend to divest themselves of their land. Free people of color were more likely to sell than to buy during that decade. Between 1850 and 1860, the free-people-of-color population in the parish fell by almost 40 percent, from 106 to sixty-four; the free white population also fell from 2,473 to 2,036, a more than 17 percent drop. Even the number of enslaved people fell from 10,666 to 9,571, a 10 percent drop.[65] The parish was beset by tensions over slavery, rampant yellow fever, and frequent flooding. Few free people of color bought land in the parish during that decade. In 1851, Ann Savage purchased six acres just outside of St. Francisville, but she sold the land in 1856 to Maria Wicker, who owned a hotel and restaurant in Bayou Sara. Wicker sold the land six months later to De

Record of Henry Oconnor's marriage to Ann Griggs. Grace Episcopal Church Records, St. Francisville, Louisiana.

La Fayette Stocking, a white dentist.[66] Also in 1856, Stanley Dickerson bought a lot north of St. Francisville, but he sold it at the same price six months later.[67] Gertrude and Antonio Nolasco, the children of Nelly Wooten, sold Wooten's property to white purchasers,[68] and William Chew's family sold most of the property he had bought to white purchasers or to the Grace Episcopal Church, where they worshipped and where their father had been a sexton.[69] In 1858, Betsey Morris bought a corner lot in Bayou Sara making her the only free person of color to purchase land in that town in the 1850s.[70] In 1860, Ann Maria Gray sold the seventeen acres she owned next to her daughter's property and purchased ten acres of land closer to St. Francisville.[71] She continued to own those ten acres until she died. She and her children stayed in the parish after 1850, while many other free people of color did not.

Before 1850, free people of color lived as members of the community throughout West Feliciana Parish and participated in its economic ebb and flow. They bought and sold property on the same terms white people were offered. When they sold their property, white people purchased at market prices and not at reduced prices. Free people of color borrowed money and accepted promissory notes along with other residents of the community. They litigated their disputes and received fair treatment by the courts. Free people of color were not a despised people but a part of their community. The requirements and restrictions imposed by the state legislature had little impact on their day-to-day activities. Their skin color did not determine where they lived, where they shopped, or with whom they interacted.

CHAPTER 4

Earning a Living

Free people of color could remain in West Feliciana Parish because it offered them opportunities to support themselves. The full range of economic opportunities available in a large urban setting, like New Orleans, was not present in this rural parish, but opportunities did exist, and free people of color availed themselves of them. As was typical in many other areas, most of the free people of color in West Feliciana Parish practiced skilled trades or engaged in service-related occupations. Carpenters and washerwomen predominated in the 1860 census, but the registration statements required by the 1830 act indicated that free people of color pursued other occupations as well. Nurses, seamstresses, and barbers found their way to the parish. A midwife, a shoemaker, and a brick molder registered in the parish. Some free people of color owned large tracts of land that they farmed; others owned businesses.[1]

Many of the skilled laborers in the parish received their training through an apprenticeship. Apprenticeship placements allowed children to learn a trade or profession to enable them to support themselves as adults. For free orphans of color, apprenticeship also provided for their care during their minority. In addition to learning a trade or occupation, apprentices were given food, drink, lodging, and apparel by their instructors. The apprenticeship placements of young free people of color indicated the limited occupational expectations for them in the parish compared with the opportunities open to white children in the parish. Additionally, black apprentices were not promised the same education that was promised to white children. Nevertheless, apprenticeship did offer a path into the skilled or service trades and an opportunity to avoid employment as a laborer.

Louisiana's 1825 Civil Code defined an apprentice as one who engaged to serve a master in order to learn some art, trade, or profession from the master. A child under age twenty-one could become an apprentice only with parental consent or by order of a parish judge or city mayor. The child would be bound to continue as an apprentice until age twenty-one if male or until age eighteen if female. An adult could agree to become an apprentice but for no more than five years. The master was bound to maintain the apprentice, to instruct the apprentice in the master's art, trade, or profession, and to teach the apprentice or cause him or her to be taught to read, write, and cypher.[2] No statute made the conditions of apprenticeship different for black children than for white children.

In October 1826, John Stirling, a white plantation owner, told a judge that there was a free girl of color at his house named Ann Eliza, aged nine years and six months, the daughter of Ann Maria Curtis, a deceased free woman of color. He reported that Ann Eliza was an orphan without a tutor or guardian or means of support. Stirling was willing to take Ann Eliza as an apprentice until she turned twenty-one on April 25, 1837. He promised to provide her with comfortable clothing, board, washing, lodging, and all necessary medical aid and attendance and to cause her to be instructed as a seamstress, servant, and housekeeper.[3] The judge allowed the placement, even though, by law, the apprenticeship should have ended when Ann Eliza turned eighteen. The 1830 census reported no females in Stirling's household in Ann Eliza's age group, free or enslaved.

In 1827, Aseriais C. Dunn, who was white, offered to take Valcourt Vessin as an apprentice until Vessin reached age twenty-one on July 1, 1838. Dunn bound himself for Vessin's "care and to teach him to read, write, and cypher and to instruct him in the art of his profession or occupation, generally Tavern Keeper but more particularly that of a House Servant and cook."[4] That same year, Benjamin Collins, also white, committed to teach John Henry Vaughn to "read, write, cypher and the duties of [a] house servant or waiter."[5] In 1828, William Huntstack, a white man, agreed to take Isaac and Ferdinand, two brothers whose mother had just died, to be instructed in the duties of servants or waiters.[6] In 1835, Eugene Remondet, who was white, was anxious to have two orphaned mulatto children bound to him—Charles, who was eight, and Margaret, aged five—"to be taught to be servants as far as they are capable."[7] He promised to protect them from oppression and ill-use but did not promise to teach them to read. Free orphans of color could expect training to become a seamstress, servant, housekeeper, tavern keeper, house servant, cook, or waiter. Most of these apprentices could expect to be taught to read, write, and cypher, but not all.

In 1835, William Norrell, also white, held slightly higher expectations for three mulatto children of a deceased enslaved woman because, as he stated, he "entertained feelings of affection" for the children. Shortly after their mother's death, Norrell placed the children as apprentices. Norrell directed that they be set free when they reached adulthood, at age eighteen for the girl, Milly, and at age twenty-one for the boys, Robert and Ben. Norrell bound Milly to be taught everything appertaining to housewifery and bound Robert and Ben to be taught "a useful mechanical business or art and to work in a trade or profession from age 16 to age 21."[8] Norrell did not specify which trade or profession the boys should be taught. He only specified that it be useful. He wanted the boys to be able to support themselves without resorting to working in the fields or to the role of servant. He wanted Milly to be prepared to care for a household and husband. Norrell's concern for the welfare of these children suggests that he was their natural father.

The contractual terms of white apprenticeships with their white masters were quite different. In 1829, fourteen-year-old Lotan Gordon Watson asked to be an apprentice to John Lennox to learn to be a blacksmith. Lennox promised Watson "a good English Education."[9] In 1834, when Benjamin Lavergne became an apprentice to Dr. Henry Bains, Bains promised him "a good English education sufficient for the ordinary affairs of life."[10] The mother of eleven-year-old Jacob Collins consented to bind Jacob until age twenty-one as an apprentice to Joseph Buatt to learn the trade of saddler. Buatt would furnish food, meat, drink, and apparel and would teach Collins to read and cypher. Nancy Roberts bound her son Jefferson Roberts to John Heart Hand for instruction in the trade of carpenter. At age twenty-one, Roberts was to get two suits of clothes, one for winter and one for summer, and fifty dollars with which to buy tools. John C. Morris of New Valencia accepted James Mitchell Jr. of New Orleans for a term of four years to learn to be a merchant or clerk in Morris's store. John McMin, with his mother's approval, indentured himself to Thomas Nesmith "to learn the art, trade and mystery of letter press printing."[11]

White apprentices could expect a good English education and training to become a blacksmith, doctor, saddler, carpenter, merchant, or printer. They might expect two suits of clothes, one for winter and one for summer, and fifty dollars at the end of their apprenticeship. In general, white apprentices could expect training for a more prestigious and likely more lucrative craft and could expect a much better education than that promised to children of color. This difference in opportunity reflected the expectations for the proper social-economic position of people of color in the parish but did not prohibit free people of color from reaching beyond those expectations. The apprenticeships available to free children of color were not dissimilar from the positions held by people of color who were enslaved: housekeeper, cook, servant. Free people of color were limited to these apprenticeships but not limited to these means for making a living.

In West Feliciana Parish, the only apprenticeship opportunities in the skilled trades made available to free children of color, whether orphans or not, was carpentry, and only male children were given that opportunity. In 1829, Fanny, a free woman of color, apprenticed her son Samuel to James A. Coulter, a white man, to learn the trade of carpentry. Coulter obligated himself "to use the said Samuel kindly at all times."[12] The other male children who became carpenter apprentices learned the trade from Drury L. Mitchell, a free man of color who had lived in the parish since 1816. Mitchell had an excellent reputation for training apprentices in carpentry.

In 1833, Mitchell bought seventeen acres of land on Woodville Road. In 1836, Mitchell sold less than an acre of that land to John West, a white man, and in 1838, Mitchell purchased another six or so acres adjacent to what he already owned, giving him about twenty-three acres of land on Woodville Road. When the West Feliciana Rail Road Banking Company wanted to lay their tracks across his land, Mitchell sold only a twenty-five-foot-wide path, where the railroad would cross through his property, a total of 9,518 square feet.[13] He continued to live, farm, and raise hogs on the remainder of his property.

As a master carpenter, Mitchell worked on business structures and on plantation homes. Both white people and free people of color hired him for their carpentry work. In 1830, Mitchell built a two-story, framed building in Bayou Sara for John Swift, a white barkeep. The upstairs portion of the building became a tavern, while the downstairs portion was used for storage. Mitchell charged Swift one thousand dollars plus an additional $436.51 for extra work done on the thirty-foot-by-fifty-foot structure. Swift complained about the quality of the work Mitchell had done and refused to pay him. Swift's complaint about Mitchell's workmanship was probably a ruse to avoid paying as promised. To get the money due to him, Mitchell sued Swift. The court that heard the case concluded that Mitchell had done the job satisfactorily and that his charges were fair. The court ordered Swift to pay Mitchell for his work but offset the amount Swift owed to Mitchell by the $96.02 debt Mitchell had accrued at Swift's store.

In 1832, Mitchell built Orange Hill for George Douse. Mitchell charged Douse for four gallery posts, four doors, five windows, framing, flooring, and shingling. When Douse was slow to pay, Mitchell sued to collect. Douse and Mitchell amicably settled the lawsuit, and it was dismissed after a few months.[14] In 1840, Mitchell charged Charles McDermott, a white lumber salesman, four thousand dollars to build a gin house and mill and charged McDermott $315.24 to build a hewed log house. When McDermott failed to pay, Mitchell sued to collect. The court ruled in Mitchell's favor, and the sheriff seized McDermott's property and sold it to pay the debt to Mitchell.[15] The local district court decided these cases on their merits rather than on the skin color of the litigants.

Not all of Mitchell's cases were decided in Mitchell's favor. Mitchell became a defendant in lawsuits whenever he did not pay a promissory note or a supplier's bill promptly. Often, when he was sued, he simply failed to appear in court and a default judgment was entered against him.[16] He did not contest a demand for payment when he knew the payment was due. He paid his just debts when he had the resources to do so. These court decisions and his occasional difficulty paying his debts did not stop people from loaning money to him. Nor did it stop people from employing him to work for them or from asking him to train their children to become carpenters.

In 1835, Phillip Piper, who was white, emancipated a nineteen-month-old mulatto boy named Ruffin and bound him to Mitchell to learn carpentry. Piper had "feelings of affection and good will" for Ruffin but continued to hold Ruffin's mother, Nelly, in slavery. That same year,

Mitchell agreed to the apprenticeship of Henry Oconnor and John Chervis, both seventeen years old, to learn the art of carpentry and ginwright for three years. By 1847, Oconnor was able to purchase six arpents of land and to purchase his wife and five children out of slavery. John Chervis fell from a horse in 1851 and died from the fall.[17] In 1838, Mitchell accepted twelve-year-old Hardesty Chervis as his apprentice. In permitting that apprenticeship, the parish judge characterized Mitchell "as a fit and proper person to be the master of said boy."[18] When Hardesty Chervis died in 1849, he owned carpenter planes and a handsaw.[19] In his 1841 will, Moses Horn, a white man, directed that his "colored Boy," probably his biological son, should remain with Drury Mitchell until March 1845 and then would be free.[20] Mitchell was considered good at his craft and worthy of trust.

The community's high regard for Mitchell led to his selection as the under tutor to guard against the waste of the estate Lewis Hutchinson inherited from his mother. In 1839, Leucy Hutchinson died leaving behind property valued at $2,315.31. Hutchinson had owned Bayou Sara lot 304 valued at seventy-five dollars; the right to lease a plot of land for three years ending April 30, 1841, valued at one hundred dollars; and a rifle, shot gun, musket, house logs and cords of wood, four smoothing irons, silver teaspoons, fine decanters, champagne glasses, a gold heart, two pairs of earrings, a breast pin, and a chain strung with coral beads.[21] She had held in slavery a mulatto man, Bob, valued at one thousand dollars, and a Negro woman, Charlotte, valued at eight hundred dollars, both of whom she had purchased from Lewis C. Hutchinson, the white father of her child.[22]

After Leucy Hutchinson's death, Lewis C. Hutchinson declared that he was the natural father of her son, born January 4, 1836. Hutchinson became the legal tutor for his son and was authorized to manage Leucy Hutchinson's estate. Mitchell was appointed as Hutchinson's under tutor to ensure that Hutchinson did not waste the property. By August 1839, Mitchell had lost all confidence in Hutchinson. Mitchell filed a petition with the court asserting that Hutchinson was "totally incapable of administering the estate" and alleging that Hutchinson was insolvent and was "a man of wasteful, extravagant + depraved habits."[23] Mitchell argued that Hutchinson was trying to dispose of his son's property without the court's permission.

The court allowed Mitchell, a free man of color, to assert these claims against Hutchinson, a white man, and sided with Mitchell. By April 1840, Hutchinson had left town. Mitchell told the court that Hutchinson left the state to avoid criminal prosecution, and Mitchell was named tutor for the minor child. By then, Leucy Hutchinson's estate was valued at only $790.[24] Mitchell had taken his responsibility seriously and was not too timid to go before a judge to condemn a white man for his malfeasance. Mitchell's reputation in the community and the factual accuracy of his assertions caused the court to accept his arguments and to rule against Hutchinson. Mitchell was not as successful when handling his own affairs.

The Panic of 1837 and the years afterwards impacted everyone in the parish. The increased production of cotton coupled with a lower demand led to lower prices. With less income to spend, people in the parish were less likely to pay for new constructions or to pay for renovations. In 1843, Mitchell filed for bankruptcy. He surrendered the twenty-three acres of land on Woodville Road with its improvements, two ploughs, and a small stock of hogs to pay his debts. John C. Morris, a white merchant in Bayou Sara, purchased the property for $325 at the sheriff's sale. In 1844, Morris sold the property back to Mitchell for $756.82, payable in two payments: $372.21, due January 1, 1845, and $384.61, due January 1, 1846. In February 1846, Mitchell sold the land to Ann Maria Gray for nine hundred dollars.[25] Morris may have agreed to accommodate Mitchell by purchasing Mitchell's land at the sheriff's sale with the intent to sell it to Mitchell when Mitchell had the funds to redeem it. The land was valuable and could have been sold to someone else for a higher profit.

Mitchell's name did not appear in the 1850 census. By 1860, Mitchell was living in Bayou Sara with Clara Simms, a midwife born in Washington, DC. W. Leslie, a carpenter, and three carpenter apprentices, T. Cook, Alfred Piper, and M. Piper lived with them.[26] Mitchell continued to work. In 1860, Mitchell built Hampton Whitaker's China Grove Hotel and billed him for framing, shingling, flooring, columns, and handrails. He presented white plantation owner Pierce Butler a bill for twenty-six days of his labor at $2.50 per day for work done at Butler's house. He also charged for the labor of five apprentices, Thomas, Alphrable, Washington, Ephram, and Joseph, each of whom worked fewer days and earned less pay per day than did Mitchell. In 1861, white plantation owner Ann Butler paid Mitchell $1,159 on one occasion and two hundred dollars on another for work done on her house.[27]

Mitchell died in January 1864, leaving no known descendants or collateral relations to accept his succession and leaving no immovable property. His estate included two claims for work he had done and for which he had not yet been paid, valued together at $1,550.[28] Because he had no heirs, his estate representative was paid, and the remainder of his estate was turned over to the state.

Mitchell came into West Feliciana Parish already free. He brought with him skills he had developed elsewhere and found them useful in his new community. His talent and integrity went unquestioned, but his fortunes were tied to those of the community. When it prospered, he prospered; when it did not, he suffered along with it. He faced obstacles well known to any carpenter: getting business and getting paid for his work. As a master carpenter he left a legacy of apprentices who supported themselves and their families with the skills he taught to them.

Apprenticeship allowed a child to learn a trade or profession, but it also offered a safe place for a child to receive care when a parent was unable to provide that care. In 1841, Aggy Waltz bound herself for five years and bound her two daughters until age fifteen and her four sons until age eighteen to Simeon T. Newman, a white man, who promised to maintain and support them. In 1860, Milly Norrell apprenticed her children, Roy William (fourteen), John (nine), Elizabeth (five), and Fanny (four), to Francis M. Roberson, who was white. Roberson promised to supply food, meat, drink, and clothing and to pay physician bills and otherwise support the children.[29] These apprenticeships probably reflected the inability of these parents to provide for their children rather than the intent that the children learn a trade. The agreement did not specify the training the children were to receive, but it detailed the care they would receive. Poverty forced these parents to choose the food, drink, and lodging offered by an apprenticeship rather than see their children hungry.

In 1827, when Thomas Purnell, a white landowner from Maryland, planned to return temporarily to Maryland, he used the framework of apprenticeship to provide for his children and their mother while he was away. Mary Doherty, a white woman, accepted his children as apprentices until their majority and accepted their mother as an apprentice until Purnell's youngest daughter became eighteen years old.[30] In fact, Purnell's children and their mother were still enslaved and not eligible to become apprentices. Purnell wanted to protect and provide for them while he was out of the state and used the ruse of apprenticeship to create a relationship between them and Doherty.

Apprenticeship placements provided skilled workers for communities. Some of the free people of color who were skilled laborers in West Feliciana Parish may have learned their skills as apprentices. West Feliciana Parish could count three seamstresses and three barbers among its free-people-of-color population. Ann Maria Bouton and Ann Eliza Wilkins, both of whom came to Louisiana in 1818, were seamstresses. Bouton had been born in Baltimore, Maryland, in 1799. Wilkins had been born in 1813 in Edgecombe County, North Carolina. P. Carbour, who was twenty years old in 1860, was a Virginia-born seamstress.[31] Albert Prince, George Murry, and Norman Davis were barbers. Prince declared that he had been in Louisiana since 1818 and was "well known in the Parish as a well-behaved and reputable man, a Barber by training." Murry, born in Fauquier County, Virginia, had been in Louisiana since 1817 or 1818. He purchased himself in 1822 and was thirty-seven years old in January 1831 when he registered with the parish judge, as free people of color were required to do. Davis was twenty-nine years old on the date of his enrollment and had been born in King William County, Virginia, in 1802.[32] None of these seamstresses or barbers, most of whom were born in Upper South states, claimed to have been born free. It is likely that they came to Louisiana as a part of the domestic slave trade that sold nearly a million enslaved people out of Virginia, Maryland, and North Carolina for work on southern plantations. They probably became free after arriving in Louisiana.

Thomas Phelps was born free and lived in Annapolis, Maryland, before coming to Louisiana. He declared himself a shoemaker, five feet, six inches tall, thirty-five to forty years old, when he registered.[33] John Clay declared himself a brick molder by trade when he registered. He had been born in Feliciana Parish before it was divided into East and West Feliciana, was eighteen or nineteen years old, and could read and write.[34] The 1850 census of West Feliciana Parish listed seven free men of color who were carpenters, some of whom had been apprentices of Mitchell.[35] In 1850, carpenter John Purnell charged fifty-five dollars for making a coffin for Hardy Perry. Perry's estate paid Purnell for the coffin and paid him another twenty-five dollars that Perry owed Purnell for work Purnell had completed before Perry's death.[36] The 1860 census listed three other carpenters—W. Leslie, William Hendrick, and William H. Gray—and the three carpenter apprentices who lived with Mitchell.[37]

Although some free people of color in the parish were skilled laborers, many more were unskilled laborers. Some free women of color supported themselves with domestic duties. Betsey Kemper, Julia Kemper, Betsey Jackson, and Judique Lacour took in washing and cared for people who were ill. Lacour earned enough money from her work to purchase a home in St. Francisville in 1816.[38] At his death, Robert H. Hewit, a white doctor in the parish, owed Lacour and Jackson twenty dollars for nursing and attending to him in the fall of 1815 during his last illness. They were paid on December 12, 1816. On November 28, 1817, the estate of white attorney Walter McClellan paid Betsey Kemper sixteen dollars for washing clothes for three months, June 8 to September 8, 1817. On April 15, 1818, the estate of James H. Ficklin, a local white merchant, paid Julia Kemper $62.75 for washing blankets. On August 28, 1818, Betsey Kemper submitted a bill for twenty-eight dollars for various services provided to Ficklin during his last illness in October and November 1817. In 1840, Mary Maurice attended to the dead corpse of Kesiah Middleton and aided in cleaning her house. She was paid fifty dollars from Middleton's estate.[39] The 1860 census listed seven free women of color as washerwomen and one as a servant. It listed four other occupations for free women of color: dairy woman, midwife, cook, and gardener.[40]

William Chew, who purchased himself and his family members, was a drayman, as were his two sons, Wilson and George.[41] Chew also served as sexton at Grace Episcopal Church in St. Francisville and was responsible for the care of the buildings and grounds of the church. Two other free men of color—Henry Oconnor and Dempsey Turner—served as sextons for the Grace Episcopal Church.[42] C. Johnson and B. Muse were also draymen.[43] Other free men of color found work as handymen or field hands. Thomas Banks planted a garden and did some carpentry work for Betsy Archer, a white woman. Not having ready cash available, Archer gave Banks a note to take to George Mathews, a white resident of St. Francisville: "Sir, You will please pay Thomas Banks $8 + you will oblige yours—Betsy Ann."[44] Archer could expect Mathews to loan her the money to pay Banks because borrowing was such a common practice in the parish.

An unskilled laborer, Aaron Griggs, agreed to work on A. P. Walsh's Cecilia Vale plantation "as one of the hands" from February until August 1823.[45] Griggs was expected to go out to the fields at the same hour as those enslaved on that plantation and was to be paid eleven dollars per month. The work Griggs did as a free man was not very different from what he would have done had he been enslaved. Walsh, who was white, paid his overseer four hundred dollars per year, almost three times what Griggs would have earned if he worked all year. The overseer reported that Griggs missed twenty-nine days of work during that February-to-August period. On twenty-one of those days, Griggs was sick.[46] Griggs failed to show up for work on eight days when he was not sick. His labor was his own, and he could decide when and how to employ it. He lost pay for missing work, but he was not whipped, and no one challenged his claim that he was sick. Five other men—John Fogglemont, William H. Gray,

Occupations of Free People of Color, West Feliciana Parish, Louisiana

	Self-declared*	1850 Census	1860 Census
Domestic	1		1
Laborer	2		5
Drayman3	2	3	
Carpenter	1	7	6
Dairy Woman		1	
Washerwoman	2		7
Nurse			2
Servant			1
Midwife			1
Seamstress	3		1
Cook			1
Gardener			1
Housekeeper			2
Woodcutter			1
Waiter			5
Barber			3
Shoemaker	1		
Brick Molder	2		
Restauranteur	5		

*The 1830 statute, which required free people of color to register their free status, asked them to provide their occupations. Other occupations were discerned from their commercial interactions.

Caesar Bailey, John Sandy, and Paul Batton—were listed as laborers in 1850, although Gray was listed as a carpenter in 1860. John Tillotson was listed as a laborer in 1860; S. Meyers was a woodcutter.[47] These skilled and unskilled laborers provided needed services to their community.

In the 1860 census, two free women of color were listed as housekeepers. Each of them lived with a white man. One of the men was a clerk born in Prussia, and the other was a carriagemaker born in France. In a third household, a free woman of color, listed as a cook, lived with a white woodcutter, born in Louisiana. All three households contained mulatto children; none had a white female present. The census taker could have left the occupation of the women blank, as he did for the white women in households headed by white men, but instead, he chose to explain the presence of a female of color in a white man's household when no white woman was present by labeling her a housekeeper or a cook. He, nonetheless, duly recorded the mulatto children

Earning a Living

Map showing Bayou Sara lots owned by Nelly Wooten, 1853.

in the household, giving evidence of a probable concubinage relationship between the white male and the free woman of color in the household. The general acceptance of free women of color and white men living together as man and wife had ebbed by 1860. The census taker believed that some more acceptable explanation was needed.[48]

Five free people of color in West Feliciana Parish had significant success as restaurant and boarding-house owners. They were able to parlay their service-related training and experiences into proprietorships and, although owners of their businesses, stood in relationship to their white customers as cooks and stewards. Their roles were not incompatible with the expectations their white clientele had for people of color. White people patronized their businesses and were not threatened by their successes. Neither in 1850 nor in 1860 did the census takers list any free people of color in the parish as restauranteurs or hoteliers. This absence might have resulted from a personal disbelief on the part of the census takers who refused to accept the ownership information given to them or might have resulted from an official policy to demean the successes of free people of color by failing to document them. Other records provide details concerning these ventures.

Nelly Wooten operated a popular tavern and inn at the mouth of Bayou Sara Creek from about 1817 until shortly before her death in 1853. She initially rented the building but eventually purchased it.[49] Wooten's tavern served river traffic and plantation gentry. Wooten's restaurant and boarding house was successful enough that she was able to purchase eight additional lots in Bayou Sara and to buy a 220-acre farm where she grew cotton and corn.[50]

Born around 1787 in Virginia, Nelly Wooten was transported from her place of birth to what is now West Feliciana Parish but was then a Spanish territory. In August 1809, a white planter, Henry Stirling, sold Wooten to John Rous, a white merchant from Genoa, Italy, for eight hundred pesos. The 1809 sales document described Wooten as a twenty-two-year-old mulatto and reported that her eight-month-old son, William, was sold with her.[51] Wooten's older daughter, Caroline, was not sold with her. Wooten's sale was an isolated sale. Rous chose Wooten at the behest of his cousin and business partner, Antonio Nolasco, who also was from Italy. Nolasco's 1817 will declared, "he had never married, but that he had two children of color born to Nelly."[52] He clearly claimed Wooten's eight-month-old child as his own.

Rous, in partnership with Nolasco, operated a dry-goods store in Bayou Sara at the mouth of Bayou Sara Creek where it met the Mississippi River. Rous and Nolasco sold a broad range of everyday items, including flannel, linen, calico, cotton shirting, cheese, fish, gin, and candles. An inventory after Rous's 1811 death valued the goods in their store at $18,029.29, a significant sum in the early days of this settlement. Nolasco also transported cotton from St. Francisville to market in New Orleans in conjunction with James Nolasco, a cousin to both Antonio Nolasco and to Rous.[53]

Wooten may have been a fancy girl purchased for her potential to provide sexual pleasure to her enslaver. Such purchases were not uncommon in the parish. When white Dr. Warren Stone of West Feliciana Parish purchased Caroline, a thirteen-year-old, bright mulatto girl, for sixteen hundred dollars, her deed of sale read, "To have and to hold the said above-described negro girl Caroline with all the rights, titles, privileges, claims, and demands of and to the same belonging or in any wise appertaining unto the only proper use benefit and behoof of him the said Dr. Warren Stone his heirs and assigns forever."[54]

When able-bodied men were selling for eight hundred dollars each, Dr. Stone would not pay sixteen hundred dollars for thirteen-year-old Caroline, then send her to the fields to pick cotton or chop sugar cane.[55]

How Wooten and Nolasco came to know of each other and where they consummated their relationship is sheer speculation. Wooten may have been a house servant sent to pick up goods at Nolasco's store. Or she may have been chosen by Nolasco at Stirling's invitation from a stable of enslaved women available to visitors at the Stirling plantation.[56] Historian Emily Clark wrote, "Some slaveholders found a new vocation as pimps."[57] She reported that Hope H. Slatter of Baltimore, Maryland, assembled a group of teenage girls to transport to New Orleans for sale.[58] Wooten may have invited Nolasco's attentions as an alternative to those of Henry Stirling who may have fathered her older daughter. Perhaps, she wanted to choose the father of her subsequent children. Notably, once she became pregnant, Wooten convinced Nolasco that he had fathered her infant child. Her notice to Nolasco prompted him to send Rous to purchase Wooten and their child from Stirling. Rous brought Wooten and her infant to Nolasco.

In his 1811 will, Rous explained that he had been in New Feliciana for nine years. In addition to his partnership in the dry-goods store, his estate included the lot where his store and home were located, lot one in square one and a lot next door where the Nolascos lived, lot two in square one. Rous left one-quarter of his estate to James Nolasco and left the remainder of his estate to Rous's minor son, John Rous Jr. Rous asked that Antonio Nolasco be the executor of his will and that Antonio manage his son's property during his son's minority. Rous asked that John Stirling, a brother to the Henry Stirling from whom Rous had purchased Wooten, act as the guardian for Rous's son during his minority.[59] The Rouses, the Nolascos, and the Stirlings were well known to one another in this small community.

After Rous's death, James Nolasco joined his cousin Antonio in the dry-goods business. In October 1816, Antonio Nolasco purchased lot three in square one, next door to where he lived on lot two in square one with his cousin James Nolasco, Nelly, and the children.[60] In January, three months later, Antonio Nolasco died in New Orleans. In his will, Nolasco described Wooten as "heretofore my slave, now free, now pregnant." Nolasco explained that he owned Wooten's children, eight-year-old William, valued at $350, and five-year-old Marguerite, valued at $275. He directed that they be freed, and he left one thousand dollars to them to share. He left twenty-five cows and forty hogs to Wooten, and left Wooten the recently purchased lot three in square one in Bayou Sara. Wooten was already operating a tavern on the lot, and she developed it into a popular restaurant and boarding house. Nolasco left the remainder of his estate to John Rous Jr. and James Nolasco.[61]

James Nolasco died later that year, in December 1817. In his will, he asked that Nelly or Ellen Wooten, a free mulatto woman, be allowed to remain in the house she occupied on lot two until John Rous Jr. became of age. Nolasco left one thousand dollars to Wooten and divided the balance of his estate, leaving one-half to John Rous Jr. and one-half to Wooten's children.[62] On June 6, 1818, the executors of the Nolascos' estates confirmed Wooten's emancipation. Shortly thereafter, the estates of Rous and of both Nolascos were combined and were placed under the administration of James Turner, a white resident of West Feliciana Parish.

Turner was responsible for distributing the property in the estates according to the terms of the wills each man left and for managing the money that belonged to the minor child, John Rous Jr., who was attending a boarding school. Turner sold the property belonging to the estates, including lot two, where Wooten and her children lived. At the sale of the property, Wooten purchased a bed and other furniture and purchased an enslaved woman named Mary for four hundred dollars.[63] In accordance with the request in James Nolasco's will, Wooten was allowed to remain in her home, however, beginning in 1818, Wooten leased the lot where she lived from the estates of John Rous and Antonio and James Nolasco.[64] The lot was valued at four hundred dollars, and she paid her rent quarterly.

On May 22, 1819, Turner gave Wooten the one thousand dollars James Nolasco left to her and the one thousand dollars Antonio Nolasco left to her children. Wooten took an oath as tutrix for her children and bound herself to preserve their funds for their use. Charles McMicken, a white land speculator and merchant in the parish, was her guarantor. The act of tutorship, however, named as her three children Marguerite, born 1812, Gertrude, born 1813, and Antonio Nolasco, born 1817. William, who was eight years old in 1817, was not mentioned and may have already died. The 1820 census showed Wooten living with only one male child under age fourteen and one enslaved woman between fourteen and twenty-five. Neither Gertrude nor Marguerite appeared on that census. According to testimony in subsequent probate proceedings, Marguerite had been taken to Cincinnati and had died while there.[65] Perhaps Gertrude was with her at the time of the census.

It is also curious that Gertrude was not mentioned in Antonio Nolasco's 1817 will. Nolasco left money to eight-year-old William and to five-year-old Marguerite and noted that Wooten was pregnant. Wooten's son Antonio Nolasco was born in 1817. Gertrude was four years old when Nolasco wrote this will, but Nolasco did not mention her or claim to be her father. When his cousin James Nolasco died, James left money and property to both Wooten and to Wooten's three children but did not name them. Perhaps James was four-year-old Gertrude's father. Note that Wooten's children were known by the last name of their father: Nolasco. Wooten did not adopt that name. She continued to use her full name, Nelly Wooten, although it sometimes appeared in the public records as Ellen Wooten.

On December 29, 1821, John Rous Jr. died at the boarding school, leaving no known relatives. His belongings were sold, and the proceeds from the sale were added to the Rous Sr. and Nolasco estates under the administration of James Turner. Three years later, the combined estates were still under Turner's administration, and Wooten's children had not received any additional money. Wooten believed she had been patient enough. On September 6, 1823, Wooten filed suit against Turner claiming that, now that John Rous Jr. was dead, her children were entitled to the whole of the money Turner held.[66] Wooten asserted that because Marguerite also was now dead, she, as her mother, was entitled to receive the portion that would have gone to Marguerite.

The district court ruled against Wooten, but Wooten appealed. In 1828, the Louisiana Supreme Court recognized her claim and ordered Turner to give Wooten an accounting for the money he had handled. The court instructed Turner to give to Wooten, as tutrix for her children, all the money and other property left in the estates.[67] The law firm of Watts and Lobdell had represented Wooten in her claim against Turner. On August 20, 1833, the law firm filed suit against Wooten to recover its four-hundred-dollar fee. Wooten paid the fee on April 29, 1833, and the suit was then dismissed.[68]

Rather than deliver the money and other property he held, Turner resigned as administrator of the estates. Turner may have refused to dispense the money from the combined estates to Wooten because he objected to transferring funds from the estates of white men to a woman of color, or Turner, simply, may have been greedy. While he held the funds, Turner could invest them to his own purposes while charging a fee to administer the estates, a double benefit. Turner's resignation left the estates without an administrator. Wooten turned to John Morris.

On June 6, 1828, John Cosby Morris began to administer the Rous and Nolasco estates.[69] Morris, a white native of Dublin, Ireland, operated an upscale general store and kept a warehouse in Bayou Sara. He also bought, sold, and rented out real estate there. Morris's store carried goods that were more luxurious than those found in the Rous and Nolasco store. He sold slippers, white cotton gloves, calfskin shoes, diamond, silver, and gold jewelry, Irish linen, Irish whiskey, Spanish cigars, and fancy bouquet paper.[70] Morris so often sold on credit at 10 percent interest that he had promissory note forms preprinted for his customers to complete.

In 1828, Wooten cared for Morris while he was ill. Morris, a bachelor, may have lodged in Wooten's boarding house because he was too ill to live alone. It may be that, during this time together, Morris learned of Wooten's claim against Turner and agreed to take over the administration of the Rous and Nolasco estates. It is also possible that they knew one another long before Morris became ill. On April 24, 1829, after he recovered from his illness, Morris executed a document purporting to sell four enslaved people to Wooten for four hundred dollars: John, a black youth about fourteen, Lewis, a black man about twenty-six, Deck, a black man about twenty-four, and Sophy, a Negro youth about twelve. He was leaving the parish for some time and left these enslaved people in her care. He may have believed that their value would repay Wooten for the services he had received while he was ill. He wrote:

> Moreover, Should I never return, I give, grant, and bequeath to the said Nelly Wooten forever the above-named negroes and their increase warranted slaves for life. This I do in consideration of the debt I owe said Nelly Wooten, free woman of color, for my board, lodging, washing, and attendance during my sickness in 1828 and also in gratitude for the kind attention I received during the time of my illness. N.B. I also sell to said Nelly improvements put on her lot consisting of a 2-story dwelling house unfinished with the furniture I possess: chairs, bedsteads, bed, and bedding, etc. for $300.[71]

The note at the end of this writing indicates that Morris had paid to build a two-story building on Wooten's lot and had occupied one of its rooms. He may have paid the costs to convert her tavern and inn into a fancier restaurant and boarding house and may have been a long-term resident of her boarding house. Morris waited until 1841 to add a notation to this 1829 document. He declared in 1841 that he had paid his debt to Wooten and that the deed he executed selling the four enslaved people to Wooten was now null and void.[72] He claimed ownership of the four people held in slavery but did not negate the sale of the two-story dwelling house he had built on her lot. By 1841, the relationship between Wooten and Morris may have soured, or more likely, Morris felt that he had done enough to repay Wooten.

Morris returned to Bayou Sara sometime before October 22, 1829, and, as the administrator of the Rous and Nolasco estates, sued James Turner on

Wooten's behalf to demand an accounting of his administration of the estates. Morris succeeded in his suit, and it was Morris who finally gave Wooten the inheritance belonging to her children.[73]

While fighting for her children's inheritance, Wooten continued to operate her tavern on the lot left to her by Antonio Nolasco. Wooten's tavern was a highly regarded establishment. In 1830, Anne Royall, a white widow who had traveled from Washington, DC, and was visiting the southern states, arrived in Louisiana. She described Bayou Sara as a low swamp with a few houses, two or three warehouses and stores, and two taverns. She noted that one of the taverns was kept by white men and that the other, kept by Wooten, was better. Royal stayed in Wooten's establishment and recorded that the table was set for dinner when she arrived. She found her bedchamber "quite neat and comfortable with bars to keep out the mosquitoes." Mosquito bars, in use before window screens were available, held mesh netting or fine muslin that could be draped over a bed, window, or door to protect from flying insects. Royall was concerned when she saw no other white people around the tavern, but her steamboat companion who had arranged for her room assured her that she was perfectly safe there.[74] On May 19, 1838, the diarist and plantation owner Bennet H. Barrow took his wife, mother-in-law, and children to Bayou Sara and "dined at Old Nelly's."[75] His reference to "Old Nelly's" showed his familiarity with the restaurant and its owner.

Wooten's tavern was in a good location. As Bayou Sara grew into a bustling river town with retail stores, taverns, boarding houses, warehouses, and horse stables, its streets were filled with riverboat crews, travelers, merchants, cotton factors, and farmers looking for a place to stay and for refreshments to eat. The parish's cotton, indigo, and sugar cane were loaded from its docks. Passengers traveling the Mississippi River stopped to visit. By 1850, Bayou Sara was the largest port on the river between Natchez and New Orleans and was the commercial hub for a large rural area extending into Mississippi.[76]

Despite having been enslaved herself, Wooten readily purchased enslaved laborers to help her in her boarding house and restaurant business. In June 1831, she traveled to Hinds County, Mississippi, to buy Charlotte. She purchased Moses and William there in December 1831.[77] Surrounded by slavery, Wooten may have given little thought to her own personal history or to the plight of her daughter left behind, enslaved by Henry Stirling. Slavery was pervasive in West Feliciana Parish and deeply imbedded in the economy of the parish. Wooten was doing what other people around her had done. She employed the uncompensated labor of others for her own advantage.[78]

In March 1834, at a probate-sale auction, Wooten purchased another lot in the same Bayou Sara square for her hotel. She paid $68.75 cash at the time of the sale and promised to pay $206.25 in two installments of $103.12 and one-half cent each on March 18 in 1835 and in 1836. She installed a horse stable on this lot and may have transported her guests from the railroad station or from the docks to her hotel. She may have used a buggy to carry people and baggage up the steep hill to the town of St. Francisville. In August 1834, Wooten paid Morris three hundred dollars cash to build a frame house on a lot he owned next to her horse stable at the corner of Calle de Sol and Calle de Comercio. Morris wrote, "said lot I bargain and sell for the full term of her natural life."[79] Wooten would own the house but not the lot, however, she could use the property for the rest of her life. The transaction was dated August 1, 1834, but it was not filed in the conveyance records until March 15, 1850, two months after Morris's death. By filing the document in the conveyance records, Wooten hoped to be protected from eviction by Morris's heirs.

In June 1836, Wooten purchased another lot from Morris for one thousand dollars. This lot was two blocks away from her restaurant and had a dwelling house and other improvements on it. Wooten paid Morris one hundred dollars in cash June 14, 1836, and promised annual payments of three hundred dollars at 10 percent interest due on June 27 each year until 1839.[80] It is not clear how she used this building to generate income, whether as rental property or to operate another tavern. She did not move onto the property but continued to live next door to her restaurant and hotel.

In 1840, Wooten purchased Willis and Easter from Harrison Jordan, a white resident of Williamson County, Tennessee, who was probably a regular trader in enslaved people. The very next month, she purchased her granddaughter Margaret and Margaret's son Augustine from Mary Stirling, the widow of Henry Stirling, her former owner.[81] In 1809, when Rous purchased Wooten and her eight-month-old son, William, from Henry Stirling, Caroline, Wooten's daughter, was left behind. Margaret was Caroline's daughter, and Augustine was Caroline's grandson. Wooten took Margaret and Augustine to Cincinnati to free them there. By 1840, people freed in the state could not remain in the state, but they could return to Louisiana if they were freed in a state that did not permit slavery.[82]

In March 1841, Wooten purchased three more lots in Bayou Sara for three thousand dollars cash. She had not yet learned to sign her name and continued to make her mark. Again, it is not known to what purpose she put these lots. Wooten now owned lots in square one, square thirteen, and square twenty-seven, all in Bayou Sara. On March 9, 1842, Nelly Wooten bought 220 acres on the waters of Bayou Sara south of the bayou for $3,500. Her vendor, again, was John C. Morris who had paid $3,300 for the land when he purchased it on January 18, 1841.[83] To pay for the land, Wooten gave Morris a two-thousand-dollar promissory note originally issued by Andrew Skillman and made payable to Ira Smith, two white men. Ira Smith endorsed the note to Wooten. Wooten now endorsed the note to Morris. Skillman's promissory note passed from one hand to another as if it were cash. In addition, Wooten gave her own promissory note payable to Morris and due in twelve months for the remaining fifteen hundred dollars of the purchase price. In these transactions, Wooten was participating in the credit economy of the parish, giving and receiving promissory notes along with cash to make purchases. She was passing notes and incurring debts like the other members of her community.

On her 220 acres, Wooten grew cotton and corn. From February 3 to July 12, 1848, Wooten accrued a bill of $26.75 with James Rudman, the town blacksmith, a white man. He had put shoes on a black horse for her, sharpened her ploughs, and put tires on a wheelbarrow. Wooten also purchased large hooks and large nails from Rudman.[84] In January 1848, she hired Daniel Wicker, a white man, as her overseer. He worked until October 21, 1848, and when he asked for his wages, Wooten did not pay him. Wicker sued Wooten for $228.32 plus interest. He claimed that he had raised a good crop; the cotton had been ginned, baled, and shipped off, and the corn was rapidly being consumed by her farm animals. He asked the court to sequester her crop until he received his wages, and the court complied. Wooten paid him his wages, and the suit was dismissed on December 23, 1848.[85]

This was not the first time Wooten was sued to pay someone's wages. Twenty-four years earlier, Jean Gambo, also a white man, had sued Wooten for wages. He asked the court to seize her property and sell it so he could collect his pay. In Wooten's answer, she denied that she had any contract with him and claimed that his services were not worth more than the cost of his board and lodging while he lived in her boarding house. She explained, "She took him destitute and fed him, naked and clothed him."[86] The court ruled in favor of Wooten. Gambo received no pay.

In January 1850, John Morris, from whom Wooten had purchased so much of the property she owned, died at age fifty-four. The inventory of his personal property was valued at $27,029.23 and his real estate was valued at $18,810 for a total of $45,839.23. Wooten was among many local residents who owed money to Morris at the time of his death. Morris had never married. In his will, he left the use of three lots with their improvements to Thomas Jefferson, who he described as "a free colored boy," but Morris gave no indication of his relationship to Jefferson. He left the remainder of his estate to his white half-sister, Rebecca Harrison. Harrison did not live long after her brother died. Her husband, George Harrison, administered the property inherited from Morris for their children until the children became adults.[87]

In December 1850, Wooten and her daughter Gertrude Nolasco purchased from Harrison lot two in square one, where they lived next door to Wooten's hotel and restaurant. The lot had been owned by Morris before his death in 1850. Wooten and Gertrude paid four hundred dollars in cash and gave Harrison two promissory notes of five hundred dollars each for a total of fourteen hundred dollars.[88] Since 1809, when Rous purchased her, Wooten had lived on the property and had leased it in 1818 after the Nolascos died. Wooten may or may not have paid rent to Morris.

In March 1852, Wooten bought a slice of land seven feet, four inches by 120 feet next door to the lot on which her hotel sat: "Said line passing about two inches from the lower front corner of the said Ellen Wooten's hotel, running parallel with the vendor's line."[89] Apparently, her hotel extended beyond her property line, so she purchased a portion of the neighboring lot, seven feet deep, to correct that encroachment.

By June 1853, Wooten was willing to give up her hotel business. Her son was living in New Orleans, and her daughter showed no interest in running a hotel. Wooten sold Nelly's Hotel to William H. Glass, a white man born in Kentucky, for $3,500. Glass paid five hundred dollars down and promised to pay three thousand dollars in four installments of $750 each.[90] Wooten was again participating in the parish's credit economy She signed notes to pay in installments for her purchases and accepted notes to be paid in installments for purchases from her.

Glass was an experienced restauranteur. In 1851, in a newspaper ad, Glass thanked his community for their "gracious support."[91] In 1852, he had advertised his Oyster Saloon and Restaurant. It had a renovated room adjoining the bar room and offered oysters from New Orleans and the finest wines. In August 1853, Glass advertised the new furniture, beds, and linens in the Planter's Exchange Hotel, another establishment that he owned. Glass converted Nelly's Hotel into Glass House, and in February 1854, Glass advertised Glass House. He described it as a "new house, newly furnished, for the use of a family . . . kept in conjunction with the Planter's Hotel." He noted that a first-rate livery stable was attached. Nelly Wooten had established this horse stable in 1834. Glass proved unable to pay his notes, and Wooten's surviving children, Antonio and Gertrude Nolasco, sued Glass to collect on the unpaid notes. The property was auctioned off, and the Nolascos jointly reacquired the property in July 1854.[92]

Wooten had moved to New Orleans shortly before her death on August 6, 1853, and was buried in Girod Street Cemetery there. Before Wooten died, she sued John Morris's heirs for an accounting of Morris's handling of the Rous and Nolasco estates and to collect on a promissory note Morris had signed in her favor. She argued that more money was due to her children from the estates and that Morris owed money to her when he died. She did not live to learn that the Louisiana Supreme Court, in 1854, ruled against her. The court noted that Morris had filed a final accounting and had been discharged from his responsibilities as the estate administrator in 1830. Morris's account of the Rous and Nolasco estates specifically noted that Wooten had been paid. The court refused to reopen Morris's administration more than twenty years later.[93]

As to the promissory note dated January 9, 1846, the court accepted the defendant's argument that the note Wooten presented was a disguised donation to a concubine for which there was no valid consideration. Louisiana law prohibited gifts between concubines and paramours. The promise of any such gift would not be enforced by a court. In Wooten's suit, the court announced, "The evidence tends quite strongly to the conclusion that the relation of concubinage did once exist between the plaintiff and Morris."[94] This finding of a marriage-like relationship between these two unmarried people helps to explain the abundance of financial interactions between Wooten and Morris. Morris may have acted as an intermediary for Wooten, helping to negotiate a better price than she would get on her own, or he may have purchased the properties and transferred their ownership to Wooten without accepting any payment from her. The transactions in the conveyance records may represent gifts from Morris to Wooten disguised as sales or may accurately report purchases for which Wooten paid. The court noted that, according to the conveyance records, Wooten had made payments to Morris for land purchases after the date of the note Wooten was now presenting. She could have offset the monies she owed to Morris for purchasing the properties by the monies Morris owed to her on the promissory note. Instead, she purportedly paid Morris for the properties, even though she held this note evidencing a debt due from Morris to her.

More than twenty years earlier, traveler Anne Royall had reached a conclusion about the relationship between Wooten and Morris similar to that of the court. Royall wrote that Morris was "smitten with her charms and her property, made love to her, and it was returned, and they live together as man and wife." Royall commented that Wooten was "the ugliest wench I ever saw, and, if possible, he was uglier—so they were well matched." She added, "This madam and her Irish gallant have an expression of horror about them."[95] Apparently, Wooten did not retain the attractiveness that caused Antonio Nolasco to send Rous to purchase her.

After Wooten died, Gertrude Nolasco, Wooten's daughter, appointed De La Fayette Stocking, a white dentist born in France, as her agent to handle her mother's estate. She explained that she was a resident of West Feliciana Parish, the wife of Emile Populus of New Orleans, but was separated from him and currently visiting in Brooklyn, New York. Gertrude Nolasco had married Populus on November 26, 1846, in West Feliciana Parish. They left the parish to live in New Orleans, but she returned to West Feliciana Parish while he remained in New Orleans. Gertrude's brother, Antonio, who also lived in New Orleans, asked to be appointed the provisional guardian of Wooten's property while Gertrude was in Brooklyn.[96]

The September 1, 1853, inventory of Nelly Wooten's property showed that she owned "Edie Place," her 220-acre residence just south of Bayou Sara Creek valued at three thousand dollars, and eight lots in Bayou Sara valued at eight thousand dollars. Her personal property, valued at $3,790, included mules, horses, oxen, cattle, promissory notes, a wagon, and cotton and corn. The fifteen people she held in slavery were valued at $12,600 making her total wealth at her death $24,390.[97] Wooten had transitioned from an enslaved woman to a well-to-do woman, who enslaved others.

In a petition filed after Wooten's death, Margaret Smith, Wooten's granddaughter, sought to share in Wooten's estate. Smith declared that her mother, Caroline, had been born to Wooten while Wooten was enslaved by Henry Stirling. Consequently, Caroline was enslaved, and Smith, a child of Caroline, was enslaved. According to Smith, Wooten purchased her and took her to Cincinnati to free her. Smith's act of manumission was recorded with a notary public in New Orleans. Smith claimed that she and Wooten visited one another frequently, and Smith felt entitled to a portion of Wooten's estate.[98] Smith's suit was not frivolous. Her mother, Caroline, had died while enslaved, but Smith was free when Wooten died. Louisiana's laws allowed a free child of an enslaved person to inherit from that person's parents, even though the enslaved person could not.[99] Smith could inherit from Wooten, although Caroline could not. Smith must have had difficulty proving her relationship to Wooten as it appears that she did not receive any of Wooten's property. Gertrude and Antonio E. Nolasco divided Wooten's property between them and sold it over the ensuing eighteen years. In 1858, when the Nolascos sold the lot where Nelly Wooten's hotel once stood, the hotel had already burned down.[100]

Wooten began her life enslaved. By the age of twenty-two, she had had two children by two different fathers. The father of her second child took her into his home and arranged for her to own and operate a tavern, which would serve to support and enrich her. Her role in conditioning him to commission her purchase cannot be known. Neither can we know how Wooten entered into a concubinage relationship with the wealthy merchant John Morris. Whether he came to her hotel and found her there or came to her hotel for her will remain a mystery. Conveyance records show property transactions, not romantic interactions. Those records show that Morris facilitated many of her property purchases. Because Morris left nothing for Wooten in his will, it is probable that Morris made lifetime gifts to Wooten. Those land transactions may have been gifts and not sales.

Wooten could neither read nor write, but she was proactive in securing her future. With her freedom after the death of the Nolasco brothers, she became the mistress of her own fate. She managed a well-regarded hotel and restaurant and managed a large farm. She left a substantial estate to her children when she died. Wooten was one of five free people of color who owned restaurant and hotel businesses in West Feliciana Parish before the Civil War.

From 1831 to 1842, George Douse owned an inn and restaurant north of St. Francisville on Woodville Road. Douse's Orange Hill offered three meals a day and could provide champagne, ice cream, Havana cigars, and brandy.[101] When he complied with the 1830 statute that required free people of color to register at their local courthouse, Douse declared himself "a free man of Colour, aged Forty-One Years, this 9th day of March 1831, of Yellow complexion, a mariner by trade, born in the City of Philadelphia, in the State of Pennsylvania, in the year Ninety."[102]

On May 25, 1831, Douse purchased three arpents of land on Woodville Road about three and a half miles north of St. Francisville. The land was bounded on the north by land he had purchased earlier and on the east and south by land belonging to Charles McMicken, a white land speculator and merchant. Douse used his land to construct Orange Hill, an inn and "house of entertainment frequented by plantation gentry."[103] Anyone traveling from Baton Rouge or St. Francisville would pass Douse's Orange Hill on their way to Natchez, Port Gibson, or Vicksburg in Mississippi. Where Nelly Wooten's inn catered to river and railroad traffic, while inviting all who would come, Douse's Orange Hill catered to a more demanding clientele, those who were traveling by road and the financial elite who could afford what he had to offer.

Douse's Orange Hill provided lodging for travelers and boarding for horses. It was a favored site for dinners, parties, and balls. A February 1836 letter to Lewis Sterling Jr., the white owner of Wakefield Plantation, mentioned two parties scheduled at Douse's, one of which was well attended and one of which was forthcoming.[104] The Feliciana Volunteers Fire Department held a July Fourth dinner there in 1836.[105] Diarist Bennet H. Barrow went to a ball there on April 9, 1839, and declared it "dull for want of good music."[106] Barrow noted, in July of the following year, "preparations for great doings at Douce's to day [sic] Barn dance" and commented that he would not go.[107] In 1840, he did attend "a party given by John Harbour at Douce's" and found it well-attended and very pleasant.[108] Barrow complained that people in the parish submitted to amalgamation in its worse form, but he was not reluctant to patronize businesses owned by people of color, even those with a yellow complexion.[109]

On July 5, 1831, Douse purchased "1 Negro Boy Named Simon for $550 . . . to be a Slave for Life," and on March 6, 1832, he purchased a "Negro man named Mike, aged about 50 years, slave for life, for $125."[110] Douse probably used their help in running his inn.

In 1835, Douse paid Charles McMicken five hundred dollars cash for about four acres of land adjacent to land he already owned. Then, in 1837, Douse purchased an additional 22.5 acres of land, also from McMicken. For this sale, McMicken required a mortgage on all the property Douse owned, not only the 22.5 acres Douse was then purchasing. Douse began the construction of a large building on the land, placing eighty-eight feet of brick pillars beneath it and adding a double brick chimney thirty-one and a half feet high. His bricklayer charged him for 3,850 bricks and three barrels of lime. Douse spent more than four hundred dollars for flooring plank, weather boards, shingles, and other building materials at the firm of Barclay and Tenney, lumber salesmen in Bayou Sarah Landing.[111]

Unfortunately, Douse incurred these debts at the wrong time. The nation entered a major depression in 1837 that would last for seven years. The price of cotton dropped precipitously, and as happened to Drury Mitchell, Douse's business suffered. Little money was available for expensive luxuries when more urgent needs could not be met. In 1837, Henry Baines, a white resident of West Feliciana Parish then living in New Orleans, wrote to his wife in West Feliciana Parish: "Chickens are very hard to get and expensive here, you had better send a few down by Douse and anything else you think of that would be of service."[112] Douse was known to travel with some frequency between Bayou Sara and New Orleans, perhaps to collect supplies for his restaurant, and was trusted to reliably transport the property of his neighbors. Douse might charge a little for transporting chickens and other things between Bayou Sara and New Orleans but could not charge enough to finish his new building. Scarce and expensive chickens were only one sign of the economic depression.

In November 1837, Ann Lobdell, the daughter of wealthy plantation owner Sarah Turnbull Stirling and the wife of wealthy lawyer and plantation owner John Lobdell of West Feliciana Parish, all of whom were white, wrote to her brother in New Haven, Connecticut, asking him to "try to be very economical." She explained that her father had a good crop, but it was selling badly because the prices were not high. She concluded, "Papa has some heavy debts to pay."[113] Douse also had some heavy debts to pay. With bank closures and bankruptcies, he had fewer patrons and had difficulty paying his vendors. Two of his vendors sued him. They alleged that Douse was "on the eve of leaving the state forever" and asked the judge to stop Douse from leaving the parish before he paid them what he owed. Douse did eventually pay these two vendors and their cases brought against him were dismissed at their cost.[114]

Also, in 1837, Douse hired an enslaved woman named Nancy from McMicken for twelve months. Douse agreed to provide her with clothes and to pay her physician's bills. His promissory note for one year of her services was due on January 1, 1838. When he failed to pay for Nancy's services, McMicken filed a lawsuit to collect. He asked for the costs due for Nancy's services and he foreclosed on the mortgage Douse had given him on Douse's property, including Orange Hill. Douse's nearly thirty-five acres with all its improvements were appraised at five thousand dollars. In March 1842, at the sheriff's sale, McMicken paid $2,300 for the land and for Simon and Mike, the two men Douse had enslaved. The sheriff noted ten other more recent mortgages that burdened Douse's property to explain the low purchase price for the land.[115] Douse had overextended himself, and when his business slowed, he could not meet his obligations.

Douse remained at Orange Hill even after his property was sold. On April 2, 1842, Douse sent a note from Orange Hill to Sidney Flowers Jr., a white customer, asking that Flowers pay Douse the $2.50 he owed for a bottle of Madera wine.[116] No longer landowners, George and Eliza Douse arranged to have Brisbane Marshall, a white man who bought and sold lots in Bayou Sara, execute for them an affidavit of their freedom.[117] Douse probably met Marshall on the Mississippi River when Douse worked on the steamboat *Brilliant*. Marshall had helped to organize the Bayou Sarah Steam Boat Company in June 1830 and may have been Douse's employer at one time.[118]

George and Eliza wanted documentation of their long-term Louisiana residency and wanted proof of their free status to protect them in the face of statutes designed to prevent free people of color from entering and remaining in the state.[119] George and Eliza Douse were aware of the ease by which they could be reduced to slavery, especially now that they were no longer landowners. In his statement, Marshall declared that he knew Douse had come to the parish as a free man in 1824 with his wife, Eliza Douse, and his two sons, John T. Douse and George P. Douse. He knew that Richard Douse, Elizabeth Douse, and Daniel Douse had been born in the parish since 1824 and that Amanda Douse had been buried on August 22, 1840, at age seven, at Grace Episcopal Church.[120] According to Marshall's statement, Douse and his family had not entered Louisiana after January 1, 1825, in violation of the 1807 statute that prohibited the entry of free people of color, so they were permitted to remain in the state. Douse died September 6, 1843, Eliza Douse died November 28, 1846, and the Douse children moved to New Orleans shortly thereafter.[121]

Enticed by his earlier mariner travels to West Feliciana Parish, George Douse moved there with his family to set up a first-class establishment for a wealthy clientele. He used his experience as a steward on a steamer to develop a popular venue for both parties and travelers. He knew which wines and cigars to buy and how to please his customers. His early success generated an optimism that led him to indebtedness and then to the eventual loss of his business. His failure was not due to bad service but to bad timing and overconfidence. Falling cotton prices led to a decline in his business at a time when he had just incurred a significant load of debt. The loss of his house of entertainment probably contributed to his death and to his children leaving the parish to seek opportunities in New Orleans. The other free people of color who owned and operated boarding houses and restaurants did so in the busy port town of Bayou Sara where Wooten owned her business.

Maria Wicker ran a boarding house and restaurant business on the Bayou Sara lot she purchased in 1845.[122] On May 26, 1842, at age thirty, Maria Battiste Wicker purchased her freedom and the freedom of three of her children, eleven-year-old Bettis, four-year-old William, and two-year-old John, from Daniel Wicker. The act of sale recited a "consideration of the sum of Twelve Hundred Dollars, cash to me in hand paid, the receipt of which I hereby acknowledge" but does not say who paid the cash.[123] Wicker may have moved the money from his right hand to his left. Or it may be that no money changed hands at all. The recitation of a dollar amount may have masked a manumission as a sale. An 1850 census taker recorded that Maria Wicker, Bettis Wicker, William Wicker, and John Wicker were still living in Daniel Wicker's household, as were two younger children, Rachel Martha Wicker and Benjamin Wicker, who had been born free.[124] The substantial consideration recited as payment for the emancipation of Maria and her children ensured that their freedom would not be considered a gift from a paramour to a concubine. This emancipation could not be reversed by Daniel Wicker's creditors or his heirs.[125]

In 1845, Maria Battiste purchased a lot in Bayou Sara. She paid $350 down and owed $350. To enable her to make that purchase, Daniel Wicker, her former enslaver and the father of her children, endorsed her note as surety for her payment. Battiste subsequently used his name, Wicker, as did her children. Daniel Wicker, who had worked as Nelly Wooten's overseer in 1848, died of yellow fever in 1853 at age fifty-eight. A notation in white Lewis Sterling's plantation diary recorded that twenty people in Bayou Sara died of yellow fever that summer.[126] Maria Wicker was left alone to care for her family. Her hotel and restaurant business provided their support.

By 1855, Wicker had earned from her business the $1,669 she needed to purchase her second and third sons, Albert (twenty-four) and Edward (twenty), who were then enslaved in New Orleans. She had appointed John Holmes of New Orleans as her agent to search for them. Holmes located them and had John F. Valentine of New Orleans purchase and hold them until Wicker could pay their purchase price.[127] Now that their price was paid, she was reunited with her sons as their enslaver. Wicker did not emancipate these sons. An 1852 law required newly emancipated people to leave the state within twelve months unless the state legislature allowed that person to stay. An 1855 state law would require Wicker to file a lawsuit against the state of Louisiana to secure their emancipation and post a one-thousand-dollar bond for each of them as security while she petitioned the legislature to allow them to remain in the state.[128] Wicker could not be sure the legislature would grant her request. Instead, Wicker gave her sons "full permission to hire themselves out, as servants or otherwise in hotels, on board Steam Boats or other places where their vocation may call them" and to keep any money they received from their work.[129] That was as close to free as she could get them and still keep them near her. Wicker did not want to again be separated from her sons.

In 1856, Wicker bought the lot adjoining her restaurant and expanded her business.[130] By then, Wicker was successful enough to act as a real-estate holding company for Ann Savage. In 1851, Savage had purchased six acres on the bluff in St. Francisville abutting the road that led downhill to Bayou Sara. In 1856, after she married Edward Purnell, she sold the land to Maria Wicker so that Savage and Purnell could leave town. Six months later, Wicker sold the land to De La Fayette Stocking.[131] Stocking would live there with Gertrude Nolasco until his death. Wicker had purchased land she did not need as a courtesy to Savage and held onto it only until she could sell it.

In 1857, having reunited her family, Wicker formally acknowledged her eight children: Bettis (twenty-seven), Albert (twenty-six), Edward (twenty-two), William (nineteen), John (seventeen), Rachel Martha (twelve), Ben Franklin (ten), and Andrew (one). Three of her children had been freed with her when she was freed, two had been born to her after she was freed, as she continued to live with and have children by Daniel Wicker, and two were her property.[132] The paternity of Andrew, born three years after Daniel Wicker died, is unclear. She may have claimed a grandchild as her child.

According to the 1860 census, four of Wicker's children worked as waiters. She was listed as a dairy woman probably because she kept cows to provide milk and butter for her restaurant. The census taker valued her real estate at fifteen hundred dollars and her personal property at six hundred dollars. Wicker's business survived the Civil War, and in letters to their nephew in Rhode Island, both George F. and William R. Greene, who were white, proclaimed their pleasure at eating at Wicker's Hotel. In 1866, George wrote, "Ate an excellent dinner at Maria Wicker's Hotel. . . . Maria is an old darky, and she keeps a first-rate house, and she thinks a 'heap' of us as William has stopped there so often."[133] In 1867, William wrote, "I left my baggage at the Railroad Depot and proceeded to the modest hotel of Aunt Maria Wicker's, which is a model of neatness and good living, and as we have been liberal patrons of Aunt Maria's (especially in my courting days) she always takes particular care of us."[134] William Greene had come to the parish many times to visit his intended bride and had eaten at Maria Wicker's restaurant during those visits.

At her death in December 1867, Wicker's restaurant and boarding house, including her cistern, was valued at $450. This post-war valuation reflected the damage the parish had suffered during the Civil War. Wicker had owned a twenty-dollar cooking stove, six cane-bottom chairs, other chairs, and three tables. She had a sideboard, a looking glass, straw carpets, a portrait of Henry Clay, an eight-day clock, a featherbed, a mattress, and a twelve-dollar bedstead. She owned a book stand with books and a pony, buggy, and harness. All this personal property was valued at $633.25.[135] She left behind four adult sons—William, who had moved to St. Louis, Missouri, Bettis, Albert, and John—and two minor sons—Ben and Andrew. Her daughter, Rachael Martha Wicker, had died at age fourteen in 1858.[136] Her son Edward must have also died.

In 1880, Albert Wicker was living on Custom House Street in New Orleans with his wife, Frances, who had been born in Alabama. His brothers, John and Benjamin, and his children, Maria and Albert Jr., lived with them. The three men worked on steamboats. The children were in school.[137]

Maria Battiste Wicker had children to feed. Although she did not voluntarily enter into her relationship with Wicker, she gave birth to his children and needed to take care of them. Watching her two sons being sold away from her and taken to New Orleans probably motivated her to convince Wicker to buy her and set her free, perhaps with a promise to stay with him afterwards. As an overseer, Daniel Wicker was not a wealthy man. Maria Wicker saw an opportunity to use her skills to better care for their family. After Daniel's death, she continued to work and was able to purchase the sons who had been sold away from her. Family was important to her. She took care of her children, and then after her death, her older children took care of her younger children.

Wicker's restaurant was next door to a restaurant owned by Henrietta Coleman. In 1856, Coleman, who had been born in Kentucky, purchased the lot next to Wicker's restaurant and built a boarding house she called Henrietta House.[138] Coleman's Henrietta House had seven guest rooms and two servant rooms. Each guest room had at least a bedstead, two mattresses, and an ewer and basin. Her Gent's Double Room contained a table, a sideboard, a lounge, a washstand, an armoire, a looking glass, two bedsteads, four mattresses, and a dinner bell. Other bedrooms held a foot tub, a looking glass, a washstand, chairs, a settee, a cedar foot tub, an iron wash kettle, a feather duster, a brush tray, an armoire, or a bureau. One had a pianoforte valued at twenty-five dollars. Coleman's Parlor Room had nine parlor chairs, a sofa, three rocking chairs, a what-not cabinet, an armoire, vases, a looking glass, five pictures on its walls, and a Brussels carpet and rug on the floor. Coleman's furnishings suggest the class of clientele she hoped to attract.

Henrietta House featured a dining room with an extension table and a variety of serving dishes, including soup tureens, goblets, a cut-glass fruit stand, a glass cake stand, sixteen cake pans, a preserve dish, and a cream pitcher. Its kitchen had two tables, a cooking stove, and a brass preserve kettle. A storeroom held a refrigerator valued at eight dollars. In addition, Coleman had seven head of cattle.[139] Despite the size and luxuriousness of her boarding house, Coleman was listed in the 1860 census as a washerwoman with real estate valued at one thousand dollars and personal property valued at five hundred dollars.[140] The boarding house, with its exquisite accoutrements, was clearly undervalued. Henrietta Coleman ran a first-rate establishment with many of the amenities expected at a fine hotel. In 1876, her hotel, perhaps the best in Bayou Sara, was selected by federal officials for the citizen interviews they held after a series of lynchings in the parish.[141]

There is no record of either Maria Wicker or Henrietta Coleman owning people, but Hampton Whitaker, who also owned a restaurant in Bayou Sara, did. On April 9, 1857, Hampton Whitaker paid two thousand dollars for lot twenty-five in square three in Bayou Sara with an existing hotel building on it. His hotel sat right on the Mississippi River. Whitaker purchased an enslaved woman named Louisa a few months later, probably to help him in his business.[142] Whitaker advertised his hotel in the *Pointe Coupee Democrat*, a newspaper printed on the west side of the Mississippi River, and in the *Phoenix Ledger*, published in Bayou Sara. He anticipated that customers would cross the river to stay at his hotel or would need a hotel once they came across. His January 15, 1858, *Democrat* advertisement read, in part: "The proprietor respectfully informs his friends that in addition to his Restaurant he has now established a first-rate hotel. . . . He is prepared to furnish gentlemen and families with comfortable rooms, and all the luxuries that can be had at any other hotel."[143] The ad ran again on January 30, 1858, and on February 6, 1858. His January 16, 1858, *Phoenix Ledger* ad promised: "This house will be found the most desirable in town for the convenience of families, having been selected expressly for his lady patrons."[144] Whitaker pitched his hotel as family friendly, an important characteristic in this river town of merchants and mariners. Ladies and children would find refuge in his rooms.

On January 1, 1859, Whitaker purchased the lot next to his hotel for seven hundred dollars. He expanded his hotel and made plans to leave it. Later that year, he leased the two lots and the building then known as China Grove Hotel to Jackson C. Banff for three years at the price of one thousand dollars per year. The lease allowed Banff, a white man, to operate the hotel while Whitaker lived elsewhere. For fifteen hundred dollars, Whitaker sold Banff all the furniture and furnishings in the hotel except the contents of the room Whitaker had occupied. In January 1860, Whitaker sold his enslaved man, twenty-three-year-old Wilson, for sixteen hundred dollars. In March 1860, he gave a power of attorney to William Leake, a white attorney in the parish, to collect his rent, to sell the property if there was a buyer, and to collect the insurance on the property in case of a fire.[145] He sold Louisa ten days later.[146] Whitaker probably left West Feliciana Parish immediately thereafter. The parish had become increasingly hostile to people of color. Having left Leake with the authority to collect his rent and to sell the property, Whitaker could move out of the parish and have his money sent to him.

Free people of color in the parish left records of other kinds of businesses. Jordan Ritchie was a merchant. When he died in 1835, he left behind sixty gallons of molasses, 394 pounds of pork, 853 pounds of lard, 152 pounds of wool, twenty-six deer skins, twenty coon and beaver skins, 530 pounds of bulk pork, 562 pounds of bacon, eighty-three sacks of corn, cooking utensils, and bedding. It seems that Ritchie brought this stock of goods with him from Woodford County, Kentucky, to sell in Louisiana and became ill in Bayou Sara shortly after arriving. He lived long enough to leave a will instructing his administrator to sell his house, free the enslaved woman he owned in Kentucky, give her the proceeds from the sale of his home, and help her to move to Indiana. He left the remainder of his estate to his mother and stepfather.[147] It is unlikely that Ritchie planned to move to West Feliciana. He saw an economic opportunity there and brought goods to sell there. Had he not died, he may have continued to conduct trade between Woodford County and West Feliciana Parish.

Kesiah Middleton participated in two different businesses, neither of which was a restaurant. On March 31, 1825, Antonio Piccaluga, a white man, purchased Kesiah Middleton for $450. He paid $220 in partial payment for her and owed $230 more.[148] Piccaluga operated a flatboat that served as a grocery store and boarding house for the local community and for travelers on vessels traveling up and down the Mississippi River. The boat had three doors and two windows and housed the shop from which goods and liquor were sold, a bedroom, and two back rooms for lodging.[149] Piccaluga probably purchased Middleton to help him in his business. Kesiah was a long-term resident of West Feliciana

Parish. In 1831, James and Thomas Fair, two white brothers, stated that they had known Kesiah Middleton for about twenty years because their mother had held her in slavery. That would place Middleton in West Feliciana Parish in 1811. Their mother, Sarah Fair, died in 1825. Fair owned only four people in 1820, three males and one female. James and Thomas Fair would know and recognize Kesiah Middleton. Middleton was probably sold in the settlement of their mother's estate.[150]

Piccaluga emancipated Middleton in 1827 and wrote in her act of emancipation that she was over age thirty and was now "authorized to act and demur herself as free persons are entitled to do agreeably to the Laws of this State."[151] Although she was now free, Middleton stayed in Piccaluga's household, but she did not bear children for him. In the 1830 census, Middleton appeared in Piccaluga's household as a free woman of color between the ages of thirty-six and fifty-five. Piccaluga's age was given as between forty and fifty.

Piccaluga died in 1833. In his November 1832 will, he declared that he had no wife, no children, and no living relations that he knew of. He left all his property to Middleton, noting that she had "rendered him important services, and [had] conducted herself as to entitle her to his gratitude and friendship."[152] He designated her as his sole and only heir. Middleton accepted his succession, which included the flatboat, with groceries and furniture in place, his household goods valued at $458.30, and a lot valued at fifty dollars.[153]

Middleton employed a white man, Samuel Stevenson, as her clerk to manage the flatboat's business for her and agreed that he would receive half the profits from his sales. When she asked him to provide an accounting to her, he refused. When she asked him to leave, he again refused. Middleton filed suit and obtained a court injunction that instructed him to leave. Again, the courts in West Feliciana Parish considered the merits of the case rather than the skin color of the litigants when reaching its decisions. Middleton had believed she could trust Stevenson. When she learned she could not, she trusted the judicial system to be fair, and she was not disappointed. In February 1834, Middleton sold the flatboat and its contents to Cecilia A. Thompson, a white woman, for eight hundred dollars.[154]

Shortly after Piccaluga's death, Im La Keep, a white man, sued Middleton for $179. Keep claimed that he had been Piccaluga's attending physician during his last illness, December 6, 1832, through January 6, 1833. Because Middleton was Piccaluga's only heir, Keep wanted her to pay the costs of Piccaluga's last illness out of the monies she received from Piccaluga's estate. Keep alleged that Piccaluga had stayed with him for twenty-seven days before his death and that Keep had provided him with food, firewood, pantaloons, and a handkerchief. In addition, Keep had seen to Piccaluga's decent burial.

In Middleton's answer, she argued that Keep had not been called to care for Piccaluga but had offered his services on his own accord. According to Middleton, Keep had come to see Piccaluga uninvited. He promised to cure Piccaluga and had promised that Piccaluga would not be charged for any medical care if he was not cured. Because of those promises, Piccaluga agreed to go with Keep to the rural area where Keep lived. Middleton admitted that Keep had permitted Piccaluga to stay in one small building belonging to Keep, a building that previously had been occupied by people Keep had enslaved. Middleton also admitted that Keep had provided one cord of firewood not costing more than five dollars to Piccaluga and had provided Piccaluga with a worn-out cravat not worth twelve and a half cents. Jonathan Ellsworth, a white man, provided testimony in favor of Middleton. Ellsworth had been present when Keep offered to care for Piccaluga and when Keep promised he would not charge Piccaluga if Piccaluga was not cured in five weeks. The court accepted the assertions of Middleton and Ellsworth and ruled against Keep for the medical costs, but it rendered judgment against Middleton for thirty-six dollars to pay for Piccaluga's burial.[155] Again, West Feliciana courts considered the merits of the case before them rather than the characteristics of the litigants.

It is not clear why Ellsworth was at Piccaluga's house when Keep arrived. Ellsworth and Piccaluga may have been friends, or they may have been business acquaintances. At the trial, Ellsworth testified in support of Middleton, a free woman of color, and against Keep, a white man, then remained in contact with Middleton. In May 1834, Middleton purchased a Bayou Sara lot from Ellsworth for three hundred dollars. She paid in cash. Two years later, Middleton and Ellsworth together purchased about eight unimproved acres of land on Cat Island in the Mississippi River near Bayou Sara for two thousand dollars. Middleton used her Bayou Sara lot as security for the purchase, and she and Ellsworth stretched their payments over the next two years. Middleton signed her name to the act. Ellsworth was a brickmaker, and Middleton became his partner in the brickmaking business. They lived together on their land, and their mortgage was paid in full by 1837. Middleton sold her Bayou Sara lot a few months later. She had purchased it in 1834 for three hundred dollars and sold it in 1837 to John Riley, a white man, for $850.[156]

In 1838, Ellsworth transferred his one-half interest in the Cat Island property to Middleton, making Middleton the sole owner of the property. In that same year, she became very ill. In 1839, with Ellsworth acting as her agent, Middleton sold the Cat Island property to Marcia Carmouche, a white woman living across the river in Pointe Coupee Parish, for four thousand dollars, double its purchase price five years earlier. Carmouche paid eight hundred dollars down and promised to pay eight hundred dollars each year for the next four years.

Middleton died without a will in April 1840 after a long and lingering illness diagnosed as dropsy. Mary Blackburn was paid fifty dollars from Middleton's estate for attending to Middleton's corpse and helping to clean her house.[157]

Three white men—Dr. Samuel A. Jones, who had been Middleton's primary physician, James Fair, the son of her former enslaver, and Ellsworth—each applied to become the curator of Middleton's estate. The court appointed Doctor Jones because his application had been filed first. Jones had filed as a creditor to recover money owed to him for medical care provided to Middleton. The court also appointed a local white attorney, Cyrus Ratliff, to look for any relatives of Middleton. The inventory of Middleton's estate included the three notes owed by Carmouche for the Cat Island property valued at $2,400, household goods and personal items, a Negro woman named Charlotte about forty years old, and a bundle containing Middleton's free papers.[158] Middleton had carefully preserved evidence of her freedom. Ellsworth disputed the inventory of the household goods and claimed that he owned some of the property inventoried as belonging to Middleton. The judge allowed Ellsworth to keep the property he claimed, recognizing that Middleton and Ellsworth had been living together and had intermingled their personal property.[159] That a white man lived openly with a free woman of color was not an issue of concern in 1840 West Feliciana Parish.

Ellsworth gave an account of the business partnership he had had with Middleton, sorting out what belonged to him and what belonged to her. He asked for reimbursement for the monies he spent on her behalf over the prior two years while she was ill. He had paid to send her to New Orleans for medical care and paid her expenses while she was there. Samuel Vanderhoofs, a white associate of Ellsworth, testified in support of Ellsworth's claims. He said that he knew Ellsworth and Middleton had been business partners and that he agreed with Ellsworth's business accounting.[160] Thomas Turner, another white man, testified that Ellsworth had lost a great deal of time from his work attending to Middleton during her illness. The testimony of these two men spoke to the entanglement of the lives of Ellsworth and Middleton. She was not a passive beneficiary of his largesse, but a companion and contributor to their joint success. Her property ownership supported their mortgage when they bought the property for their business. He cared for her during her subsequent illness. The community response to their relationship was not tinted by prejudice against Middleton because she was a woman of color.

Ellsworth had no difficulty finding doctors to examine and provide care for Middleton. None were dismayed or dissuaded from providing service because she was Ellsworth's business partner and shared a home with him. At the sale of her estate property, white people purchased sheets, towels, clothing, a parasol, and a chest that had belonged to Middleton. As in earlier estate sales, white people were not reluctant to purchase personal items that had belonged to a person of color.

Before her death, Middleton had been sick for two years. She had had three operations, and four different doctors submitted claims for the medical attention they had provided. Middleton's medical expenses consumed two-thirds of her estate.[161] After Jones, the estate curator, sold Middleton's property, collected the money owed to Middleton, and paid Middleton's debts, including those to himself, her estate was worth only $1,489.94. On July 31, 1841, Cyrus Ratcliff appeared with Hannah Bettis to claim Middleton's estate.

Hannah Bettis was a maternal aunt of Middleton. As her nearest relative, Bettis was entitled to the remainder of Middleton's estate. Bettis objected to some of the payments Jones had approved, particularly the one hundred dollars paid to R. H. Horn for, reportedly, consulting with Jones, and asked to receive Middleton's estate. Jones argued that Bettis was not free and could not inherit Middleton's property.[162] Bettis was required to prove her free status. She produced a copy of the will of John Bettis, her white, former enslaver. The will directed that Hannah Bettis be emancipated one year and six months after John Bettis's death.[163]

In 1847, the parish district court ruled that Bettis was free at the time of Middleton's death and could inherit Middleton's property. It ordered Jones to pay to Bettis $1,281.75, the value of Middleton's estate less a fee owed to Jones as curator of Middleton's estate, and to pay interest at 5 percent from September 10, 1841, until paid.[164] Jones did not pay. Instead, he moved to Caddo Parish, Louisiana, and Bettis had to locate him and then pursue him there to collect the money owed to her. Bettis's 1847 judgment was recorded in Caddo Parish on November 3, 1855, and Jones finally gave Bettis a mere $150 to satisfy her claim to Middleton's $1,281.75 estate.[165] Middleton had been dead almost sixteen years by then. Middleton's aunt, Hannah Bettis, showed considerable tenacity in pursuing Dr. Jones to Caddo Parish for her inheritance. Free people of color expected fair treatment from the state's courts and expected court decisions to be obeyed. Bettis may have settled for $150 because Jones could not afford to give her more.

Middleton did not have a choice when she was purchased by Piccaluga, but once she sold the flatboat he had left her, she had eight hundred dollars in her pocket. She could have caught a steamboat north and left Louisiana, but she stayed. Louisiana had been her home for most of her life, and she may have been reluctant to leave it. She may have already begun her relationship with Ellsworth and been reluctant to leave him. Ellsworth may have been anxious to use her resources as start-up money for his brickmaking project, or she may have suggested that the parish had a need for bricks and Ellsworth agreed to help her start that business. Her story is atypical in that she shared her life with two different white men and had no children for either one of them. Children had often been the catalyst for men to emancipate the mothers of their children. She produced no children for Piccaluga but was given her freedom anyway. The care Ellsworth exhibited in taking Middleton for medical attention and the fact that their personal belongings were intermingled suggest that, despite the absence of children, their relationship was not only a business relationship. Also atypical was the type of business she pursued. Most of the free women of color in the parish were seamstresses, restauranteurs, housecleaners, or washerwomen. Middleton had been a merchant and a brickmaker.

Middleton and Piccaluga purchased their acreage for their brickmaking business, but they probably used some portion of their property to grow produce. Although cotton, corn, and sugar cane were the cash crops in the parish, farmers also produced foods for local sale and consumption. Many of the free people of color who lived within the two towns had gardens and may have sold some of their produce to generate income. Free people of color who owned or lived on larger tracts of land outside of the two small towns were most certainly farmers, although none could be called a planter. None owned more than a few hundred acres, and none held more than a few people in slavery.

In 1821, Jesse Wilson bought more than five hundred acres. In 1824, he sold four hundred acres and kept the remaining one hundred acres. Caroline Perry owned one hundred acres valued at two thousand dollars. Ann Maria Curtis had 240 acres, which she sold in 1822 shortly before her death. Nelly Wooten owned 220 acres. Mary Ann Curtis owned about forty acres, and Ann Maria Gray owned fifty-three acres valued at fifteen hundred dollars.[166] Many of the people who owned sizable tracts of land held others in slavery.

Slavery was endemic in West Feliciana Parish. Both free people of color and white people saw the enslavement of laborers as an economic advantage and as a sign of social status. For free people of color, the enslavement of others signified their allegiance to the slaveholding culture and protected them from the suspicion that they would support a slave rebellion. It also helped to augment their incomes.[167] The presence of enslaved laborers in the households of large landowners suggests that crops were grown for sale, not just for consumption. In 1839, Ann Maria Gray acquired fifteen people from the father of her children. They had been mortgaged by Gray, so she lost them to his creditors after his death, but she benefited from their labor up until that time.

In 1845, Ann Maria Gray's daughter, Josephine Gray, traveled to New Orleans to purchase Betsey, aged about thirty, from a regular trader in enslaved people. According to the record of her sale, Betsey only recently had been introduced into the state. In 1848, Ann Maria Gray purchased twenty-five-year-old Mary Ann from the same trader. Josephine Gray signed as a witness for that sale. In 1850, Josephine Gray bought an enslaved fourteen-year-old for herself.[168] In 1833, Norman Davis purchased twelve-year-old Rhody, and in 1835, he bought thirteen-year-old Titus. He would later buy ten acres of land on the Mississippi River.[169]

Elsey Scott, the laundress who moved into the parish from New Orleans, owned two enslaved people. Thirty-year-old Dorcas may have helped Scott in her laundry business. Scott sold Dorcas in 1833 on the same day that Scott bought five acres of land on Woodville Road. Scott may have used the money from Dorcas's sale to pay for her land. In 1840, when Scott sold forty-five-year-old Dicey, she also sold her five acres of land to the West Feliciana Rail Road Banking Company. Dicey had probably helped Scott enhance the value of her property from its six-hundred-dollar purchase price to its $2,500 sales price and was rewarded by being sold to another enslaver.[170]

Caroline Perry bought and sold men, women, and children from 1844 until 1857.[171] In 1850, when Hardy Perry sold one hundred acres of his property to Caroline Perry, he exchanged the land, in part, "for the hire of her three negroes, viz: Mary, Olivia, and Handy, for 6 years."[172] In addition to selling her the land, Hardy Perry gave Caroline five more enslaved people.[173] Caroline had been enslaved but was now an enslaver.

Other free people of color bought and sold enslaved people. In 1837, Leucy Hutchinson purchased Bob and Charlotte, both twenty-four years old. In 1838, George Britton sold Dave to Mary Ann Britton, a white woman. She held onto him for only two years before selling him in 1840. In 1848, when Catherine Collins purchased a lot in Bayou Sara, she paid for it with a fifteen-year-old, enslaved female valued at $450 and a promissory note for $79.88.[174] Free people of color, even those who themselves had been enslaved, took advantage of the unpaid labor and enhanced status that the ownership of others brought to them.

West Feliciana Parish provided ample opportunities for both entrepreneurialism and employment as it grew rapidly in the early nineteenth century. Free people of color had a variety of options when choosing how to make their living. White residents of the parish showed no reluctance to patronize or purchase businesses owned by free people of color, and there was no apparent concern that a white man and a black woman owned a business together. As historian Warren E. Milteer Jr. pointed out, free people of color were important to their community's economy wherever they lived.[175] Skin color was less important to acquisition decisions than what the seller had to offer.

West Feliciana Parish provided an environment in which people of color could flourish. The color of their skin was not a barrier to their success. Despite the discriminatory laws intended to make free people of color feel unequal to white people, free people of color found their way. They may have learned a trade or engaged in an occupation or may have worked as unskilled laborers or washerwomen. Apprenticeships for carpentry seemed readily available, although other, more lucrative opportunities were not. Free people of color found employment, purchased land to farm, or started businesses. They were able to contribute to the economic development of the parish and to provide needed services while caring for themselves.

While their businesses grew and their incomes soared, free people of color were dependent on the white community for customers. An insular economic community of free people of color could not be sustained. There were too few free people of color in the parish to support these businesses without white customers. Free people of color contributed to the parish community, and the parish community accepted them and their contributions. They found a place in the West Feliciana Parish community where they could belong.

CHAPTER 5

Black-White Personal Relationships

In West Feliciana Parish, prior to the 1850s, free people of color interacted regularly with free people raced white. Most of their interactions were cordial and respectful. They were friends and neighbors. They bought and sold property to one another. They borrowed and loaned money from and to one another. They helped one another. Historian Kimberly Welch wrote, "interpersonal relations of small communities presented free blacks with opportunities to be evaluated as human beings."[1] Free people of color were a part of their community.

In 1820, white plantation owner A. P. Walsh sent a servant to purchase a bull from Julia Lacour. In his letter requesting the bull, he asked Lacour how she was and when her husband would return to the parish from Washington, DC. Lacour sent the bull with the servant and, in her response, told Walsh that Reuben Kemper, her husband, had written recently and would be with her in six or eight weeks. "I am looking out for him every day. I am well at present and I hope that these few lines will find you the same."[2] The tone of the letter and the exchange of personal information transformed this transaction from a business relationship between a buyer and a seller to a personal exchange between friends.

In 1822, when Amos Hoe signed the promissory note as surety for Jacob Potter, a white man loaning money to another white man accepted a free person of color, who had formerly been enslaved, as surety on the loan.[3] Hoe's prior status did not dissuade James Calvin from making the loan.

In 1836, when Frank and his wife Nancy purchased their home in St. Francisville, they were not yet legally free. They paid cash and were identified as free people of color in the recordation of the transaction. That recordation did not show a last name for Frank and Nancy.[4] It may be that no one asked about their status when they presented themselves ready to purchase the lot. It is more likely that no one cared. So long as the institution of slavery was not challenged, free people of color and these enslaved people could conduct their affairs without the animosity that the color of their skin would later evoke.

Frank and Nancy remained enslaved homeowners until October 1838 when David Bradford, a white man, applied to free them from slavery. Bradford placed the required legal ads in the local newspaper, and no opposition was filed.[5] Between 1836, when Nancy and Frank purchased the lot, and 1850, when Frank Bradford sold it, Nancy died, Frank acquired the last name of Bradford, and Frank mortgaged the house and lot to Daniel Turnbull, a wealthy, white plantation owner.[6] In 1850, when Bradford sold his lot to Hannah Fouty, a white woman, Bradford reserved for himself the right to occupy the kitchen in the yard for the remainder of his natural life. Fouty purchased the lot by paying the one-hundred-dollar balance due on the mortgage held by Turnbull and by promising to take care of Bradford. Fouty's white husband did not object.

Relationships between free people of color and white people were such that Fouty's husband was not bothered by Fouty's promise to care for a person who had been enslaved just twelve years earlier. There was no clamor raised about a free person of color living in the backyard of the white couple. The Foutys and Bradford may or may not have been friends. They certainly were tolerant of each other's close company. In 1854, Fouty was ready to sell the property. She contacted Bradford, who had left Louisiana, to ask that he free her from her obligations to him. Bradford agreed, and Fouty paid Bradford fifty dollars for the release. Fouty sold the property to a white buyer for five hundred dollars shortly thereafter.[7] There was no stigma attached to the property, and Fouty had no difficulty selling it. Other transactions evidenced even closer personal relationships between people of color and white people.

In 1816, after his father died, Joseph Buatt, who was white, was apprenticed to be trained as a saddler and harness maker.[8] In 1835, he took $250 from Peggy Russell, who was then sixty years old, in exchange for her freedom. A year after purchasing her freedom, Russell bought two lots on Royal Street for three hundred dollars. She paid $105 down and promised to pay the remaining $195 over the next year.[9] In February 1840, when Russell wrote her will, she named her executors and asked that her estate be divided equally among her then living children:

Charlotte, as near as she recollects about 33 years old living with Thomas Hooper in the Parish of Rapides; Susan, between 32 and 33 and living with Archibald P. Williams in the Parish of Rapides; Marcus, a son about 30 living with a sister of Emile Dolton, deceased, on the Manchac . . . Adam about 27 living with William Chapman in the Parish of East Feliciana; also her two children Amy about 18 and Charles about 19 living with Mr. James Turner of this parish.[10]

None of Russell's children lived with her, and none of her children were free. She knew their names and ages and believed that she knew where they lived. She wanted to leave to her offspring whatever she had at her death, but the laws of Louisiana would not allow that bequest.

At some point, someone must have informed Russell that her enslaved children could not inherit her property. Russell was obliged to write a new will. Her October 1840 will revoked her earlier will and left her property to Buatt, her former enslaver. In exchange for the property, Buatt promised to care for Russell and her home and to make any needed repairs. Buatt agreed to provide Russell with "the conveniences of life" and to bury her at her death. Russell's children could not help her, and she could not help them. Their sale away from her severed the familial bond that would have provided for her care and for their inheritance. In her final years, Russell turned to someone else that she knew. Russell relied on Buatt to see to her needs, and Russell left to Buatt her property. Russell died a month after the agreement, in November 1840.[11]

Russell was not the only free person of color to leave property to a white person at her death. Julia Gardner's 1842 will left her estate to Amelia Maria Mumford, the white daughter of Capt. Robinson Mumford, a white landowner in West Feliciana Parish. Gardner had been born free in Salem, Massachusetts, and could read and write. She was placed under the protection of Joseph Pierce at age five and moved west with Pierce. At a probate sale in February 1835, Gardner purchased a house on a one-acre lot in St. Francisville. She rented the house to one white person and rented a portion of the land to use as a garden to another white person. It is not clear where she lived. She may have lived in Mumford's household.

When Gardner purchased the lot, she executed a note and mortgage for the property with Mumford as her cosigner. Some personal relationship between Gardner and Mumford emboldened Gardner to ask Mumford to cosign the loan for her. The details of their relationship are not evident from the records. Under the provisions of Gardner's will, Mumford's daughter would inherit the property at Gardner's death.[12] The bequest to Mumford's daughter may have been a condition for cosigning for the loan, or it may have been further evidence of the friendship Gardner shared with Mumford. Gardner died in April 1843, and her note was paid in full on July 28, 1843, probably by Mumford. Mumford had helped Gardner acquire the property, and Gardner reciprocated by leaving the property to Mumford's daughter. The Gardner-Mumford relationship was not unusual in a parish where free people of color often had personal relationships with white people.

In 1837, Elsey Scott purchased three improved lots in square two on Royal Street in St. Francisville. Her 1835 will left her property to be equally divided between her daughter, Josephine Matilda Scott, and Catherine Eliza Hall, the daughter of Nicholas C. Hall, a white man. Scott's decision to leave a portion of her property to Hall evidenced her close relationship with Hall and his daughter and evidenced her concern about the financial security of Hall's daughter. In 1842, shortly before her death, Scott changed her will to make her daughter, Josephine Scott, her sole and universal heir.[13] Catherine Hall had married into the wealthy Barrow family in September 1840 and had no need for Scott's property.

In 1837, Betsey Givins of Pointe Coupee Parish bought four acres of land, along with its improvements, located one mile north of St. Francisville on Woodville Road. In 1838, she sold a portion of that property, thirty-nine feet along Woodville Road and back 150 feet, to Simeon Chefer, a white man, and required him to enclose his lot with a good picket fence. Chefer was to pay one hundred dollars on January 1, 1839, and fifty dollars on January 1, 1840. Instead, in March 1839, Chefer conveyed the property back to Givens. In 1876, Givens donated these four acres to Mary Thornsberry, a white woman whose husband had been interdicted as an incompetent on October 11, 1870. In the act of donation, Givens wrote that she gave the land to Thornsberry because of the love and affection she bore for her. Thornsberry needed permission from the court to accept the donation because her interdicted husband could not give his consent.[14]

It is not clear how Givens and Thornsberry became such good friends. In 1876, tension between white people and people of color was very high in West Feliciana Parish. Their friendship, evidently, surmounted that tension. In June of that year, federal officers came to the parish to investigate the lynching of thirty or so people of color there. White men complained to these officials about the elected officials in the parish. Many had been enslaved a decade earlier and had not yet learned to read.[15] Yet, Gibbons and Thornsberry were friends. Like emancipation in the parish, personal relationships between free people of color and white people were just that: personal. Individual people made individual choices about who they selected as a friend.

In 1838, William and Ann Jones purchased a lot in square nine on Royal Street from the white, real-estate speculator Charles McMicken for $250 on credit.

McMicken did not require a down payment, a rare occurrence. Most sellers of land wanted some portion of the purchase price to be paid immediately, while the remainder could be paid over the next two to four years. McMicken asked for nothing. William Jones had been born free in New York. Ann Jones, his wife, was technically still enslaved when they signed the promissory notes for the cost of the property at 10 percent interest. In 1836, when Ann was seventeen, James Fair, a white man, had given her his name, Fair, and given her the right to be free at age twenty-one. This right to be free at some specified time in the future gave Ann the status of *statu liberae*. She was legally capable of receiving gifts of property from the date she became *statu liberae* and would retain her right to freedom at age twenty-one even if she were sold to someone else. In 1838, when she and William Jones bought the Royal Street property, she was only nineteen. William Jones signed his name; Ann Jones signed with an *x*. In August 1840, when Ann Jones turned twenty-one, Fair officially set her free.

In 1841, when the Joneses wanted to sell the property, McMicken facilitated the sale by arranging for a buyer from New Orleans and by ensuring that the sale, at $350, was at a profit.[16] This assistance with the sale, coupled with McMicken allowing the purchase without requiring a down payment, reflected a personal rather than a business relationship between the Joneses and McMicken. McMicken, a shrewd and successful businessman, took the risk because he knew Ann and William Jones as individuals.

Russell turned to Buatt, her former enslaver, in her old age. Mumford cosigned for Gardner, and Gardner left property to Mumford's daughter. Givens donated land to Thornsberry, whose husband had been interdicted. McMicken facilitated a purchase and a sale for the Joneses. Friends and neighbors, free people of color interacted with white people as people. They met, spent time together or not, asked each other for favors or not, looked out for each other or not, depending on their personal choices and not on societal mandates that separated people who might otherwise become friends. There was both a general practice and a general acceptance of personal relationships between white people and free people of color in prewar West Feliciana Parish. These friendships and others across color lines were documented. No doubt many more undocumented friendships existed. General acceptance, however, did not mean 100 percent acceptance.

An 1835 newspaper article reported that white attorneys John B. Dawson and Cyrus Ratliff promoted a resolution in favor of planting a colony for free blacks in Texas. The resolution sought a federal constitutional amendment that would authorize a state to expel any free people of color living within its borders and sought a federal appropriation to support the Texas colony. Both Dawson and Ratliff served as judges in the parish. They took this public position, although it was inconsistent with their personal decisions. They continued to conduct business with and for free people of color in the parish without reluctance or discrimination, and free people of color lived in their households. Ratliff's household included four free people of color in 1830 and two free people of color in 1840. He had freed Ann and posted a five-hundred-dollar bond for her in 1830 and appeared before Dawson in 1834 to record the birth and freedom of Ann's child, Andrew Jackson. Dawson's household included one free person of color in 1830 and none in 1840.[17] As judge in the parish, Dawson had received the registrations of free people of color required by the 1830 act and the acts of emancipation filed during his term of office.

The public position of Dawson and Ratliff on the presence of free people of color in the state did not alter their private treatment of the free people of color they knew or with whom they came into contact. It may be that Dawson and Ratliff asserted their public opposition to free people of color to further their political careers rather than because of any personal animosity toward them. Conversely, they may have wanted to distance themselves from the free people of color they did not know, although they were comfortable keeping close to them those they did know.[18] Relationships between people in the parish were personal. Political positions on controversial issues were not.

Personal relationships of a different kind were common in West Feliciana Parish. The institution of slavery, wholeheartedly embraced by parish residents, enabled the sexual exploitation of enslaved people. As historian Brenda Stevenson wrote, "Sexual contact between slave masters and their bonded female 'property' was a common practice in the Atlantic World."[19] By law, the body of an enslaved woman was owned by her enslaver, and he or she could send an enslaved woman to the fields, force her into a bedroom, or share her with friends. An enslaved woman could not reject the advances of her enslaver. She had no right to exercise consent and could neither say yes nor no to her enslaver's demand for sexual relations. An 1817 Louisiana statute prescribed the punishment of death for any enslaved or free person of color who attempted to rape the body of any white woman or girl.[20] No punishment for rape protected a black woman. A free black woman might successfully resist, although an 1806 law ordered free people of color to yield to white people on every occasion. An enslaved woman had no recourse. She was the property of her slaveholder, and the slaveholder's property rights were sovereign over her right to control her body. Many white slaveholders across the state fathered children with their enslaved women of color. Their acts of rape were not considered crimes under the then current laws.[21]

Ofttimes, enslavers felt entitled to exploit the reproductive capacity of their enslaved women and counted their offspring as the natural increase of their investment in the enslaved women. In 1860, of the 9,571 people held in slavery in the parish, the census taker classified 1,208 of them as mulattos, the children of sexual relationships between a white person and a black person, usually between a white slaveholder and a woman he held in slavery. The fathers who sired these mulatto children with enslaved women felt no compulsion to free their children. The census taker counted only fifty-two mulattos who were free.[22]

Some white fathers did free their children. Some also freed the mothers of their children. Lucy had been enslaved by Barthelemi Bettelany. In 1832, when Bettelany freed thirty-year-old Lucy and her two children, he explained that he had purchased Lucy with the intent to sell her but that the situation changed.[23] Bettelany had free rein over Lucy and could decide in what ways she would be used. Bettelany may have planned to use Lucy to give birth to children he could sell at a profit. Instead, he was now giving Lucy and their children freedom. Lucy and the children, aged fifteen and nine, would not be sold to benefit his estate. Instead, Bettelany allowed his investment to walk away free. Lucy may have played a part in changing Bettelany's intent, but the final decision rested with Bettelany. Between 1825 and 1842, twenty-three children of white slaveholders in the parish were freed by their fathers.[24]

A few white slaveholders created families with their offspring and the mother of their children. The parents of the children could not legally marry, but they could live as a family unit with their children. Stevenson wrote that the practice of concubinage was underestimated in the smaller cities, countryside, and frontier territories. In many small communities, men and women lived together without entering a formal marriage. Personal relationships between slaveholders and the women they enslaved did not usually begin as friendships. They reflected the authority the enslavers held over the enslaved women.[25] Law-school dean Camille Nelson called this "captured agency" and explained it as agency encumbered by socio-legal norms "calculated to result in submission" of that agency to those in authority. She wrote:

> The law's conception of slaves as an amalgamation of person and property thus not only dishonored their essential humanity and inherent agency, but also facilitated manipulation, coercion, compulsion, coaxing, and other forms of abuse. . . . Slave women were alternatively forced, coerced, or manipulated into practices that allowed the slave-owning class to appropriate the most intimate features of their persons for profit and pleasure.[26]

Enslaved women, who could not walk away, sometimes embraced the opportunity to benefit from a sexual relationship with their owner. They might feel that their sacrifice of themselves would allow them to protect their children or others they cared about from slavery. Some white slaveholders rewarded the cooperation of their enslaved mistresses with freedom.

Josias Gray had married twice but had no children from either marriage. His first marriage ended with his wife's death, and his second bride, who he married in Baton Rouge, refused to move to West Feliciana Parish to live with him. Gray fathered four children with "his Negro woman slave Ann Maria."[27] He freed Ann Maria and his children, publicly and formally acknowledged his children, and lived openly with them and their mother as a family.

On June 13, 1825, when Gray emancipated Ann Maria, he described her as "aged about thirty years, about five feet ten inches high, of rather a light complexion."[28] Maria had already given birth to two of his children and was pregnant with a third. After the birth of that third child, Gray appeared before the parish judge to say "there was born on the plantation of the said Josias Gray, known as Mulberry Hill Farm . . . on the 28th day of December last (1825) a male child named William Hargis Gray, the mother of whom, is, and was at the time, a free woman of color named Ann Maria."[29] In this document, Gray gave his name to William and asserted William's status as a free person of color because his mother was free at the time of his birth. On July 4, 1826, Josias Gray emancipated Thomas Hardy Gray, aged four, and Josephine Gray, aged about two, again giving them his last name. He acknowledged these "bright mulattos and children of a colored woman named Ann Maria" as his illegitimate children.[30] By acknowledging them, Gray gave them the right to inherit his property and the right to require him to support them.[31]

On August 4, 1827, Josias Gray bought fifty-three acres of land from his white neighbor, William Draughan, for $345 using three promissory notes of $115 each, the first due on June 16, 1828.[32] In November 1827, Gray transferred ownership of that property to Ann Maria Gray.[33] Ann Maria assumed Gray's debt for the property and gave a horse to Draughan valued at one hundred dollars in partial payment for the land. She issued a promissory note to Draughan payable in three months for $250. Gray used this act of sale to again acknowledge his three children, Thomas Hardy, Josephine, and William Hargis Gray.

Although she had been emancipated and was now a landowner, Ann Maria remained in Gray's household and continued to have his children. Ann Maria's fourth child, Virginia, was born August 4, 1828, and Gray acknowledged her as his child at that time.[34] The 1830 census shows five free people of color living in Gray's household: one female between ages twenty-four and thirty-six years, Ann Maria, two females under ten years of age, Josephine and Virginia, and two males under ten years of age, Thomas and William. The household also included two white males, one between twenty to twenty-nine years old and another forty to forty-nine years old, the elder of which was Gray.[35] Gray held 111 people in slavery in 1830. The presence of free people of color in his household did not cause Gray to reconsider his use of unpaid labor for his and their benefit.

On July 11, 1839, fourteen years after her emancipation, Ann Maria Gray purchased fifteen enslaved people from Josias Gray for thirteen thousand dollars: a husband and wife, both fifty years old, younger men and women aged ten to twenty-two years old, and three children, who were the children of a nineteen-year-old. The act of sale reported that the enslaved people were paid for in cash and by Ann Maria's services rendered "in the capacity of a housekeeper since her emancipation."[36] By reciting her position of housekeeper in his home, Gray confirmed that Ann Maria continued to live with him, although as an owner of land from which she could make her living and now as the enslaver of laborers with which to work the land, she could have supported herself. There is no reason to believe that any money changed hands in this transaction. Had Ann Maria been paid as a housekeeper for fourteen years, she might have earned three hundred dollars per year for a total of $4,200.

The thirteen-thousand-dollar payment recited in the act reflected the market prices of the people sold and acted to ensure that the transfer would not be deemed a gift. Louisiana law restricted gift giving between persons who were living together as a married couple while not married to one another.[37] A gift from Gray to Ann Maria could be negated by his creditors or by any relatives of Gray. A sale could not. In fact, the enslaved people Gray sold to Ann Maria had been mortgaged and may have had a net value—their value less the amount of the mortgage—closer to $4,200. The sale might have been a legitimate sale for a fair price. More likely, the transfer of ownership was a gift.

On November 6, 1839, Josias Gray and Ann Maria Gray together entered a declaration into the parish conveyance records regarding the free status of their children. They declared that Josephine Gray, William Hargis Gray, and Virginia Gray were the children of Ann Maria, a free woman of color, and were Gray's illegitimate children. They noted that William and Virginia had been born since the emancipation of their mother.[38] No mention was made of Thomas Hardy Gray, their first child, who would have been seventeen years old at that time. He may have died or may have been sent out of the state for education or training. The 1840 census showed Josias Gray was the only free white person in his household. Ann Maria and their three younger children lived with him, as did 138 enslaved people.[39] Despite freeing his children and their mother, Gray continued to acquire people whose labor he could exploit and continued to hold in bondage the children of other mothers. His emancipations were personal and not a refutation of slavery.

Gray died in 1842. His will had left a large bequest to his nieces and nephews and left the remainder of his estate to his acknowledged children. His estate included fourteen tracts of land, animals, farming equipment, and "valuable Acclimated Negroes . . . among whom [were] a carpenter, a blacksmith, other mechanics, and house servants."[40] His property, valued at between $128,000 and $130,000, was sold on December 19, 1842. Unfortunately, Gray's debts amounted to $163,000. Because he was insolvent at the time of his death, Gray's children inherited nothing from his estate. However, his will made clear that Ann Maria owned the fifty-three acres he had sold to her and owned the house that sat in his front yard. The fifteen mortgaged enslaved people Ann Maria had purportedly purchased in 1839 were lost to Gray's creditors.[41]

Like Gray, Thomas Purnell lived with the family he created with a woman who had been held in slavery. Born in 1798 into a prominent land and slaveholding family in Snow Hill, Maryland, Purnell came to West Feliciana Parish in 1817 with Thomas R. P. Spence, also a resident of Snow Hill and probably Purnell's uncle. On November 13, 1822, acting as attorney in fact for Spence, Purnell paid five thousand dollars for three tracts of land amounting to about 550 acres on the west side of Little Bayou Sara fronting the bayou. He continued to live in West Feliciana Parish, buying and selling land and people both as the agent for Spence and for himself until 1860.[42]

Purnell and Spence had traveled to Louisiana with Mary Martin, who had been born in 1802 in Maryland and who was enslaved by Spence.[43] In 1820, Purnell lived in Feliciana Parish with Spence and thirteen enslaved people. Two of them were women between the ages of fourteen and twenty-five, one of whom was Mary Martin. By 1826, Martin had borne Purnell three children: Matilda, born 1822, John, born 1824, and Mariah, born 1825. His children and their mother were the property of Spence, who did not plan to remain in Louisiana. In 1827, Purnell prepared to return temporarily to Maryland with Spence. Acting as the agent for Spence, Purnell entered into an agreement with Mary Doherty, a white resident of West Feliciana Parish, to provide care for his children and their mother during his absence. Doherty agreed to accept Martin and the children as apprentices: Matilda until she was eighteen or until November 1, 1840, John until he turned twenty-one on May 1, 1845, to be trained as a carpenter, and Mariah until 1843 when she would be eighteen. Their mother, Mary Martin, was conveyed to Doherty for a term equal to that of Mariah's so that Martin and her youngest daughter would be discharged together. The agreement required Doherty to treat them in a lenient manner, and it allowed Purnell to take them back if he heard they were being mistreated or if he gave six to nine months' notice of his intention to remove them from the state.[44]

This agreement between Doherty and Purnell affiliated enslaved people owned by Spence to a local white family but in a quasi-legal way. Free people, white or black, surrendered their freedom for a term to enter an apprenticeship, usually to learn a skill or trade. Purnell's family had no papers to show that they were free, so they had no freedom to surrender. They were, in fact, enslaved. Perhaps Purnell intended for people to believe Mary Martin and her children were free when they were not. Perhaps he merely sought to prevent them from being treated in his absence as the enslaved people they were. In 1830, after Doherty's death, her husband and son disclaimed all rights to Martin and the children. They acknowledged that the agreement with Purnell was an artifice entered into for the benefit of Purnell so that his children and their mother would be safe while he was away. Doherty noted that the children had since gone back to Purnell and had been emancipated.[45]

By an act dated July 27, 1829, Thomas Purnell, again acting for Spence, emancipated Martin and their children, Matilda, John, and Edward Purnell.[46] The act was not recorded until July 18, 1842. Mariah must have died before July 1829 as her name does not appear in the act of emancipation. Nor does it appear in the 1830 census record. The 1830 census showed two free colored males, both under age ten, and two free colored females, one under age ten and one between twenty-four and thirty-six years of age, in the Purnell household.[47] Edward, their fourth child, was born in 1829. Thomas Purnell and Mary Martin lived together as husband and wife until Purnell's death and would parent five more children: Sarah E., born 1832, Alexander, born 1834, Ann Maria, born 1836, William, born 1841, and Eugene, born 1843. John, Edward, and Alexander would become carpenters. Ann would become a schoolteacher and Charles Hatfield's grandmother.[48]

Purnell's open acknowledgement of his children did not make him a pariah in the parish. There was no stigma attached to his choice of Martin for his lifelong mate. He retained his status as a respected member of his community. Purnell served as the under tutor for the white children of Dr. Robert Duer after their mother died.[49] He endorsed a note for a white neighbor, Albert G. Howell, and paid it when Howell did not. Howell transferred one hundred acres to Purnell to repay Purnell for paying the debt.[50] Purnell still went out with Bennet Barrow, the white local diarist and owner of a neighboring plantation, and others to look for runaways.[51] His status as the father of publicly acknowledged illegitimate children of color did not diminish his standing in the parish.

On February 3, 1833, Purnell purchased 120.1 acres of land, about eight miles from St. Francisville, again acting as the agent for Thomas Spence. This land was adjacent to land owned by Purnell in his own name. On July 15, 1843, Purnell conveyed those 120.1 acres to Martin for six hundred dollars cash. Purnell had now arranged for Martin to become a landowner. As a landowner, Martin was less likely to be mistaken for an enslaved person and would have a place to call her own. Purnell probably provided the money for the purchase as Martin had been a housewife with no source of income, but the property was purchased in her name and was eventually sold in her name. Martin continued to own this 120.1-acre tract until she and Purnell moved to Baton Rouge in 1860. Purnell showed a similar concern for their sons. In 1851, Purnell sold a little over seventy-two acres to his two oldest sons, John and Edward, for $350. The sons bound themselves to reserve for their mother five acres of land from the northern corner of the tract fronting their dwelling house. Four years later, John and Edward sold the land to their younger brother, Alexander, for the same price.[52]

On May 23, 1857, Martin formally acknowledged her children to establish their legal relationship to her.[53] Because they had been born while she was not married, they were considered illegitimate, but they could be acknowledged. Only six of her nine children reached adulthood: Matilda, John, Edward, Sarah, Alexander, and Ann Maria. William had died July 21, 1850, of brain fever. In her acknowledgement, Martin noted that she was a free woman of color better known in the community as Mary Purnell. She and her children used the last name of the children's father despite the absence of a legal marriage or of his formal acknowledgement of the children. Their oldest daughter, Matilda, married William Hargis Gray, the son of Ann Maria and Josias Gray, on August 24, 1848.

In March 1860, Thomas Purnell and Mary Martin left the parish and moved to Baton Rouge. Martin sold her 120.1 acres to John J. Barrow for sixteen hundred dollars, and for $334, Purnell and Martin sold Barrow all their interest in the stock on the land, together with the mark and security brand used to identify the stock. Two weeks later, on March 29, 1860, Martin, purchased a sixty-four-by-ninety-foot lot on the corner of Royal and Europe Streets in Beauregard Town, Baton Rouge, Louisiana. The neighborhood around Royal and Europe Streets was like the neighborhoods in West Feliciana Parish. People of all shades of skin color lived next door to one another. Sarah and Ann Maria were still living at home in 1860 and moved to Baton Rouge with their parents. Purnell died April 23, 1861.[54] By 1870, Sarah had moved out and Alexander had moved in and was living with his mother and remaining sister, Ann Maria. When Mary Martin Purnell died on April 12, 1884, at the age of eighty-one, a newspaper article noting her death stated that she was a native of Snow Hill, Maryland, but had lived in Louisiana sixty-seven years, twenty-four of them in Baton Rouge. Her obituary stated, "No name, among our free colored citizens, stands higher than that of Purnell."[55]

Any sexual relations between a slaveholder and an enslaved woman were necessarily coercive at their inception, but Ann Maria Gray and Mary Martin continued to live with and have children by their former owners long after they were freed. Each of them owned land and could have chosen to escape their relationships, yet they stayed.[56] These initially coercive relationships, begun between an enslaver and his female captive, evolved into permanent relationships akin to marriage. These couples formed family units in which to raise their children and stayed together until death parted them. Emily Clark found in her research that white bachelors often coupled with free women of color for life: "Their attentiveness to the large families they created with their free black partners paralleled what was expected of contemporary white patriarchs."[57]

It is likely that Ann Maria Gray weighed her options and decided to stay with wealthy Josias Gray to enjoy the comforts he could offer to her and her children. He had provided for her well, had given her freedom and land, and had publicly acknowledged their children as his own. Ann Maria Gray had reason to believe that Josias Gray would leave some portion of his vast estate to her children as he had no other children. She could not have anticipated that his extravagant living would deplete his estate. Reflecting upon her options as she perceived them, and with a concern for the security of her children, Ann Maria Gray may have consciously decided to remain in a relationship with which she was familiar rather than risk her fate otherwise. Showy, flamboyant Gray may have been hard to love, but Ann Maria Gray knew she and her children could have been picking cotton instead. Her life could have been much worse. It presents an example of Camille Nelson's "captured agency." Ann Maria Gray made a choice between the options she believed were available to her at the time she made her decisions. She may have chosen differently had she visualized other options.

Mary Martin's relationship with Thomas Purnell was probably very different. Although Purnell was a substantial landowner, he was not a large slaveholder. The 1830 census reported that Purnell, who freed his family in 1829, held only one man in slavery. By 1840, however, the Purnell household held fifteen people in slavery.[58] Martin had traveled with Purnell from Maryland in 1817, yet it was not until 1822 that their first child was born. Purnell's care and concern for his family in placing them in quasi-legal apprenticeship positions while he was out of the state demonstrated his sincere interest in their welfare. That Martin and Purnell continued to have children and eventually left the parish together suggests a marriage-like relationship of mutual love and respect. Their relationship might have been coercive at first instance, but Purnell demonstrated a depth of commitment that was probably reciprocated.

Louisiana's laws prohibited marriage between free people of color and free white persons and prohibited marriage between all free people and those enslaved. These laws precluded couples like Purnell and Martin, who chose to live as husband and wife, from forming legal families.[59] Nonetheless, Purnell and Martin stayed together, and Ann Maria and Josias Gray stayed together, as did other black-white couples despite laws that would not allow their marriage.

Their relationships provided examples of the concubinage Brenda Stevenson said was underestimated in frontier communities.

Not everyone in the parish approved of these relationships. The diarist Bennet H. Barrow, who attended balls at Douse's Orange Hill and ate dinner at Nelly Wooten's restaurant, lived next to Purnell's property. In November 1839, he complained that his white friend Mr. Riddell handed "T Purnell's Mulatto boy" something to eat and invited him to join their group. Riddell's actions reflected the attitudes of many parish residents that free people of color should not be ostracized. Barrow allowed Purnell to eat with the group. He emphasized that only his respect for Riddell kept him from protesting Purnell's presence. Barrow was forced to accept that some of the other white people in the parish were more receptive to engaging in some level of social equality with people of color than he was. He lamented, "so goes this world."[60]

Barrow took other opportunities to vent his annoyance with mulatto children. In August 1840, Barrow recorded his encounter with fourteen-year-old William Gray, who had dared to pass through Barrow's land to visit with the Purnells.

> There is a great deal of talk through the country about abolition & yet the people submit to Amalgamation, in its worse Form in this parish. Josias Grey [sic] takes his mulatto children with him and to public places & and receives similar company from New Orleans, fine carriages & horses. . . . [Y]esterday Grey's [sic] son with two of his visitors from the city had the impudence to pass here & through my Quarter, on a visit to see Purnell's family. I ordered the Negros if they returned this way to stop them. . . . Alfred [enslaved by Barrow] suffered them to enter one Gate then shut both and had them completely Enclosed . . . dressed as fine as could be. . . . As I rode up to them with a stick in my hand, and asked how dare they pass here & through my quarter, I never [saw] anything humble as quick as they did, forgot all their *high breeding* and self-greatness. . . . I told them to take the road as fast as they could and never to pass this way again.[61]

In this one entry, Barrow expressed his discontent with talk of abolition, not surprising coming from a slaveholder, with amalgamation, with Josias Gray appearing in public with his mulatto children, and with Gray entertaining mulattos from New Orleans. He is unhappy with the fine carriages and horses they ride, with the fine dress they wear, and with their fine breeding. He is also angry about, and could do something about, the trespass across his land. It is not clear which of these affronts angered him the most.

Barrow had allowed one of Gray's enslaved men to use a short cut across his land to get to Purnell's land. Barrow was not willing to extend that courtesy to Gray's son. After chasing Gray and his friends off his property, Barrow hit

Gray's guide with a stick. Barrow bragged about his mistreatment of Gray and his friends, but nonetheless, when he wondered what Purnell's daughter would think of her suitor if she saw him trapped, surrounded, and afraid, Barrow respectfully referred to her as "Miss Purnell."

Two years later, when "Old Grays Mulatto family passed" by his property, Barrow "made my negro get as many horses as they could & gallant them from End of the Lawn through." Barrow gloated that his act of dusting up the Gray party of riders was "no doubt the greatest indignity I could have offered them." Although he was powerless to do anything more to discourage Gray from appearing in public with his family, Barrow was convinced, "they will never pass here again."[62] Barrow may have objected to the showiness of Gray traveling in public with his children, or he may have been just a curmudgeon who took pleasure in aggravating others.

Annoying the offspring of white men and their once-enslaved women did little to stop the tide of these relationships. Hardy Perry, a white planter, also lived as part of a family unit with a free woman of color. In 1842, Perry allowed thirty-three-year-old Caroline to go to Cincinnati, Ohio, to become free and to return to Louisiana "if she thinks fit."[63] Perry's note implied that Caroline was free to stay in Ohio or to travel to anywhere else, but Caroline returned to Louisiana, and Perry recorded her Ohio certificate of emancipation in West Feliciana Parish two months later.[64] In 1850, sixty-five-year-old Perry was the head of a household that included Caroline Perry, still age thirty-three, and a free child of color, Augustus Perry, age eleven. It may be that Perry sent Caroline to Ohio without her son, and her son drew her back to Louisiana. Perhaps she was not willing to abandon her child. It may be that Perry promised her land and enslaved people to work the land to induce her to return. In 1850, Perry sold one hundred acres taken from the north end of his property to Caroline Perry. He exchanged the land "for her service as housekeeper for me from August 1842, the date of her return from Cincinnati, and for the hire of her three negroes, viz: Mary, Olivia, and Handy, for 6 years."[65]

In addition to transferring the land to her, Perry gave Caroline more enslaved people: Ginny (age fifty), Boy John (mulatto, eighteen), Boy Clark (black, fifteen), Big George (black, twelve), and Boy Jacob (black, ten). Thomas Purnell, the father of free children of color, witnessed the donation.[66] Caroline Perry continued to hold people in slavery, buying and selling men, women, and children from 1844 until 1857.[67] In September 1858, she sold her land for fifteen hundred dollars to John Scott, a white, adjoining landowner. In January 1859, she left West Feliciana Parish and bought 165 acres on Bayou Grosse Tete in Pointe Coupee Parish.[68] Given the option to remain free in a state without slavery, Caroline chose to return to Louisiana, where she received gifts of land and enslaved people from her former enslaver.

Hardy Perry did not formally acknowledge Augustus Perry, Caroline Perry's son, as his son. Few white fathers in the parish formally acknowledged their children. Admissions of paternity were generally much more subtle and were often cloaked in other actions. On April 30, 1827, when William Hendrick took Fanny and her children to Hamilton County, Ohio, to release them from slavery, he described Fanny, age twenty-six, as mulatto in color and described her children as quarteroon in complexion. The label "quarteroon," or "quadroon," was affixed to the offspring of a mulatto and a white parent. By describing Fanny as mulatto and her children as quarteroon, Hendrick identified the children's father as a white man. In his act of emancipation, Hendrick named the children: "my colored girl Cintheana now aged three years two months," Samuel, between the age of eight and nine years, and William Augustus, two years old.[69] It is likely that Hendrick was the father of at least the two younger children, whose ages he knew with some precision. He may have sired all three children. When Hendrick used the word "my" in the phrase "my colored Girl Cintheana," he may have been claiming ownership of the child, but more likely, Hendrick was claiming paternity. Hendrick did not formally acknowledge the children as his own, but he hinted at their paternity in the document he drafted that freed them.

Fanny Hendrick adopted Hendrick's last name when she returned to Louisiana after she and her children were freed, but she did not stay with William Hendrick. In April 1829, Fanny apprenticed her son Samuel, then ten, to James A. Coulter, a white man, to learn to be a carpenter. Coulter promised to use Samuel kindly and to furnish him with good and sufficient apparel, board, washing, and tools, including pliers, a saw, a hatchet, and a compass.[70] In 1831, when Fanny registered as a free person of color, Coulter swore that he knew Fanny Hendrick had been emancipated since 1825 despite the record that her emancipation took place in 1827.[71] His error with respect to the date of her emancipation may have been due to her acting and being treated as an emancipated woman as early as 1825, right after William Augustus was born, despite her continued enslaved status.

As a free woman, Fanny Hendrick had two more children, May Thomas and James Edward Tillotson. She cohabitated with John Tillotson, a white man and the probable father of these two free-born children. In 1836, Tillotson donated the partial Bayou Sara lot on which they lived to May Thomas, still a minor child. Tillotson stated that he gave the lot and its improvements to Thomas in consideration of the friendship he had for Thomas. The gift came with the condition that Thomas could not alienate or encumber the property while Hendrick lived and that Hendrick was to manage the property.[72] Like Gray and Purnell, Tillotson provided a place for his children to live that was under the control of the children's mother. In case of Tillotson's death, Hendrick and her children would have a home free from the clutches of Tillotson's creditors or relatives.

In 1838, Hendrick's older daughter, Cintheana, purchased two lots in Bayou Sara two blocks away from Hendrick. She sold Hendrick one of the lots in 1842. In 1844, Hendrick purchased an additional lot near her home.[73] It is not clear to what use Hendrick put these lots, but it is likely she put them to some commercial use in this busy port town. She continued to live on the partial lot Tillotson had given to Thomas. By July 1849, May Thomas had died. The lot Tillotson had gifted to her reverted back to him. He then sold the lot to Hendrick for twenty-five dollars but reserved for himself "the use and enjoyment of a room in the building" for the rest of his life.[74] Like Gray and Purnell, Tillotson lived openly with his children and their mother.

In November 1849, Tillotson donated an adjacent lot to his son, James Tillotson, also then still a minor. The donation was given "in consideration of the natural love and affection he bears towards his son" and came with the condition that Hendrick and her children would keep and nurse John Tillotson "in his days of sickness."[75] With her purchases and this donation from Tillotson, Hendrick now owned or controlled three contiguous lots and another lot some distance away, all in Bayou Sara. Tillotson never formally acknowledged his children, but he lived with them, provided for them, and expected them to care for him in his old age.

Tillotson and Perry likely had less confidence in their relationships than Gray or Purnell had with the mothers of their children. Tillotson reserved a room for himself in his donation of the property and required, as a condition for the gift, that his son care for him in his old age. Perry held Caroline's child in Louisiana when she traveled to Ohio to become free. Gray and Purnell did not feel a need to coerce further cooperation. The mothers of their children envisioned no other options. All four men lived with their children and their children's mothers as family. Their open cohabitation suggests a general, even if not universal, acceptance of intimate relationships between white men and free women of color in West Feliciana Parish.

Other mulatto children lived in households headed by white men. The 1850 census was the first to record the skin color of members of each household, whether white, black, or mulatto. Previous censuses had only recorded whether people were free white, free black, or enslaved. At the time of the 1850 census, four households headed by a white man included mulatto children and no white woman. Daniel Wicker, Hardy Perry, and Thomas Purnell were joined by Henry Robertson, the father of a one-year-old child. Josias Gray had died in 1842. In three of those households, the adult woman was listed as black; in the fourth, she was listed as mulatto.[76] Apparently, these white men in West Feliciana Parish showed no preference for lighter-skinned women of color. The presence of a free woman of color with mulatto children and the absence of a white woman suggested a concubinage relationship between the white, male head of household and the free woman of color. Many other fathers left their children in slavery; still other fathers freed their children and sent them out of the state to boarding schools or to the homes of friends. Family units such as these were probably more the exception than the rule, even in West Feliciana Parish.

No West Feliciana Parish census report in 1820, 1830, 1840, 1850, or 1860 recorded a white woman living in a marriage-like relationship with a free man of color. Such pairings, however, were evident in other areas of the South. Warren E. Milteer Jr. has documented numerous relationships between white women and free men of color in early rural North Carolina.[77] According to Milteer, North Carolina did not ban marriage between people of color and white people until 1830. After 1830, white men cohabitating with free women of color were seldom bothered by policing authorities. Free men of color cohabitating with white women, however, were often charged with fornication, adultery, cohabitating without being married, or with bastardy for creating children from these unions. The men were often forced to place bonds to guarantee they would provide support for their children.[78]

Conjugal relationships between black males and white females were tolerated early in the nation's history. Only later did they become forbidden. According to Peter Bardaglio, interracial sexual relations were extensive in colonial America. He postulated that the commitment to white supremacy fostered the antipathy toward racial mixture.[79] Winthrop Jordan reported a 1731 case in which a carpenter, Gideon Gibson, moved from Virginia to South Carolina with his family. Gibson, a free man of color married to a white woman, drew attention from the members of the House of Burgess. The governor of the colony met with Gibson and investigated his reputation. The governor learned that Gibson's father and grandfather had also been free men of color, and the governor recommended to the House of Burgess that Gibson and his family be allowed to remain in South Carolina. The governor reported, "they are not Negroes nor slaves but Free people." He intimated that a Negro married to a white woman would not be acceptable to the state, but a person who had been free for generations transcended his phenotype and was acceptable despite his skin color.[80] The House of Burgess allowed Gibson and his family to stay.

Brasseaux, Fontenot, and Oubre found only a handful of liaisons between white women and free men of color in southcentral Louisiana, an area settled somewhat later than Virginia and the Carolinas. They remarked on the level of violence in reaction to such unions.[81] By the time Louisiana was settled in the 1800s, these relationships were no longer tolerated.[82] White males were free to settle with and have children with free women of color, but free men of color could not exercise those same opportunities with white women. The environment of freedom free people of color experienced in West Feliciana Parish had its limitations.

In West Feliciana Parish, white people and free people of color had both business and personal relationships of various kinds. While slavery raged in the parish, free people of color and white people made friends with one another and cared for one another. Societal taboos did not prevent their friendly relationships. Nor did taboos discourage white men who wanted to act the part of fathers to their children from doing so. Some slaveholders who had children with their enslaved women freed their children and took steps to provide for their financial support. Others did not. Some previously enslaved women were able to form family units with the white fathers of their children despite the laws that prohibited their marriage. Others were not. In West Feliciana Parish, free people of color could live in peace with their white neighbors. That peace was shattered as war approached.

CHAPTER 6

And Then the War Came

The environment that allowed free people of color to thrive in West Feliciana Parish changed radically beginning in 1850. Up until the 1850s, white people and free people of color lived side by side, regularly interacting with one another. That openness in the community dissipated in the 1850s and 1860s. Historian Leonard P. Curry ended his study of free people of color in 1850 because the last ten years before the Civil War were different from earlier years. Free people of color in the cities he studied experienced greater hostility after 1850. The United States of America acquired a vast expanse of land after its victory in the Mexican-American War. Northerners and southerners hotly debated the question of whether the new territory would be open to slavery. Free people of color undermined arguments in support of slavery.

Free people of color contravened the dichotomy that associated freedom with white skin and enslavement with any other skin color. Proslavery rhetoric presented free people of color as anomalies antithetical to the natural order, as obliterating the distinction between white people and people of color.[1] Support for the antislavery movement in the North and fear of its success led to greater repression of free people of color in the South.[2] West Feliciana Parish no longer provided a comfortable place for free people of color to live. The Civil War and the abolition of slavery exacerbated community tensions. In the eyes of most white people in postwar West Feliciana Parish, people of color who had been free before the war became indistinguishable from people of color who had not been free before the war. The war and the anticipation of war changed everything.

The Louisiana State Legislature meeting in 1850 added a new restriction to the freedom of free people of color. A March 1850 statute forbade free people of color from incorporating for religious purposes or for creating any secret associations. It revoked the corporate status of any existing organizations of free people of color.[3] Free people of color were no longer allowed to gather in organized groups where they might discuss forging opposition to their mistreatment. In 1852, Louisiana's legislature required any person released from slavery to leave the state within twelve months of their manumission, unless the legislature specifically permitted that person to remain. Newly freed people of color were not welcome to remain in the state. In 1857, manumission in the state was forbidden altogether. Self-purchase remained available as a pathway to freedom; escape was another.[4] These new restraints and restrictions carried the message to free people of color that they were not wanted. Free people of color in West Feliciana Parish heard that message loud and clear. Between 1850 and 1860, nearly 40 percent of the free people of color in the parish left. Those who stayed receded into the background.

In 1850, twenty-nine households in the parish were headed by free people of color; in 1860, only sixteen were. In 1850, thirteen households headed by white men had free people of color present in them; in 1860, only four did.[5] Many of the free people of color who owned property in the parish sold their property. In 1853, Henry Oconnor sold his six acres to a white buyer. In 1856, Ann Savage and Stanley Dickerson each sold land that they owned in West Feliciana Parish. From 1856 to 1859, the children of William Chew sold most of their land.[6] Free people of color were no longer an integral part of the West Feliciana Parish community. Their presence was no longer generally accepted.

Other historians of Louisiana's free people of color found a similar change in relationships between people raced white and free people of color in the 1850s. In the southcentral part of Louisiana, free people of color were treated fairly by their neighbors until the late 1850s when vigilantes, originally organized to rid the area of criminals, turned their energies to ridding the area of *gens de couleur libre*.[7] In New Orleans, large numbers of immigrants willing to accept work in low-paying, unskilled jobs pushed many free people of color into poverty, and many of those free people of color left the city.[8] As the country moved toward civil war, free people of color left West Feliciana Parish.

The flight of free people of color from the parish was part of an overall loss of population in the parish. From 1850 to 1860, the total population of the parish fell almost 12 percent, from 13,245 to 11,671. The population of enslaved people dropped by 10 percent, and that of free white people dropped nearly 18 percent. The largest drop in population, however, was among the free people of color.[9]

West Feliciana Parish Population Loss, 1850–1860			
	1850	1860	percent loss
Free People of Color	106	64	39.62
White People	2,473	2,036	17.67
Enslaved People	10,666	9,571	10.267
Total	13,245	11,671	11.88

Source: West Feliciana Parish Conveyance Records, Manuscript Census, West Feliciana Parish, Louisiana, 1850, 1860, ancestry.com.

A variety of factors contributed to the parish's overall population drop. Additional factors motivated free people of color to leave. The area was beset by yellow fever in 1853, 1854, and 1855. Flooding decimated Bayou Sara in 1856 when the levee broke. The financial panic of 1857 crushed many hopes and dreams. Landownership and the ownership of enslaved people became the privilege of fewer and fewer people; smaller farmers and merchants floundered. West Feliciana Parish was one of the wealthiest parishes in the state, but that wealth became concentrated in fewer and fewer hands. In 1850, 84 percent of the families in the parish held at least one person in slavery. In 1860, only 79 percent of them did. Inklings of class antagonism could be heard as smaller landowners became increasingly aware of their relative poverty.[10]

During that same 1850–1860 period, the national antislavery movement gained momentum and aggressiveness. The Compromise of 1850 admitted California into the Union as a free state but enhanced the Fugitive Slave Law to such an extent that kidnappings became commonplace. Outrage on the part of northern abolitionists fueled the sectional divide. Louisiana lawmakers acknowledged the problem by imposing a fine of one thousand dollars on any person who brought a free person of color into the state and claimed the person was enslaved.[11] In 1852, Harriet Beecher Stowe published *Uncle Tom's Cabin*, further galvanizing the antislavery movement. Newspapers in Louisiana reported on its commercial success. News that 150,000 copies of the book had been sold in London and that the book had been translated into German and Welsh might have stoked fears that the international community would soon condemn the South for continuing to hold people in slavery.[12] Slaveholders agitated to defend their property rights. The animosity white people directed at abolitionists spilled over onto free people of color who were made to feel unwelcome in the parish and in the state.

To defend slavery and to fend off class hostility, slaveholders focused attention on the differences between free white people who could envision improving their lot and enslaved black laborers who could not. Historian Roger Shugg explained how slavery in Louisiana staved off overt class hostility. White people in power actively associated slavery with skin color and kept lower-class white people ignorant of how government policies advantaged large landowners and merchants but did little for other citizens of the state. By attributing a value to whiteness, wealthy white people in control of the state created a basis for comradeship with white members of the lower classes that forestalled class hostility. Even the poorest white person could look with contempt upon a person bound in perpetuity to labor for another. Free people of color had no place in that dichotomy.[13]

Free people of color threatened white unity by demonstrating that white skin was often irrelevant to social or financial success. Most critically, successful free people of color defied the moral arguments used to justify slavery: innate inferiority. Slaveholders who argued that people of color were enslaved because they were intellectually inferior could not explain why, once freed, people of color thrived. Initially, Louisiana's white population was not threatened by free people of color with whom they might share a real or imagined kinship. They could attribute any success achieved by a free person to the white blood in their veins. They, therefore, took fewer real steps to frustrate the progress of free people of color. With growing class conflict, legislators, many of whom were slaveholders, subjected free people of color to increasingly discriminatory and demeaning laws to foster white unity under a banner of white supremacy.[14] In 1857, the *Dred Scott* decision from the US Supreme Court gave legal sanction to notions of white supremacy and tension in anticipation of war added to the discomfort of free people of color in the parish.[15]

Some of the residents of West Feliciana Parish had contemplated going to war to protect slavery as early as 1836. In 1828, the Army Corps of Engineers sent William Henry Chase, a white West Point graduate and a talented engineer, to fortify the Gulf Coast. In 1836, Chase wrote a letter to his father-in-law, Judge George Mathews, presiding judge of the Louisiana Supreme Court and a white resident of West Feliciana Parish, warning that the abolitionists were not prostrate but "crouching for another spring." Chase advised, "We of the South ought not to trust them, but to prepare for the worst, by urging [from the US government] appropriations for strong places of arms such as Forts, arsenals, navy yards, etc. on the South Atlantic and the Gulf of Mexico."[16] He suggested that the United States build another fort and a drydock at Pensacola, Florida, and that it deepen the bar and build a levee on the Red River at Alexandria, Louisiana, anticipating their benefit for a Southern defense. In 1856, when Chase retired from the US Army, he remained in Pensacola. In 1861, he accepted an invitation from the State of Florida to become a colonel in the Florida Militia. On behalf of the Confederacy, Chase demanded that the US Army officers surrender Fort Pickens at Pensacola, and when its officers refused, he refrained from attacking it. He had built it and knew it was impenetrable.

In 1837, Louisiana's legislators expressed their willingness to go to war to protect slavery. The Louisiana Legislature concurred with then governor Edward Douglass White Sr.'s message condemning the Abolition Society. It proposed holding a convention of slave-holding states to ascertain the best means to obtain respect for slavery and authorized delegates to agree to the use of force "if they must." The resolution insisted that slavery was authorized "by the positive enactments of the Federal compact, and by the stronger law of self-preservation."[17] In 1838, a resolution from Louisiana's legislature warned that "agitating the question of slavery" would "operate to the dissolution of the Union, and a termination of our present form of government."[18] It considered slavery a matter which exclusively belonged to local legislation and applauded those congressmen who walked out of the chamber rather that listen to a debate on the abolition of slavery. Legislators in Louisiana were afraid that the federal government would enact legislation that would end slavery and upend their property interests.

In 1844, a legislative resolution asked the senators and members of the House of Representatives representing Louisiana in the US Congress "to procure the passage of such laws as will effectually prevent our citizens from being despoiled of that species of property" and to request indemnity from Texas for enslaved persons carried away to Texas.[19] Louisiana's legislators were concerned about protecting the investment the state's citizens had made in enslaving other humans. They wanted Congress to be proactive in protecting slavery. Plantation owners relied upon the unpaid labor of others for their profits and were desperate to retain that advantage.

In early 1850, Louisiana's legislators authorized then governor Joseph Walker to send a stone to represent the state as a part of the Washington Monument, which was then under construction. Per their instructions, the inscription on the stone was to read, "The State of Louisiana, ever faithful to the Constitution and the Union."[20] The purported patriotism Louisiana's politicians asserted on the stone did not reflect the legislators' true convictions as they increasingly envisioned "the Union" as a threat to slavery. This inscription masked the prosecession sentiment present in the state and contravened the 1838 resolution that threatened disunion to protect slavery.

In the 1840s, Robert C. Wickliffe, whose father had been governor of Kentucky, married into the parish's politically active Dawson family and moved to St. Francisville.[21] In 1856, he became governor of Louisiana after serving in the state senate. He was a strong defender of slavery and advocated ridding the state of free people of color whose presence, he believed, undermined the institution.[22] It was during his administration that emancipation in the state was prohibited entirely. It was during his administration that free people of color were permitted to enslave themselves.[23] In his final message to the general assembly of the state, Wickliffe bemoaned the failure of state legislation designed to prevent free people of color from entering the state even though those measures had been quite effective. The number of free people of color in Louisiana in 1850 was 17,462 and had grown only to 18,647 by 1860, while the number of white people in the state had grown from 255,491 to 354,456 during that decade.[24] Free people of color were not moving into the state.

In this final speech, Wickliffe condemned the practice of allowing enslaved people to hire themselves out. He described that "pernicious custom" as "extending to them liberties and privileges totally inconsistent with their proper condition and good government." He continued, "The influence of such example on our slave population is most ruinous, and should be checked by the most stringent laws, made to reach both master and slave."[25] Wickliffe was willing to punish white people for allowing their enslaved people to exercise a bit of self-actualization. He wanted to throttle the few opportunities open to enslaved people to generate money to buy their freedom. The Louisiana Legislature had already forbidden the practice of allowing enslaved people to hire themselves out in St. Tammany, Washington, St. Helena, and Livingston Parishes, four parishes in the northeast toe of the state.[26] It was inevitable that Wickliffe's feelings about people based solely on their perceived African heritage would discourage free people of color from remaining in his home parish.

It is impossible to know whether the free people of color who remained in the parish supported the Union or the Confederacy during the war. Those who stayed kept their thoughts to themselves. Anyone who held pro-Union sentiments would not want to draw the attention of their neighbors. The economy of the parish was highly dependent on the slave-labor system. Most white people there were decidedly pro-Confederacy and anxious to help with the war effort.[27] In 1860, only three of the sixty-four free people of color in the parish were slaveholders. Gertrude Nolasco, Ann Maria Gray, and Josephine Gray held only a few people each in slavery. Many of the free people of color in the parish had been enslaved themselves and were unlikely supporters of the institution. It is probable that they hoped for a Union victory, but it was dangerous for them to say so out loud.

There is evidence to suggest that some free people of color in the parish were pro-Union. Two of the young men who grew up in the parish but left before the war did join the Union cause. Richard Douse, whose family moved to New Orleans in the 1840s, served the Union in Mississippi. After registering in New Orleans as a free person of color in 1859, Douse moved to Baton Rouge where he worked as a plasterer. On September 11, 1862, at age twenty-six, Douse, enrolled in the Louisiana Native Guards and was mustered into that military unit on October 12, 1862, as first sergeant, Company C, Second Regiment Louisiana Infantry, Native Guards, Free Colored.[28] In January 1863, Douse's Company C was sent to Ship Island off the coast of Mississippi, where it constructed batteries, mounted nine-inch guns, built bombproof magazines, guarded Confederate prisoners, and worked to maintain the post. It saw combat on April 8, 1863, in East Pascagoula, Mississippi, after raising a United States flag on the roof of a hotel. Douse received a glancing gunshot wound during the battle and carried a one-and-one-half inch scar on his right hand as evidence. Douse remained in the service and on duty until November 14, 1865, then returned to Baton Rouge and to his occupation as a plasterer.[29] His brothers, John and George Douse, died in New Orleans, John in 1856 and George in 1863. They did not serve in the war.

John Purnell joined the Third Louisiana Native Guard Infantry and participated in the Red River Campaign and in the Union siege of Port Hudson, a well-defended Confederate stronghold ten miles south of Bayou Sara. The Native Guardsmen attacking Port Hudson received national attention for their bravery.[30] John Purnell's younger brothers did not fight but expressed a willingness to join. After the Union Army captured Baton Rouge, Edward and Alexander Purnell registered for the draft into its service.[31] The Union veterans, Douse and Purnell, survived the war but neither of them returned to West Feliciana Parish, where Confederate sentiment had been strong.

West Feliciana Parish was an important center for Civil War activity. The West Feliciana Rail Road Company had completed its track in 1842. The twenty-eight-mile track running from Bayou Sara to Woodville, Mississippi, was built to ship cotton south, out of Mississippi. For the war effort, it could send food and other needed supplies north, into the state. It offered the Confederacy free transportation for military companies and free shipping for its war materials. Bayou Sara's Mississippi River port was perfectly located to receive war materials from the west for shipment into Mississippi via the railroad.[32]

Because of its port, Union gunboats arrived early in Bayou Sara. The Union navy had reached New Orleans in April 1862, and Union gunboats arrived in Bayou Sara shortly thereafter. Confederate guerillas routinely raided St. Francisville and Bayou Sara for supplies and shelled the Union naval forces when they found them stationed in the Mississippi River. On August 10, 1862, the Union ironclad ram *Essex*, patrolling between Vicksburg and Baton Rouge, came to Bayou Sara looking for coal. Her arrival coincided with the stockpiling of a considerable store of supplies that were to be shipped by rail to Confederate troops. The supplies had been sent across the river from Pointe Coupee Parish and had not yet been loaded onto the train cars. Union commodore William D. Porter seized the supplies as contraband of war. He took what he wanted and left a gunboat at Bayou Sara to guard the rest while he and his crew continued on to Baton Rouge. On August 23, when Porter returned to Bayou Sara, both the gunboat and the supplies were missing, and Union sympathizers in the parish had been molested. Union forces disembarked from the *Essex* and came under fire. Porter ordered his men back to their ship and directed that all the buildings along the levee be burned to remove any hiding places for the Confederate guerilas. Hampton Whitaker's China Grove Hotel was among the buildings destroyed. On August 29, 1862, Union forces were again attacked, so Porter had the rest of Bayou Sara burned down.[33]

On May 22, 1863, Union general Nathaniel Prentiss Banks unloaded his men at Bayou Sara on their way to Port Hudson. As they traveled south, these Union troops foraged in the area. They took what they needed from whoever had it. Confederate guerilas regularly scavenged in the parish for food and other supplies and sometimes engaged Union troops when they encountered them. On June 30, 1863, and on January 9, 1864, in retaliation for Confederate activity in the area, Union boats fired on St. Francisville, the town on the bluff above Bayou Sara, damaging many of its buildings. The port that had been so important to the growth of wealth in the parish found itself furnishing supplies for both sides of this divisive war and suffered destruction as a result of the war. The war was costly for everyone in the parish. By the end of the war, West Feliciana Parish was in dire straits. Two armies had lived off its land. The railroad locomotive of the West Feliciana Rail Road Company had been dismantled for its copper and other metals, and the railroad, run by mule power for a time, had become useless. Historian Lawrence Estaville explained, "its right-of-way was a mass of weeds and bushes; its bridges and crossties were rotting away."[34] War had left its mark on the parish.

Attorney Cyrus Ratliff, who had represented Hannah Bettis in her suit to claim Kesiah Middleton's estate, died in 1860. After the war, his son, C. Henry Ratliff, explained what happened to his inheritance: "The negro property was freed and stolen from the estate by the laws of the Federal Government. The personal property was stolen and carried away by the troops of the United States." The dwelling houses had been burned. All that remained was the land, the gin house, and a few "negro quarters."[35] When former governor and local attorney Robert Wickliffe asked for a declaration that white parish resident William Dalton was dead, he described the wartime environment in Bayou Sara:

> During and near the close of the late war, . . . William Dalton suddenly and mysteriously disappeared and has never been heard of since. At the time of his

disappearance, [he] resided about one mile and a half from the landing at Bayou Sara on the Mississippi River then occupied by the gunboats and other vessels of the United States. The Parish of West Feliciana, particularly the vicinity in which William M. Dalton resided, was alternately occupied by lawless bands of irresponsible bodies of men known as jayhawkers and many acts of rapine and bloodshed were committed.[36]

Wickliffe believed and sought to convince the court that William Dalton did not survive the war.

The free people of color who remained in the parish suffered along with their neighbors. In January 1864, both Drury Mitchell and George Chew, William Chew's son, died.[37] It is not clear if their deaths were war related. Mitchell was sixty-four years old and had lived in Bayou Sara; Chew was fifty-seven and lived in St. Francisville. Mitchell left no wife or descendants, but Chew, whose funeral service was conducted by the rector of Grace Episcopal Church, left behind a widow, Sylvia, and a twenty-one-year-old daughter named Mary, who continued to live in the parish.[38]

Fanny Hendrick died in Baton Rouge in 1865 leaving behind lots she owned in Bayou Sara and children and grandchildren in Bayou Sara and Baton Rouge. Hendrick's son William A. Hendrick lived in Bayou Sara with his wife, Josephine Thomas, and his son, William Feliz Hendrick. Fanny Hendrick's other sons, James Tillotson and John Hendrick, lived in Baton Rouge, as did her son-in-law, Alphonce Arbour, and two granddaughters, Fannie Ann and Mary E. Arbour, children of her deceased daughter. Before distributing her property to her heirs, the judge in St. Francisville had to determine whether Fanny intended a permanent move to Baton Rouge or whether she was living there with her daughter and son-in-law temporarily, just for the duration of the war.

Restaurant owner Henrietta Coleman provided testimony on that issue. She explained that Hendrick's property was burned in the spring of 1861, the first year of the war. Hendrick never lived in Bayou Sara after that, although she did return from time to time to visit her son William. Coleman testified, "When she left, she carried her cow and calf and furniture with her, and she never brought it back."[39] Once repaired, Hendrick's residence was rented out or was shut up while she was in Baton Rouge. Coleman reported that, after Hendrick's daughter died, Hendrick had talked about returning to Bayou Sara but Hendrick herself died before she had the opportunity to return. The court concluded that Hendrick intended to return to Bayou Sara at the time of her death and that her stay in Baton Rouge was due solely to the war.

Matthew Reilly, who was white, had begun to administer Hendrick's estate and had sold some of her real estate even though she owed no debts. Hendrick's heirs challenged Reilly's decision, and the court ruled that Reilly's sales of Hendrick's property were improper. It reversed the sales.[40] Hendrick's children and grandchildren inherited her property. Hendrick's son, William, died in 1867. His wife, Josephine Thomas, continued to live in Hendrick's Bayou Sara property.[41] Thomas, like so many of her neighbors, tried to recover from the war.

Recovering from the war was not an easy task. The two armies battling in the parish had destroyed its economy. Capital had been exhausted in support of the war, and the agricultural workers were now free. West Feliciana Parish planters were concerned about finding the labor they needed to plant and harvest their crops and restore their fortunes. White plantation mistress Emily Baines eloquently expressed the general sentiment: "Tis so hard to have to submit and give up our property and oblige to pay them wages."[42] The shift from using unpaid labor to having to pay those same laborers was disquieting. White planters John and Ann Lobdell had taken their enslaved laborers with them to Canton, Texas, during the war. Writing to her mother in 1865, Ann Lobdell complained that the laborers all wanted to go home. She worried that they would not stay with her and her husband after being transported back to Louisiana. She felt discouraged by the lost war and lamented: "They can never again talk of Southern chivalry. I feel that it is buried in the dust."[43] Her husband negotiated a deal with the laborers. He promised to transport them back to Louisiana if they agreed to work for only food and clothing until January of the next year and then to work for another year for wages after they arrived home. Any laborers who did not agree would have to pay their own way back to Louisiana.[44]

White planter Scott McGehee of the parish promised his laborers one acre of land for their use as a church or school to keep them from leaving him.[45] He even supplied the lumber for the building. In early January 1866, Greenwood Plantation overseer Philip B. Key, a white man, complained that his laborers had left during the holidays "not so much for a fancied improvement in conditions, as it was with the purpose to drive me into terms with them."[46] The newly freed laborers knew that their cooperation was necessary for the recovery of the South and used the power that knowledge gave them to improve their lives. They were willing to work, but they wanted to be treated fairly. Those who employed them were not disappointed. Later, in January 1866, overseer Key reported, "the conduct + good behavior of the hands is in remarkable contrast to the ways of the old set." He assured Penelope Mathews, the white owner of Greenwood Plantation, that there was no limit to the amount of work that could be done.[47]

While most enslaved people in West Feliciana Parish had been engaged in agricultural production, slaveholders had relied on unpaid laborers to complete other tasks. In 1869, finally accepting the reality of her situation, white resident

Emily B. Maynard wrote to white plantation mistress Margaret Butler, "I am learning to sew."[48] Harriet Mathuro, a white resident of the parish, told Butler, "This is the first time this week I have had a servant to send up to see how you all are."[49] White plantation mistress Martha Turnbull complained to her diary, "When I ordered Celine to scrub my kitchen she walked off; Stepsy was impudent and would not cook; Augustus said he would not cut wood to put in my woodhouse."[50] Disobedience became an option for paid laborers; it had not been for people enslaved. White people and people of color were adjusting to a change in their relationships.

The officials who recorded property transactions also had to make an adjustment. Before the war, they had been required by law to indicate when the buyer or seller of property was a free person of color. They wanted to continue to comply with the law after the war but were unsure about what the law now required. In 1866, when Ellen Chadwick, a white woman, sold two lots in St. Francisville to Moses Lamb, Lamb was labeled "a freedman of the parish."[51] This recorder wanted to distinguish people of color who had been free before the war from those who had not. In 1867, when Horace Hill, who was white, leased property to William Brown and Bosen Green, Brown and Green were labeled "freedmen," but in the margin, the recorder wrote, "they being both free men of color."[52] This recorder remained aware of and noted the distinction between those newly freed and those who had been free before the war but was unsure what labeling was proper. In 1868, when Sylvia Chew, the widow of George Chew, sold a lot on Prosperity Street to Dempsey and Ann Turner, the act of sale indicated that Sylva Chew was a free woman of color, that Dempsey Turner was a free man of color, but that Ann Turner was a freedwoman.[53] Chew and Dempsey Turner had been free before the war; Ann Turner had not. The law requiring this labeling was eventually repealed. In 1872, when Sylvia Chew leased her house and lot to Joseph W. Armstead for five years, the transaction did not indicate the skin color or the prewar status of the parties.[54]

Although, for some years after the war, the recorders of property transactions continued to distinguish antebellum free people of color from people of color freed because of the war, other people in the state did not. An 1870 broadside from the People's and White Man's Reform Party made clear that it applied to "the Colored Race, born free or enfranchised." It read:

> It is proposed to organize throughout the State of Louisiana a People's and White Man's Reform Party, which shall be; Opposed to Radicalism and to Negro Rule ... Opposed to any system of public education that may bring about the mingling of White and Black Children in the same schools ... In favor of White Immigration to the State ... Finally, to unite all true White Men in the state in one strong

body . . . It is distinctly understood in advance, that the objects of this party are to be carried out ONLY by peaceful and legal means; and that there is no intention whatever to interfere with the vested rights of the Colored Race, born free or enfranchised. . . . [The People's and White Man's Reform Party simply wanted] to prevent them from control.[55]

While acknowledging the historical distinction between people born free and those who were not, the People's and White Man's Reform Party advocated extinguishing that distinction and drawing a black-white line to separate people raced white from people of color, whether born free or enfranchised, rather than the free-enslaved line that had predominated in the parish prior to 1850. Free people of color were no longer perceived as individuals welcomed to become a part of the community. Instead, they became a threat to the community, part of "the Colored Race" that interfered with control by white people. By opposing "the mingling of White and Black children in the same schools," the People's and White Man's Reform Party precluded opportunities for their children to learn to distinguish members of "the Colored Race" from one another. Their children would not have personal relationships with people of color but, instead, be continually separated from them or have regulated interactions with them that would support white supremacy. By encouraging white immigration into the state, the party hoped to ensure a continuing numerical superiority of people raced white over people of color in the state to ensure their political power. The People's and White Man's Reform Party wanted to exclude people of color from everyday interactions with white members of their community and to exclude them from political rule.[56]

The Civil War forced a division in the community and made skin color of paramount importance. People of color who had been free before the Civil War found themselves economically marginalized and conceptually subsumed within the class of newly freed people of color. Skin-color discrimination infused itself into the economic, social, and political life of the parish. The cordial interaction between free people of color and white people had ended.

People of color who had been free before the war did not reject this new conception of their position in the local community. There had not been a large enough number of them in the parish to form a discrete free-people-of-color community, and many of them were not far enough distant from their own enslavement to think of themselves as separate and distinct from the people newly freed because of the war. Before the war, Louisiana's laws sought to limit interaction between free people of color and enslaved people, but the free people of color in the parish had not previously distanced themselves from people who had been enslaved. They had interacted and intermarried with them. In at least two cases, free men of color married enslaved women before they were freed. Henry Oconnor, whose mother had been free in 1820, was married to Ann Griggs by the rector of Grace Episcopal Church almost nine years before he was able to purchase and free her. William Jones, who had been born free in New York, married Ann Fair, three years before her enslavement officially ended.[57] Before the war, free people of color freely associated with one another whether they had been born free or had just recently become free. After the war, free people of color continued to choose friends and marriage partners without regard to their previous condition of servitude.

Although large numbers of free people of color left the parish before or during the war, two ladies with thriving businesses remained. Maria Wicker, who owned a restaurant and boarding house in Bayou Sara, remained in the parish with her family. In July 1866, her son, Albert Wicker, leased four lots in Bayou Sara for sixty dollars per month for two years, hoping to open another successful restaurant and boarding house. In March 1867, Wicker purchased a lot in Bayou Sara for two thousand dollars, but he sold the property for the same price in June 1867.[58] Maria Wicker died in December 1867, and by 1880, Albert Wicker and two of his younger brothers, John and Benjamin, were living in New Orleans.[59]

Henrietta Coleman continued to operate her restaurant and inn next door to Wicker's. In June 1876, federal officers investigating the lynching of thirty or so black men in the parish held interviews with parish residents at Henrietta Coleman's Henrietta's House.[60] Henrietta's House was both spacious enough and of high enough quality to accommodate the needs of those federal authorities. When Coleman died in 1877, her estate, valued at $1,624.86, was left to her grandchildren, Henrietta Stuart in Kentucky and Alexander Williams in Baton Rouge, the children of her deceased daughter Sarah, and to her niece, Henrietta McMillan. Coleman was buried at Grace Episcopal Church in St. Francisville on June 10, 1877.[61]

Only one of Nelly Wooten's children remained in the parish. Her son Antonio Nolasco moved to New Orleans before Wooten died in 1853. He married Annie Ellen and worked as a barber until he died of cancer on January 11, 1889, at the age of seventy-two.[62] After Wooten's death, Antonio and Gertrude Nolasco divided her estate and, over the next eighteen years, sold her Bayou Sara lots, her 220-acre farm, and the people she had enslaved. By 1872, all of Wooten's land holdings in West Feliciana Parish had been reduced to cash.[63]

In the 1860 census, Gertrude Nolasco was listed as thirty-two years old and living in West Feliciana Parish with two children. L. D. Nolasco was five years old, and E. Wooten was four years old. Nolasco was actually forty-seven years old by then. The children may have been children of a deceased son. Nolasco had not yet sold all the property she inherited from her mother and owned real estate valued at $2,700 and personal property valued at $5,400. No occupation was listed for her.[64] The 1870 census reported that Gertrude Nolasco, now only age thirty-seven, was living on six acres of land just outside of St. Francisville in West Feliciana Parish with two children, Leon Nolasco, age sixteen, and Ella Nolasco, age fourteen. Nolasco had aged five years while the children living with her had aged ten. She was a schoolteacher, and the children attended school. Her real estate was valued at three thousand dollars, and her personal property was valued at three hundred dollars.[65]

In 1857, De La Fayette Stocking, a white dentist, purchased six acres of land near St. Francisville from Maria Wicker. Stocking had been Gertrude Nolasco's agent after her mother died. Stoking and Nolasco had probably lived on the six acres from 1857 until Stocking died in 1872. In August 1872, Nolasco purchased the six acres from Stocking's heirs. By October 1872, Nolasco had leased the land to Alfred Gastrill, a white man, for twenty-five dollars per month, providing Nolasco with a monthly income.[66]

By 1900, Nolasco was living in Baton Rouge with her granddaughter Angela Taylor. She gave her age as seventy-three and her birthdate as April 1827. She declared herself a widow who had had two children, one of whom was dead. She stated that her father had been born in Spain, not Italy, and her mother had been born in the West Indies, not in Virginia. Nolasco was a schoolteacher who could read and write and owned her home free of a mortgage. Her granddaughter had been born May 1882 and, at age eighteen, was still single. She also could read and write.[67] Gertrude Nolasco died in Baton Rouge on May 6, 1902, at age eighty-nine from cancer.[68]

Sylvia Chew, the widow of George Chew, remained in the parish throughout the war. In 1858, Sylvia Chew had purchased some of the property her in-laws had sold out of their family ownership.[69] In March 1868, Sylvia sold one of those lots on Prosperity Street to Dempsey and Ann Turner. Turner was then the sexton at Grace Episcopal Church, as both William and George Chew had been. The lot Sylvia sold to the Turners was adjacent to church-owned property. The sale, at a low price, stipulated that the property would return to Chew's estate free of costs after the Turners died.[70]

In 1871, Chew filed a claim for five hundred dollars with the US Southern Claims Commission asserting that, in June 1863, the Fourth Regiment, Wisconsin Cavalry seized a horse, a saddle, and two sets of buggy harnesses from her. She claimed that the Fourth Regiment, Illinois Cavalry came through the parish in March 1864 and seized yet another horse from her. The Claims Commission disallowed her claim. In 1872, Chew sold lots ten and eleven in square eleven in St. Francisville to Rev. Alexander O. Bakewell of the Grace Episcopal Church for five hundred dollars. William Chew had purchased these lots in 1841.[71] Like Gertrude Nolasco, Sylvia Chew benefitted from the opportunity afforded to people of color once they were free to generate wealth they could pass on to their heirs. Chew, in turn, could pass that wealth to her daughter when Chew died in the parish in August 1880 at age eighty.

Ann Maria Gray and her children stayed in the parish. In 1846, Gray had purchased twenty-three acres of land from Drury Mitchell. In 1860, she sold that acreage and purchased ten acres in another part of the parish.[72] She continued to live on her ten acres until her death sometime before the end of 1872. William H. Gray, her son, married Matilda Purnell in August 1848 and, after Matilda's death, married Rachel Griffin in August 1866.[73] Gray broke his leg in 1872, and his physician, Dr. P. G. A. Kaufman, sued him to collect a fifty-dollar payment for bandaging Gray's compound fracture. Gray did not pay, and the sheriff seized his interest in the ten acres of land that had belonged to his mother. In 1880, when Gray was fifty-five and Griffin was sixty-two, Gray listed his profession as a carpenter, and Griffin kept house.[74]

Like both her parents, Josephine Gray was a slaveholder. She held three females in slavery in 1850: Betsey, purchased in 1845, Martha, purchased in 1850, and one other. Gray sold Betsy in 1852.[75] In 1860, Gray lived on property next door to her mother on Woodville Road with four children aged four to sixteen. In 1870, she lived there with two grandchildren, Cora and James Gray, aged nine and five. Gray did not pay her 1875 taxes. In 1880, Gray sold the land she owned to Newton Payne, and Payne paid the 1875 taxes. Gray was then a schoolteacher living with fourteen-year-old James Gray, her grandchild. In 1900, Gray was still in West Feliciana Parish and had moved to live in her son-in-law's household.[76]

Gray was not the only person to have trouble paying taxes in the 1870s. When Priscilla Davis died in 1874, her two lots in St. Francisville were sold to pay her 1873 taxes.[77] Fanny Hendrick's daughter-in-law, Josephine Thomas, and her grandson, William Feliz Hendrick, continued to live in the house where Hendrick and Tillotson had lived, but Thomas had difficulty paying the taxes on the property. She finally lost the property in 1879 after failing to pay taxes in 1875 and 1876.[78]

Their difficulty in paying these taxes was not because taxes were unreasonably high, but because people of color had been frozen out of the economy. Davis's tax bill was $18.70; Thomas lost her property for $11.09 in unpaid taxes.[79] Where they had been partners in the economic growth of the parish before the war, their role after the war was limited to being laborers and it was difficult for the former free people of color to find employment or patronage for their businesses.[80] Their social and economic exclusion was almost universal.

Coleman and Wicker stand out as exceptions, but after Wicker's death, her sons moved to New Orleans, and Coleman left no family in West Feliciana Parish at her death. The exclusion of the former free people of color from the economy carried over into politics. Men of color were elected to local and state offices in West Feliciana Parish, but none of those elected had been free there in 1860.[81]

People of color who had been free before the Civil War had had an opportunity to purchase land, start businesses, or leave the parish. Those certainly were advantages enslaved people had not shared. Those advantages, however, were eroded in the postwar period when people of color, whether born free or freed by the war, were lumped together to become a despised "Colored Race" considered an obstacle to white political power. Having lost a war to Northerners, Southern white people were not about to lose what self-respect they had left to those they had enslaved or to others who looked like them. The characteristics that had made West Feliciana attractive to free people of color—its openness to their aspirations and its recognition of their individuality and the diversity of their circumstances—had dissipated. A line had been drawn separating people raced white from people raced black, and the spaces where people of color could interact with white people had closed.

EPILOGUE

In 1944, historian Rayford W. Logan edited a collection of essays on the topic "What the Negro Wants." The contributors included such luminaries as Mary McLeod Bethune, Sterling A. Brown, W. E. B. Du Bois, Langston Hughes, A. Philip Randolph, and Roy Wilkins. The United States was involved in a war to protect democracies from fascist nations and had drafted people of color in the United States to help. These essayists addressed the conundrum that black soldiers were fighting overseas so others could have freedoms that those same black soldiers could not enjoy at home. Historian and college president Charles H. Wesley drew attention to 1940 census data: 99.4 percent of people of color in the United States were native born, and 97 percent of them were born of native-born parents. "The Negro is not an alien," Wesley pronounced. "This is his country, and he knows it."[1] He argued that people of color wanted the "right to enjoy all citizenship privileges and to accept all obligations and perform all duties expected by the nation of its citizens."[2] College president Leslie Pinckney Hill wrote, "Negroes want to be accepted by our American society as citizens who in reality belong, who have the respect of their fellow man and equality of opportunity for life, liberty and the pursuit of happiness."[3] English professor Sterling A. Brown wrote simply, "Negroes . . . want to belong."[4] Instead, people of color in the United States faced legal, social, and economic discrimination.

For a short while, the free people of color in West Feliciana Parish could feel that they belonged there. The Spanish law of the parish had favored emancipation and had supported integrating a newly emancipated person into the community. It treated slavery as a temporary status and not a permanent curse. It promoted self-purchase. It permitted relationships between slaveholders and enslaved women that often led to emancipating the woman and her children and that sometimes led to these couples living together as man and wife, raising their children together. The Spanish tradition that welcomed free people of color into the community continued for a while in West Feliciana Parish after the area became a part of the United States. Free people of color were attracted to come, and newly freed people were content to remain in the parish because they believed they belonged there.

Free people of color knew what freedom meant. Their acts of emancipation gave them "permission to go where she pleases"[5] and "the liberty of doing and acting for himself."[6] A newly freed mother and her children were "free and no longer subject to bondage or servitude."[7] Free people of color could do things enslaved people could not. Some purchased lots in the town of St. Francisville. Others purchased lots in Bayou Sara. Still others purchased acres of land in the rural parts of the parish. Some farmed; others started successful businesses. Once free, a man could purchase his wife. He could locate, purchase, and emancipate his children, reuniting his family. Once free, a woman could own and operate a boarding house and restaurant to provide for herself and her family. A free person of color was neither dependent for support nor subject to the will of another. Options abounded, once a person was free.

Being free from slavery did not mean experiencing equality with people raced white. Free people of color recognized a constant threat to their freedom because they could not identify as white. The laws of Louisiana did not allow free people of color to vote or to participate in self-governing. They prescribed different punishments for the same offense depending upon the skin color of the offender. Free people of color needed to always carry proof of their free status with them, while people raced white did not. Imprisonment, enslavement, or worse lay in wait if, when challenged, free people of color could not produce proof of their freedom. Any justice of the peace could demand to see it.[8] Any other person bold enough might ask. To protect their freedom, free people of color created multiple records of their free status, made themselves known in their communities, and sought out white friends to vouch for them.

Finding white friends was not difficult in West Feliciana Parish. The number of free people of color in the parish was small. Rather than form a separate community, free people of color became a part of the larger community where they could find white friends and make white acquaintances. White friends offered a safety net. If a free person lost his or her papers or had them torn up, a white friend or two could bear witness to their free status. A white person who declared a free person of color to be a free person carried more credibility than the free person of color who declared their own free status. Any enslaved person, given the opportunity, would claim free status and hope to be believed.

A white person who attests to a person's free status surrenders the chance to claim that person as their own enslaved property. Declaring that an enslaved person was free would be contrary to their pecuniary interests.

This rural, frontier community easily accommodated free people of color into its everyday life. Free people of color could live wherever they wanted and could afford to live. Some stayed in the homes of white people; others headed their own households. Some had been given money or land along with their freedom; others had used their own money to acquire their freedom. Each of them used their talents and skills to support themselves and to contribute to the growth of the parish, and each of them reaped the benefits of their labors. Many of the women were washerwomen. Most of the men who were not innkeepers or waiters were carpenters or draymen. Using only their freedom and their initiative, free people of color operated restaurants and boarding houses. Free men of color who were merchants came to the parish, and free people of color owned small farms. These occupations and vocations reflected their training and experiences, not laws that limited their options.[9] It was not until 1859 that the Louisiana Legislature began to limit employment opportunities for free people of color.

Free people of color intermingled with white people, buying from and selling to them without regard to skin color. They borrowed from and loaned money to their white neighbors and had accounts at stores and mortgages on the same terms offered to people raced white. Louisiana's courts were open to a fair adjudication in both civil and criminal matters, and free people of color could depend on procedural due process in settling disputes. Their white neighbors afforded them common decencies and avoided most of the "thousand and one devices and artifices used to prevent the colored people's full enjoyment of citizenship rights and privileges" that journalist George S. Schuyler complained about in 1944.[10]

As the voices for abolition grew stronger, free people of color stood out as undermining the rationale supporting slavery. They disproved the argument of their innate inability to survive outside of slavery. They set an example of what was possible once a person of color was freed from slavery. Slaveholders feared that the presence of free people of color in the community would incite people held in slavery to seek their own freedom more aggressively. Wealthy slaveholders feared the loss of their cheap labor. Lawyer and labor union organizer A. Philip Randolph explained the root of skin color discrimination: "The origin of the Negro problem was economic, for it had its seat in the slave trade. The reason for subjecting Negroes to slavery was economic. It had residence in cheap labor."[11] To protect the institution of slavery and to serve their own power and financial interests, wealthy slaveholders drove people raced white and free people of color apart. For free people of color, feelings of belonging ended in the last decade before the Civil War as skin color discrimination took center stage.

Charles Wesley recognized the same phenomena in the 1940s: "Southern leaders of agriculture were playing up race prejudice to keep the workers apart and to maintain their own dominance of Southern society."[12] Wesley continued: "The doctrine of racism has no scientific foundation. It is, however, one of the most dangerous of dogmas."[13] From 1820 to 1850, in West Feliciana Parish, the danger of this dogma was mitigated by the community's acceptance of people for what they could contribute to the community. A designation as black or white was less important than the quality of the service or commodity offered, whether carpentry, food services, or haircuts. People could be friends and neighbors, landlords and tenants, and lenders and borrowers without regard to pigmentation. Separation by skin color was neither necessary nor commonplace in that place at that time. Nor is it necessary today, but it is far too commonplace. It continues to be a tool the wealthy and powerful use to divide people who might otherwise join forces to challenge their hold on wealth and power.

Benjamin Franklin's statement to the Continental Congress in 1776 is just as true today as it was then: "We must, indeed, all hang together, or most assuredly we shall all hang separately." Nationally and internationally, we must respect humanness in all people and step back from judgments based on misinformation or on superficial characteristics. We must refuse to prioritize the acquisition of wealth at the expense of other people over living in peace.

NOTES

Acknowledgments

1. Paul M. Hebert, letter to Charles J. Hatfield III, January 24, 1946, box 66, folder 22, Tureaud Papers, Amistad Research Center, Tulane University, New Orleans, LA.
2. Evelyn L. Wilson, *Laws, Customs and Rights: Charles Hatfield and His Family; A Louisiana History* (Westminster, MD: Willow Bend Books, 2004), 9ff, 59ff.

Introduction

1. *Adelle v. Beauregard*, 1 Mart. (o. s.) 183, 184 (1810).
2. 1830 La. Acts, 90, §§1, 6, 9.
3. *Adelle*, 1 Mart. at 184.
4. John Hope Franklin, *The Free Negro in North Carolina, 1790–1860* (Chapel Hill: University of North Carolina Press, 1943), 137–38, 225.
5. Franklin, *The Free Negro*, 129.
6. Ira Berlin, *Slaves without Masters: The Free Negro in the Antebellum South* (New York: Pantheon Books, 1974), 198, 49, 185.
7. Loren Schweninger, "Antebellum Free Persons of Color in Postbellum Louisiana," *Louisiana History: The Journal of the Louisiana Historical Association* 30, no. 4 (Autumn 1989): 352.
8. Leonard P. Curry, *The Free Black in Urban America 1800–1850: The Shadow of the Dream* (Chicago: University of Chicago Press, 1981), 9, 83–93, xvi–xviii.
9. Warren Eugene Milteer Jr., *Beyond Slavery's Shadow: Free People of Color in the South* (Chapel Hill: University of North Carolina Press, 2021), 14.
10. Milteer, *Beyond Slavery's Shadow*, 88.
11. Milteer, *Beyond Slavery's Shadow*, 254–55, 180, 160ff.

148   Notes

12. Emily Clark, *The Strange History of the American Quadroon: Free Women of Color in the Revolutionary Atlantic World* (Chapel Hill: University of North Carolina Press, 2013), 44.

13. Daniel H. Usner Jr., "From African Captivity to American Slavery: The Introduction of Black Laborers to Colonial Louisiana," *Louisiana History: The Journal of the Louisiana Historical Association* 20, no. 1 (Winter 1979): 38–40.

14. Alice Dunbar-Nelson, "People of Color in Louisiana: Part I," *Journal of Negro History* 1, no. 4 (October 1916): 363, 371; Alice Dunbar-Nelson, "People of Color in Louisiana: Part II," *Journal of Negro History* 2, no. 1 (January 1917): 57, 55, 61.

15. In 1850, Louisiana had 17,462 free people of color, which constituted 6.4 percent of all free people in the state. Orleans Parish had 9,961 free people of color, which was 9.8 percent of its free population. St. Landry Parish had 1,242 free people of color, which was 10.9 percent of its free population. Natchitoches Parish had 881, 13.9 percent of its free population. Manuscript census, 1850, Feliciana Parish, LA, ancestry.com.

16. Dunbar-Nelson, "People of Color in Louisiana: Part II," 61.

17. Frank Tannenbaum, *Slave & Citizen: The Negro in the Americas* (New York: Vintage Books, 1946), 53, 69.

18. H. E. Sterkx, *The Free Negro in Ante-Bellum Louisiana* (Rutherford, NJ: Fairleigh Dickinson University Press, 1972), 99, 170–73.

19. Sterkx, *The Free Negro*, 221, 175.

20. Gary B. Mills, *The Forgotten People: Cane River's Creoles of Color* (Baton Rouge: Louisiana State University Press, 1977), 194, 210–11, 227.

21. Carl A. Brasseaux, Keith P. Fontenot, and Claude F. Oubre, *Creoles of Color in the Bayou Country* (Jackson: University Press of Mississippi, 1994), 7–8, 44, xiii, 119, 73, 83, 49, 74.

22. James H. Dorman, *Creoles of Color of the Gulf South* (Knoxville: University of Tennessee Press, 1996), 170.

23. Clark, The Strange History, 39.

24. W. E. B. Du Bois, *The Philadelphia Negro: A Social Study* (New York: Benjamin Blom, [1899] 1967), 144, 390, 397.

Chapter 1. West Feliciana Parish, Louisiana

1. Free people of color purchased property in the parish at least as early as 1816. James Haggerty, sale to Mariann or Mary Ann Curtis, Book A, 318, March 18, 1816, conveyance records, West Feliciana Parish [hereafter, in citations, WFP], LA; John Johnson, sale to Judique Lacour, Book A, 383, December 12, 1816, conveyance records, WFP, LA.

2. Miriam Reeves, *The Felicianas of Louisiana* (Baton Rouge, LA: Claitor's Book Store, 1967), vii–viii.

3. Adam Sundberg and Sara Brooks Sundberg, "Happy Land: Women Landowners in Early West Feliciana Parish, Louisiana, 1813–1845," *Agricultural History* 90, no. 4 (Fall 2016): 487; Winston DeVille, *New Feliciana in the Province of Louisiana: A Guide to the Census of 1793* (Ville Platte: self-published, 1987), 8.

4. Lee Malone, *The Majesty of the Felicianas* (Gretna, LA: Pelican Publishing, 1989), 9.

5. 1811 Acts of the Legis. Council, Territory of Orleans, proclamation, 204.

6. United States Department of Commerce, *Historic Statistics of the United States, Colonial Times to 1970*, bicentennial ed. (Washington, DC: Bureau of the Census, 1976), 2:375–76, table Bb1–98.

7. Berlin, *Slaves without Masters*, 97.

Notes

8. Clayton E. Cramer, *Black Demographic Data, 1790–1860: A Sourcebook* (Westport, CT: Greenwood Press, 1997), 149.

9. Rebecca J. Scott, "Paper Thin: Freedom and Re-enslavement in the Diaspora of the Haitian Revolution," *Law and History Review* 29, no. 4 (2011): 1062.

10. United States Department of Commerce, *Bicentennial Edition*, 375–76, table Bb1–98.

11. Edmund S. Morgan, *American Slavery, American Freedom: The Ordeal of Colonial Virginia* (New York: W. W. Norton & Company, 1975), 308–10; V. Elaine Thompson, *Clinton, Louisiana: Society, Politics, and Race Relations in a Nineteenth Century Southern Small Town* (Lafayette: University of Louisiana at Lafayette, 2014), 42.

12. Alexis de Tocqueville, *Democracy in America*, trans. Henry Reeve, 4th ed. (Cambridge, MA: Sever and Francis, 1864), 2, 473.

13. "Resolutions Proposing the Emancipation of Slaves," no. 8, January 19, 1824, box 2, State Archives Series 593, Ohio General Assembly House and Senate Resolutions: Ohio History Connection.

14. 1826 La. Acts, 36.

15. Manuscript census, 1820, Feliciana Parish, LA, ancestry.com; Clerk of the House of Representatives, *Abstract of the Returns of the Fifth Census* (Washington, DC: Duff Green, 1832), 32; Department of State, *Compendium of the United States Sixth Census* (Washington, DC: Thomas Allen, 1841), 61–62.

16. Department of State, *Compendium*, 240.

17. Department of State, *Compendium*, 61–62.

18. Harry L. Coates, "Some Notes on Slaveownership and Landownership in Louisiana," *Journal of Southern History* 9, no. 3 (August 1943): 385, table "Percentage of Heads of Families Owning."

19. J. D. B. DeBow, *The Seventh Census of the United States* (Washington, DC: Robert Armstrong, Public Printer, 1853), 473, table 1; Wattine Frazier, "The Great Planter in West Feliciana Parish, Louisiana, 1850–1860" (MA thesis, Louisiana State University, 1969).

20. Anne Butler and Helen Williams, *Bayou Sara: Used To Be* (Lafayette: University of Louisiana at Lafayette, 2017), 16; Joseph C. G. Kennedy, *Population of the United States in 1860* (Washington, DC: Government Printing Office, 1864), 194.

21. Department of State, *Compendium*, 61–62; DeBow, *The Seventh Census*, 473; Kennedy, *Population*, 194.

22. DeBow, *The Seventh Census*, 473. The total US population of 23,191,876 minus 3,204,313 enslaved people equals 19,987,563 free people.

23. DeBow, The Seventh Census, 473.

24. Morgan, *American Slavery*, 328, 331, 257.

25. Carter Goodwin Woodson, *The Mis-Education of the Negro* (Washington, DC: Associated Publishers, 1933). Dr. Woodson argued that Blacks were culturally indoctrinated in their schools to become dependent and to seek out inferior places in American society.

26. De Tocqueville, *Democracy in America*, 488.

27. Adele Logan Alexander, *Ambiguous Lives: Free Women of Color in Rural Georgia, 1789–1879* (Fayetteville: University of Arkansas Press, 1991), 36.

28. E. Stout, *Laws for the Government of the District of Louisiana, Vincennes, Indiana Territory* (New York: self-published, 1804), 116–17, §23.

29. Stout, *Laws*, 107, §§4–5, 112, §12, 113, §14.

30. 1806 Acts of the Legis. Council, Territory of Orleans, Black Code, ch. 33, 188, §40.

31. H. Cowles Atwater, *Incidents of a Southern Tour: Or the South as Seen with Northern Eyes* (Boston, MA: J. P. Magee, 1857), 68.

32. Ulrich B. Phillips, "The Central Theme of Southern History," *American Historical Review* 34, no. 1 (October 1928): 31.

33. 1806 Acts of the Legis. Council, Territory of Orleans, ch. 30, 126.

34. 1807 Acts of the Legis. Council, Territory of Orleans, 28. The statute reads, "No free negro or mulatto shall emigrate to or settle in this territory." West Feliciana Parish was a Spanish possession until 1810. Louisiana's territorial laws became applicable to the parish in December of that year.

35. Dunbar Rowland, ed., *Official Letter Books of W. C. C. Claiborne, 1801–1816* (Jackson, MS: State Department of Archives and History, 1917), 4:352.

36. Rowland, *Official Letter Books*, 4:372.

37. Scott, "Paper Thin," 1062–1063, 1072, 1075. "From and after the first of January 1808, it shall not be lawful to import . . . any . . . person of colour, with intent to hold, sell, or dispose of such . . . as a slave." See An Act to Prohibit the Importation of Slaves, US Cong., 2 stat., 426 (March 2, 1807). See also An Act for the Remission of Certain Penalties and Forfeitures, and for Other Purposes, 11th Cong., ch. 8, §1 (June 28, 1809).

38. Rowland, *Official Letter Books*, 4:388.

39. Rowland, *Official Letter Books*, 4:402.

40. Rowland, *Official Letter Books*, 4:407.

41. 1808 Acts of the Legis. Council, Territory of Orleans, ch. 31, 138. Spanish records also indicated when one of the parties to an act of sale was a free person of color.

42. Berlin, *Slaves without Masters*, 93.

43. 1812 La. Acts, ch. 23.

44. 1830 La. Acts, 144, §6.

45. David Walker, *Walker's Appeal, in Four Articles; Together with a Preamble, to the Colored Citizens of the World, but In Particular, and Very Expressly, to Those of the United States of America* (Boston, MA: self-published, 1829).

46. Sterkx, *The Free Negro*, 98.

47. 1830 La. Acts, 90, §1. This act states:

Section 1st. Be it enacted by the senate and house of representative of the State of Louisiana in general assembly convened, That all free negroes; mulattoes, or other free persons of colour, who have come into this state since the first day of January of 1825, in violation of an act of the Territory of Orleans, passed on the 14th of April 1807, entitled 'An act to prevent the emigration of free negroes [sic] and mulattoes into the Territory of Orleans,' shall and may be arrested and proceeded against by warrant, before any judge, justice of the peace, or mayor in this state.

48. 1830 La. Acts, 90, §12.

49. 1830 La. Acts, 90, §§2, 17.

50. 1830 La. Acts, 90, §§7–8.

51. 1830 La. Acts, 90, §9.

52. 1830 La. Acts, 96, §§1–2.

53. 1830 La. Acts, 96, §3.

54. 1835 La. Acts, 224.

55. *Phenix and St. Francisville and Bayou Sara (LA) Advertiser*, October 27, 1835. Sometimes the newspapers do not have a heading for pieces of information it picks up from other papers. Where there is a heading, it is provided.

56. Bennet H. Barrow, diary, 232, August 15, 1841.

57. Barrow, diary, 188, August 3, 1840.
58. 1806 Acts of the Legis. Council, Territory of Orleans, Black Code, ch. 33, 188, §40.
59. 1843 La. Acts, 45, §§2–3.
60. 1846 La. Acts, 92; 1847 La. Acts, 178.
61. 1848 La. Acts, 19.
62. Milteer, *Beyond Slavery's Shadow*, 3.
63. 1850 La. Acts, 179.
64. Alexander, *Ambiguous Lives*, 36.
65. 1852 La. Acts, 16.
66. 1855 La. Acts, 377, §19.
67. 1859 La. Acts, 18.
68. Franklin, *The Free Negro*, 137; Michael P. Johnson and James L. Roark, *Black Masters: A Free Family of Color in the Old South* (New York: W. W. Norton, 1984), 266.
69. David C. Rankin, "The Forgotten People: Free People of Color in New Orleans, 1850–1870" (PhD diss., John Hopkins University, 1976), 15.

Chapter 2. Free People of Color in West Feliciana Parish

1. *Alexandria (VA) Daily Advertiser*, "Riches of Louisiana," December 4, 1806.
2. Drury Louis Mitchell, declaration of free status, book C, 333–34, June 15, 1830, conveyance records, WFP, LA.
3. Drury Louis Mitchell, declaration of free status, book H, 538, April 12, 1827, filed February 27, 1844, conveyance records, WFP, LA. John Chavis of North Carolina taught both free black people and free white people for over thirty years. Franklin, *The Free Negro*, 224.
4. Julia Cornish, enrollment, book B, 224, May 24, 1820, conveyance records, WFP, LA.
5. *State v. Julie Ann Cornish*, receipt, book B, 224, May 26, 1820, conveyance records, Office of the Clerk of Court, WFP, LA.
6. James H. Coulter, declaration, book D, 131, March 7, 1831, conveyance records, WFP, LA.
7. John Eagan, sale to Jesse Wilson, book B, 396–97, August 14, 1821, conveyance records, WFP, LA.
8. Sally Jones, sale to Jesse Wilson, book AA, 53–54, November 25, 1822, conveyance records, WFP, LA; Nancy Jones, sale to Jesse Wilson, book AA, 55, January 22, 1822, conveyance records, WFP, LA; Rachel McLanon, sale to Jesse Wilson, book AA, 54–55, December 1822, recorded November 20, 1824, conveyance records, WFP, LA.
9. Jesse Wilson, sale to Thomas N. Hosea, book AA, 53, January 8, 1824, conveyance records, WFP, LA.
10. James Sterret, Jas. Robimare, Ben. Chur, Sam Moore, I. H. Holland, B. Shaunibugh, James Thirst, Thomas Brace, and G. W. Morgan, statements [concerning Elsey Scott], book D, 139, August 15–16, 1823, recorded March 17, 1831, conveyance records, WFP, LA.
11. M. Nicholson, statement [concerning Elsey Scott], book D, 139, August 15, 1823, conveyance records, WFP, LA.
12. Probate Book, no. 9, 1841–1842, 223, March 18, 1842, WFP, LA.
13. George Douse, declaration of free status, book D, 235, June 14, 1831, conveyance records, WFP, LA. The 1856 certificate of death for John Douse states that he was born in 1818 in Louisiana. See Orleans deaths indices, 1804–1885, 32:325. That of George Douse says he was born in 1819 in Philadelphia. Orleans death indices, 1804–1885, 22:363. Family oral history says that both were born in Philadelphia.

14. Their children included Richard McKennon Douse, born August 12, 1834, Michael William Douse, born July 27, 1836, Mary Elizabeth Douse, born March 3, 1838, and Daniel Turnbull Douse, born in 1840. Brisbane Marshall, affidavit of freedom of George and Eliza Douse and their children, book H, 244, September 1, 1842, conveyance records, WFP, LA; Elizabeth Townsend, affidavit, September 24, 1904, pension file of Richard Douse, file no. C 2536643, Civil War and Later Pension Files, Records of the Veterans Administration, record group 15, National Archives, Washington, DC; Orleans deaths indices, 1804–1885.

15. William Jones, affidavit of free status, book G, 169, November 6, 1840, conveyance records, WFP, LA.

16. Jacob Kirby, letter to Samuel Jones, book G, 41, book H, 42, September 26, 1839, conveyance records, WFP, LA.

17. *Minute Record Book* 1, 1824–1828, 281–2, La. 3rd Jud. Dist. Ct., February 23, 1827.

18. The records of these prosecutions included first and last names for some defendants and only one name for others. While some enslaved people were known by both a first and last name, most records show only a single name for an enslaved person. A person known by a single name while enslaved may not have adopted an additional name until some later time after their release from slavery. Where the records show only a single name to identify a person, that single name is used in this manuscript.

19. *Minute Record Book* 1, 1824–1828, 294–97, 368–69, La. 3rd Jud. Dist. Ct., May 26, 1827.

20. Recordation of freedom papers, book F, 298–99, November 7, 1827, conveyance records, WFP, LA.

21. Bennet H. Barrow, diary, 36, November 19, 1837, mss. 2978–2014 1833–1846, Vault: 9 v., Louisiana and Lower Mississippi Valley Collections, LSU Libraries [hereinafter LLMVC, LSU], Baton Rouge, LA.

22. Barrow, diary, 36, November 19, 1837.

23. Declaration of free status, book H, p. 249, September 6, 1842, conveyance records, WFP, LA.

24. Louisiana legislators were especially concerned about seamen and mariners. An 1804 statute prohibited the master of a ship from transporting any Negro or mulatto without the permission of the person's owner. Stout, *Laws*, 107, §34. Black seamen were expected to leave with their vessels and could be imprisoned at hard labor for a year if they failed to do so. 1830 La. Acts, 90. An 1835 statute required the master of every vessel bringing a free person of color into the state to provide a five-hundred-dollar bond guaranteeing that the person would not leave the vessel without a passport from the mayor of the city or a designee. A free person of color on board without the payment of the bond or on shore without a passport would be arrested. 1835 La. Acts, Black Code, §§95–98. In 1845, the governor of Massachusetts objected to the imprisonment of its state citizens without any allegation of a crime. The Louisiana Legislature considered his protest dangerous interference with the state's laws. 1845 La. Acts, 79, §138.

25. Ellen Campbell, affidavit of free status, book H, 191, April 29, 1842, conveyance records, WFP, LA.

26. Thomas Phelps, affidavit of free status, book H, 566, May 4, [1844] recorded in error as 1839, conveyance records, WFP, LA.

27. Jordan Ritchie, will, book F, 315, November 7, 1831, conveyance records, WFP, LA; box 90, succession records, WFP, LA.

28. Lucinda Wilkins, affidavit of free status, book H, 50, August 4, 1841, conveyance records, WFP, LA.

29. Julia Gardner, affidavit of free status, book H, 145, November 24, 1840, conveyance records, WFP, LA.

30. C. Woodroof [Aaron], statement, book F, 286, May 10, 1828, conveyance records, WFP, LA; Caesar, declaration of free status, book E, 359, March 12, 1827, conveyance records, WFP, LA.

31. La. Civ. Code, art. 174 (1825). This article states, "The slave is incapable of making any kind of contract, except those which relate to his own emancipation." Under Spanish law, an enslaved person could demand that a judge set a purchase price and the slaveholder was required to grant the emancipation once the price was paid.

32. La. Civ. Code, art. 175 (1825). Emphasis original.

33. Abel, act of emancipation, book D, 525, December 31, 1832, conveyance records, WFP, LA.

34. Ira Berlin and Philip D. Morgan, eds., *The Slaves' Economy: Independent Production by Slaves in the Americas* (London: Frank Cass, 1991). This collection of papers documents and compares the opportunities given to enslaved people to earn an income in various jurisdictions.

35. Hardy Perry, succession, December 12, 1850, box 80, succession records, WFP, LA.

36. Nitty, permission to travel, book E, 254, May 23, 1834, conveyance records, WFP, LA.

37. Silvia, permission to travel, book G, p. 39, November 1, 1837, conveyance records, WFP, LA; Chauncey Pittibone, sale to Silvia, book G, 248, July 29, 1839, conveyance records, WFP, LA.

38. Heirs of Bell, sale to Amos Hoe, book B, 306, December 18, 1820, conveyance records, WFP, LA.

39. Heirs of D. Stewart, sale to Phil, book F, 43, July 6, 1835, conveyance records, WFP, LA.

40. Titus, act of emancipation, book M, 84, February 5, 1856, conveyance records, WFP, LA.

41. Daniel Davis, act of emancipation, book N, 573, May 13, 1863, conveyance records, WFP, LA.

42. William Chew, act of emancipation, book AA, 317, July 25, 1827, conveyance records, WFP, LA.

43. Reuben Adams, act of emancipation, book M, 40, February 6, 1857, conveyance records, WFP, LA; Reuben Adams, act of emancipation, book M, 548, December 29, 1857, conveyance records, WFP, LA.

44. Caroline Boyd, act of emancipation, book M, 260, February 6, 1857, conveyance records, WFP, LA.

45. Phoebe, act of emancipation, book H, 260, January 14, 1840, conveyance records, WFP, LA.

46. Peter Ambrose, act of emancipation, book D, 382, February 29, 1832, conveyance records, WFP, LA.

47. Maria Wicker purchased herself and three children. Daniel Wicker, sale to Maria Wicker, book H, 238, May 26, 1842, conveyance records, WFP, LA. Prudence purchased herself and her son Thomas. John C. Morris, sale to Prudence, book H, 75, June 23, 1841, conveyance records, WFP, LA.

48. Mary Shouler, sale to Billy Chew, book D, 266, March 8, 1831, conveyance records, WFP, LA; George Chew, Harriet Chew, Mary Chew, Arie Ann Chew, and May Lilly Chew, act of emancipation, book G, 7, June 12, 1839, conveyance records, WFP, LA.

49. Charles Smith, sale to William Chew, bills of sale 2, 254–55, April 4, 1845, WFP, LA.

50. John Hill, act of emancipation, book F, 239, March 11, 1837, conveyance records, WFP, LA.

51. Caesar, act of emancipation, book F, 290, July 17, 1837, conveyance records, WFP, LA.

52. Mary Stirling, sale to Nelly Wooten, bills of sale 1, 347, February 13, 1840, Office of the Clerk of Court, WFP, LA; Margaret Smith, petition, succession of Ellen Wooten, box 111, succession records, WFP, LA.

53. Priscilla Davis, will, book H,184–85, April 20, 1842, conveyance records, WFP, LA; Rose Ann Davis, Cassy Ann Davis, and Elizabeth, act of emancipation, book H, 225–26, July 7, 1842, conveyance records, WFP, LA.

54. Cora Guibert, sale to Celia Guibert, book 1, 513–14, December 4, 1848, conveyance records, WFP, LA.

55. William Harriet Mathews, sale to Henry Oconnor, book 1, 373, June 3, 1847, conveyance records, WFP, LA. The sale included Ann, thirty-two, yellow; and children of Ann—John, nine, yellow; Henry, seven, yellow; Sarah, four, yellow; Mitchel, three, yellow; Emily, seven months—for one thousand dollars. Act of emancipation, book K, 137, November 6, 1850, conveyance records, WFP, LA.

56. John F. Valentine, sale to John Holmes [as the agent for Maria Wicker], book L, 551, June 13, 1855, conveyance records, WFP, LA.

57. Louisiana's 1825 Civil Code required a parent to leave one-third of their property to their child if the parent had one child, one-half of their property to two children to share if they had two children, and two-thirds of their property to share if the testator had three or more children. If the testator had no children but had a living parent, the parent was to get one-third of the testator's property. These recipients were the testator's forced heirs. The testator could give the rest of their property to whomever the testator chose, unless a law forbade the gift. La. Civ. Code, arts. 1480 and 1481 (1825).

58. 1804 Laws of the District of Louisiana, 107, §23; La. Civ. Code, art. 190 (1825). This law states, "Any enfranchisement made in fraud of creditors, or of the portion reserved for forced heirs, is null and void."

59. Cramer, *Black Demographic Data*, 20.

60. 1807 Acts of the Legis. of the Territory of Louisiana, ch. 35, 96–97. The enslaved person could sue as a pauper and claim damages for assault and battery and false imprisonment. The court would appoint counsel. Under the 1825 Civil Code, an enslaved person could not be party to any civil action "except when he has to claim or prove his freedom." 1825 La. Civ. Code, art. 177.

61. *Minute Record Book* 1, 1824–1828, 413, La. 3rd Jud. Dist. Ct. (December 14, 1827).

62. James Doherty, will, September 24, 1842, box 30, succession records, WFP, LA; John Norris, will, May 8, 1815, box 65, succession records, WFP, LA.

63. Joseph David Lejeune, will, January 30, 1807, box 62, succession records, WFP, LA.

64. Joseph Lejeune, act of emancipation, book D, 65, April 5, 1830, conveyance records, WFP, LA. Louisiana's Civil Code, art. 187 (1825), required her to declare her intent to emancipate Joseph to the parish judge, then advertise the intended emancipation for forty days.

65. Constance Beauvais, will, April 26, 1832, box 9999, unsorted records, Office of the Clerk of Court, WFP, LA; Isaac Johnson, sale to Joseph Lejeune, book F, 150, July 14, 1836, conveyance records, WFP, LA; manuscript census, 1840, WFP, LA, ancestry.com.

66. William Weeks, will, May 30, 1816, succession of William Weeks, box 113, succession records, WFP, LA. See also book A, 167, October 2, 1817, conveyance records, WFP, LA. The varied spellings of names reflected the uncertainty of the notary who recorded Weeks's dictated will. Weeks could not read or write.

67. David Weeks, agreement with Hercules O'Connor, James O'Connor, and Stephen Bell, book A, 166, October 2, 1817, conveyance records, WFP, LA. These latter three men were cousins of David Weeks.

68. David Weeks, donation to Ann Maria Curtis, book A, 112, July 17, 1816, conveyance records, WFP, LA.

Notes

69. Ann Maria Curtis, sale to Levi Sholar, book AA, 10, March 14, 1825, conveyance records, WFP, LA.

70. Ann Higdon, declaration of free status, book H, 197, May 11, 1842, conveyance records, WFP, LA.

71. Moses Horn, will, July 1, 1841, box 43, succession records, WFP, LA. During his tenure in the parish, Mitchell would train more than ten apprentices to become carpenters.

72. John C. Morris, will, November 31, 1850, box 65, succession records, WFP, LA.

73. Ann Chew, will, October 21, 1820, box 24, succession records, WFP, LA.

74. John Bettis, will, June 30, 1833, succession of Kesiah Middleton, box 68, succession records, WFP, LA.

75. Samuel Kemper, will, September 28, 1814, succession of Reuben Kemper and Samuel Kemper, box 56, succession records, WFP, LA; probate record, book 1, 1811–1819, 120–21, WFP, LA.

76. Probate record, book 1, 1811–1819, 129, WFP, LA.

77. Hardy Perry, succession, January 7, 1833, box 80, succession records, WFP, LA.

78. John G. Shrim, sale to Solomon M. Brian, book AA, 123, October 26, 1827, conveyance records, WFP, LA.

79. John G. Shrim, sale to Solomon M. Brian, book AA, 336, November 15, 1827, conveyance records, WFP, LA; John G. Shrim, sale to Solomon M. Brian, November 15, 1827, conveyance records, 1811–1954, Sco-Sim, book 73, 189, WFP, LA.

80. Jim, act of emancipation, book E, 126, April 2, 1833, conveyance records, WFP, LA.

81. Peter, act of emancipation, book D, 420, June 22, 1832, conveyance records, WFP, LA.

82. Sandy, act of emancipation, book AA, 419, May 24, 1828, conveyance records, WFP, LA.

83. Norman Davis, appointment, book F, 284, April 3, 1835, conveyance records, WFP, LA; Catherine Childress, Dulcinia, Christopher, and William, act of emancipation, book G, 219, April 3, 1840, conveyance records, WFP, LA.

84. Peter, act of emancipation, book B, 47, December 19, 1797, conveyance records, WFP, LA.

85. Stout, *Laws*, 116–17, §23.

86. La. Civ. Code, art. 186 (1825).

87. 1807 Acts of the Legis. Council, Territory of Orleans, 82, §2.

88. See, for example, 1824 La. Acts, 42. Hanna, a free woman of color in St. Mary Parish, was authorized to emancipate her two children under age thirty.

89. Leah Savage, act of emancipation, book B, 77–78, June 8, 1819, conveyance records, WFP, LA.

90. Old Dinah, act of emancipation, book AA, 403, July 2, 1824, conveyance records, WFP, LA.

91. Ann Maria Gray, act of emancipation, book AA, 147, 149, June 13, 1825, conveyance records, WFP, LA.

92. 1826 La. Acts, 106. See also 1825 La. Acts, 132, 42.

93. 1827 La. Acts, 13, §1.

94. Catherine Childress, Dulcinia, Christopher, and William, act of emancipation, book G, 219, March 4, 1841, conveyance records, WFP, LA.

95. Kimberly Welch, "Black Litigiousness and White Accountability: Free Blacks and the Rhetoric of Reputation in the Antebellum Natchez District," *Journal of the Civil War Era* 5, no. 3 (September 2015): 372, 398, 378.

96. 1830 La. Acts, 90, §§10, 16; 1831 La. Acts, 98, §2.

97. 1830 La. Acts, 90, §16.

98. William Weeks, will, May 30, 1816, box 113, succession records, WFP, LA; book A, 167, October 2, 1817, conveyance records, WFP, LA.

99. Eliza Gorham, recordation of free status, book B, 470, July 2, 1820, conveyance records, WFP, LA.

100. Richard Ratliff, will, January 12, 1819, box 85, succession records, WFP, LA.

101. Fanny Hendrick, act of emancipation, book AA, 332–35, April 30, 1827, conveyance records, WFP, LA.

102. Lucy, Sarah, and Charles, act of emancipation, book E, 149, February 1, 1832, conveyance records, WFP, LA.

103. Charlotte, Alexander, and Ferdinand, act of emancipation, book F, 382–83, May 23, 1837, conveyance records, WFP, LA.

104. Caroline Perry, declaration of intent to emancipate, book H, 231, July 18, 1842, conveyance records, WFP, LA.

105. Caroline Perry, certificate of emancipation, book H, 247, September 3, 1842, conveyance records, WFP, LA; Negro Records, August 5, 1842, Hamilton County, OH, book 5, 763.

106. Purnell family, declaration of intent to emancipate, book H, 230, July 18, 1842, conveyance records, WFP, LA.

107. Purnell family, declaration of permission to travel, book H, 239, July 18, 1842, conveyance records, WFP, LA. The declaration states:

> intention to authorise and permit his slaves, as follows to wit: Woman, named "Mary" aged about forty years, of a Yellowish complexion, + her seven children, all mulattos, named + aged as follows to wit: Girl "Matilda" aged nineteen years; Boy "John" aged seventeen years; Boy "Edward" aged about fourteen years; Girl "Sally" aged about nine years; Boy "Alexander" aged about six years; Girl "Ann Mariah" aged about four years; Boy "William" aged about two years; to go to the City of Cincinnati, in the State of Ohio, for the purpose of residing there + enjoying the benefit of the laws of said State of Ohio, which confer freedom on all Slaves, who are allowed by their owners to live in said State or to return to the State of Louisiana at their pleasure, or the pleasure of their Mother Mary, who is fully authorised to take all said children to said City of Cincinnati—the said Thomas R. Purnell declaring that it is fully + absolutely his intention by this act, to emancipate all his aforesaid Slaves.

See also recordation of free status, book H, 240, August 5, 1842, conveyance records, WFP, LA; Negro Records, Hamilton County, OH, book 5, 764–65.

108. Rose Ann Davis and Cassy Ann Davis, act of emancipation, book H, 225–26, July 7, 1842, conveyance records, WFP, LA.

109. *Frank Irvin v. Thomas Powell*, civil suit, no. 1635, La. 3rd Jud. Dist. Ct. (February 6, 1837).

110. 1831 La. Acts, 98, §2.

111. Lucy, act of emancipation, book AA, 249, December 6, 1826, conveyance records, WFP, LA.

112. Lidy, act of emancipation, book AA, pp. 281–82, April 24, 1827, conveyance records, WFP, LA.

113. Rebecca and Issac, act of emancipation, book AA, 405, March 18, 1828, conveyance records, WFP, LA.

Notes 157

114. Priscilla, act of emancipation, book D, 113, May 17, 1830, conveyance records, WFP, LA.

115. Jane, act of emancipation, book 1, 476, June 5, 1848, conveyance records, WFP, LA.

116. Ruffin, act of emancipation, book E, 403, May 26, 1835, conveyance records, WFP, LA; Norvell children, act of emancipation, book E, 423, June 29, 1835, conveyance records, WFP, LA.

117. 1839 La. Acts, 78; resolution of parish police jury, book G, 7, June 3, 1839, conveyance records, WFP, LA.

118. 1846 La. Acts, 163.

119. 1852 La. Acts, 214.

120. Albert Wicker and Edward Wicker, permission to pass, book M, 416, December 29, 1857, conveyance records, WFP, LA.

121. 1857 La. Acts, 5.

122. 1858 La. Acts, 214. This act states, "It shall hereafter be lawful for any free person of African descent, over the age of twenty-one years, now residing in this state, to select his or her master, or owner, and to become a slave for life."

123. Emily West, *Family or Freedom: People of Color in the Antebellum South* (Lexington: University Press of Kentucky, 2012), 14.

124. La. Civ. Code, art. 183 (1825). This article states, "Children born of a mother then in a state of slavery, whether married or not, follow the condition of their mother; and they are consequently slaves and belong to the master of their mother."

125. Julia Cornish, declaration, book F, 121, August 23, 1836, conveyance records, WFP, LA.

126. Sarah Jackson, affidavit of free status, book K, 132, November 4, 1850, conveyance records, WFP, LA.

127. Ann Maria Gray, act of emancipation, book AA, 147 and 149, June 13, 1825, conveyance records, WFP, LA.

128. William Gray, acknowledgement of paternity, book AA, 187, May 2, 1826, conveyance records, WFP, LA; Virginia Gray, acknowledgement of paternity, book C, 242, September 24, 1828, conveyance records, WFP, LA.

129. Ann Jackson gave birth to Andrew. Ann Jackson, emancipation, book D, 83, February 16, 1830, conveyance records, WFP, LA; Andrew Jackson, declaration of free birth, book E, 278, September 12, 1834, conveyance records, WFP, LA; Andrew Jackson, declaration of free birth, book F, 287, July 8, 1837, conveyance records, WFP, LA. Leucy Hutchinson gave birth to Lewis Hutchinson on January 4, 1836. Leucy Hutchinson, affidavit of paternity, book F, 483, January 8, 1839, conveyance records, WFP, LA. Eliza Wilkins gave birth to Clara Wilkins, in 1827. Eliza Wilkins, declaration of free status, book K, 136, November 8, 1850, conveyance records, WFP, LA. George and Eliza Douse's four children born in the parish were born free: Richard McKennon Douse, born August 12, 1834, Michael William Douse, born July 27, 1836, Mary Elizabeth Douse, born March 3, 1838, and Daniel Turnbull Douse, born in 1840. Brisbane Marshall, affidavit of freedom of George Douse and Eliza Douse and their children, book H, 244, September 1, 1842, conveyance records, WFP, LA.

Chapter 3. Land Sales, Loans, and Litigation

1. Manuscript census, 1820, Feliciana Parish, LA, ancestry.com. Judigue Lacour is listed as Julia Kemper on the 1820 census. She was married to Reuben Kemper. John H. Johnson, sale to Judigue Lacour, book A, 126, December 12, 1816, conveyance records, WFP, LA.

2. Curator's account, December 12, 1816, succession of Robert H. Hewit, box 45, succession records, WFP, LA; James Ficklin, curator's account of succession, February 9, 1822, box 33, succession records, WFP, LA.

3. Judique Lacour, sale to Mary Higgins, book B, 475, October 16, 1820, conveyance records, WFP, LA.

4. Manuscript census, 1820, Feliciana Parish, LA, ancestry.com.

5. Manuscript census, 1820, Feliciana Parish, LA, ancestry.com.

6. James Haggerty, sale to Ann Curtis, book A, 99, March 18, 1816, conveyance records, WFP, LA; David Weeks, donation to Ann Maria Curtis, book A, 112, July 17, 1816, conveyance records, WFP, LA; William Weeks, will, May 30, 1816, box 113, succession records, WFP, LA. See also book A, 167, October 2, 1817, conveyance records, WFP, LA; manuscript census, 1820, Feliciana Parish, LA, ancestry.com.

7. Leah Savage, act of emancipation, book B, 77–78, June 8, 1819, conveyance records, WFP, LA.

8. Hamilton Pollock, sale to Amos Hoe, book B, 281, October 16, 1820, conveyance records, WFP, LA.

9. Heirs of Bell, sale to Hoe, book B, 306, December 18, 1820, conveyance records, WFP, LA.

10. *James Calvin v. Jacob Potter and Amos Hoe*, judgment, civil suit, no. 67, La. 3rd Jud. Dist. Ct. (April 5, 1824).

11. *Amos Hoe v. Henry Sterling*, civil suit, no. 192, Parish Court, WFP, LA (April 13, 1824); Minute Record Book 1, 1821–1828, 61, La. 3rd Jud. Dist. Ct. (December 22, 1824).

12. John C. Morris, promissory notes, box 1, folder 9, mss. 1382, [Henry A.] Lyons Papers, LLMVC, LSU.

13. *Amos Hoe v. Heirs of Kennedy*, judgment, civil suit, no. 187, La. 3rd Jud. Dist. Ct. (January 26, 1825); *Amos Hoe and Wife v. F. A. Browder*, transcript, civil suit, no. 187, La. 3rd Jud. Dist. Ct. (November 15, 1824).

14. *State v. Harrison*, 11 La. Ann. 722 (1856), 724; Kimberly M. Welch, *Black Litigants in the Antebellum American South* (Chapel Hill: University of North Carolina Press, 2018), 14.

15. "Slave Ads," Woodville Republican and Wilkinson County (MS) Advertiser, July 30, 1825.

16. Amos Hoe, sale to Sophia M. Slaughter, book D, 228, April 2, 1831, conveyance records, WFP, LA.

17. Martha S. Jones argued that free people of color in Baltimore inserted citizenship claims into their litigation to support their right to remain in the state. Martha S. Jones, *Birthright Citizens: A History of Race and Rights in Antebellum America* (New York: Cambridge University Press, 2018), 41. The citizenship of free people of color in West Feliciana Parish was not in issue. Their free or slave status mattered.

18. Jeremiah Shelton, succession, inventory and sale, August 1 and 22, 1822, box 95, succession records, WFP, LA. The inventory included one paper desk valued at twelve dollars and one lot of apparel valued at forty dollars for a total of a fifty-two-dollar net worth. What was sold to white purchasers included a paper desk ($7.25), vest ($1.25), beaver hat ($3.75), "raser" (*sic*) (thirty-one and one-quarter cents), two pantaloons (fifty cents); cloth coat ($10.50); vest ($1.62 and one-half cent); one lot of shirts ($3.12 and one-half cent); one lot of clothing (one dollar); one lot of boots and shoes (four dollars).

19. George and Jane Clark, succession, inventory, March 9, 1827, box 24, succession records, WFP, LA.

20. La. Civ. Code, art. 176 (1825). This article reads: "They [enslaved people] can transmit nothing by succession or otherwise; but the succession of free persons related to them

which they would have inherited had they been free, may pass through them to such of their descendants as may have acquired their liberty before the succession is opened." See also Henry Flowers, answer, February 20, 1827, probate suit, no. 270, succession of George and Jane Clark, box 24, succession records, WFP, LA.

21. La. Civ. Code, art. 175 (1825); Emily Bridges, petition, February 20, 1827, probate suit, no. 270; George and Jane Clark, succession, box 24, succession records, WFP, LA; La. Civ. Code, art. 176 (1825). This article states, "They [enslaved people] can transmit nothing by succession or otherwise."

22. Charles McMicken, petition, March 14, 1827, probate suit, no. 297, succession of George and Jane Clark, box 24, succession records, WFP, LA.

23. George Clark, act of emancipation, book D, 82, December 7, 1829, conveyance records, WFP, LA.

24. 1830 La. Acts, 42, §12. This act states, "George Clark of West Feliciana Parish was a slave when his parents George and Jane Clark, free people of color, died intestate. The State renounces in favor of George Clark all the rights it may have in the estate of his parents."

25. 1830 La. Acts, 90, §12.

26. Manuscript census, 1830, WFP, LA, ancestry.com.

27. John Eagan, sale to Jesse Wilson, book B, 396–97, August 14, 1821, conveyance records, WFP, LA.

28. Joseph Buatt, sale to William Marbury, book AA, 418, May 19, 1828, conveyance records, WFP, LA. The lot was twenty-five feet by fifty feet, sold for sixty dollars.

29. Manuscript census, 1830, WFP, LA, ancestry.com.

30. Joseph Semple, sale to George McIntosh, book D, 160, April 2, 1831, conveyance records, WFP, LA. Lot fifteen, square twenty-seven was sold for $279.50. David Austen, sale to Priscilla Balfour, book E, 341, January 31, 1835, conveyance records, WFP, LA. Lot ten, square seventeen was sold for $705. Charles McMicken, sale to William and Ann Jones, book F, 407–8, March 8, 1838, conveyance records, WFP, LA. Lot ten, square nine was sold for $250. Joseph R. Thomas, sale to Peggy Russell, book F, 199, December 17, 1836, conveyance records, WFP, LA. Lots four and five, square ten was sold for three hundred dollars. Julia Gardner, succession, September 6, 1843, box 40, succession records, WFP, LA; Joseph R. Thomas, sale to Elsey Scott, book F, 195, January 31, 1837, conveyance records, WFP, LA. Lots two, three, and five, square two were sold for $175. George Pease, sale to Frank and Nancy, book F, 136, October 24, 1836, conveyance records, WFP, LA. Lot three, square one was sold for $450.

31. Brisbane Marshall, sale to John F. Valentine, book E, 99, January 4, 1833, conveyance records, WFP, LA. Lot 113, square ten sold for $130. John F. Valentine, sale to John Holmes, book F, 432, February 24, 1838, conveyance records, WFP, LA. Lot 113, square ten sold for three hundred dollars. Moses Horn, sale to Billy Chew, book D, 204, March 15, 1834, conveyance records, WFP, LA. Lot six, square eleven sold for $120. Andrew C. Woods, sale to Norman Davis, book E, 201–2, February 3, 1834, conveyance records, WFP, LA. Lot ninety-four, square eight sold for two hundred dollars. Jonathan Ellsworth, sale to Kesiah Middleton, book E, 247, May 12, 1834, conveyance records, WFP, LA. Lot ninety-five, square eight sold for three hundred dollars. Brisbane Marshall, sale to Norman Davis, book E, 262, June 25, 1834, conveyance records, WFP, LA. Lot ninety-one, square eight sold for one thousand dollars. John C. Morris, sale to Ellen Wooten, book F, 144, June 27, 1836, conveyance records, WFP, LA. Lot 131, square thirteen sold for one thousand dollars. John Holmes, sale to Cynthia Ann Hendrick, book F, 251, April 5, 1837, conveyance records, WFP, LA. Lot 104, square nine sold for nine hundred dollars. John Tillotson, sale to Norman Davis, book F, 407, June 7, 1838,

conveyance records, WFP, LA. Lot 415, square thirty-seven sold for $185. Norman Davis, sale to William L. Parker, book H, 499, December 26, 1843, conveyance records, WFP, LA. Lot 415, square thirty-seven sold for fifty dollars. Heirs of John Ketchum, sale to Nelly Wooten, book E, 224, March 18, 1834, conveyance records, WFP, LA. Lot seven, square one sold for $275. Bartholomew Bettelany, sale to Madelene Cloud, book F, 271, May 1, 1837, conveyance records, WFP, LA. Lot 327, square twenty-four sold for four hundred dollars. John Holmes, sale to Cynthia Ann Hendrick, book F, 377, February 27, 1838, conveyance records, WFP, LA. Lots 336 and 337, square twenty-seven sold for nine hundred dollars. Brisbane Marshall, sale to Catherine Collins, book G, 19, July 29, 1839, conveyance records, WFP, LA. Lot thirty-nine, square four, and lot ninety-two, square eight sold for $2,100.

32. Henry Bains, sale to George Douse, book D, 233, May 25, 1831, conveyance records, WFP, LA; Charles McMicken, sale to George Douse, book E, 348, February 18, 1835, conveyance records, WFP, LA; Charles McMicken, sale to George Douse, book F, 208, February 18, 1837, conveyance records, WFP, LA.

33. Charles McMicken, sale to Elsey Scott, book E, 77, April 5, 1833, conveyance records, WFP, LA; Charles McMicken, sale to Drury L. Mitchell, book E, 78, April 11, 1833, conveyance records, WFP, LA; Charles McMicken, sale to Drury L. Mitchell, book F, 364, March 6, 1838, conveyance records, WFP, LA.

34. Drury L. Mitchell, sale to West Feliciana Rail Road Banking Company, book G, 153, July 28, 1840, conveyance records, WFP, LA; Elsey Scott, sale to West Feliciana Rail Road Banking Company, book G, 117, January 21, 1840, conveyance records, WFP, LA; Joseph R. Thomas, sale to Elsey Scott, book F, 195, January 31, 1837, conveyance records, WFP, LA. Lots two, three, and five, square two sold for $175. West Feliciana Rail Road Company, sale to Josephine Gray, book 1, 587, May 12, 1849, conveyance records, WFP, LA.

35. Jean Pierre Ledoux, sale to Jonathan Ellsworth and Kesiah Middleton, book F, 176, November 7, 1836, conveyance records, WFP, LA. Eight acres sold for two thousand dollars. Middleton used her lot in Bayou Sara as collateral for the loan. Victor Dominique Vasse, sale to Betsey Givins, book F, 293–94, July 13, 1837, conveyance records, WFP, LA; Charles McMicken and James Turner, sale to Norman Davis, book F, 494–95, January 11, 1839, conveyance records, WFP, LA. Thirteen arpents from Trudeau tract along the Mississippi River to Fountain Bayou sold for $2,600.

36. Manuscript census, 1840, WFP, LA, ancestry.com. The sixteen were Nelly Wooten, Julia Cornish, Eliza Paul, Priscilla Davis, Frank Alexander, William Chew, Fanny Hendrick, Norman Davis, Clara Nox, William Marbury, Stephen, Elsey Scott, Caesar, Charity Britton, George Douse, and Drury Mitchell.

37. Moses Esquire, sale to William Chew, book G, 212, April 13, 1841, conveyance records, WFP, LA. Lots five, seven to eleven, square eleven sold for $425. Benjamin Lavergne, sale to William Chew, book H, 313, February 4, 1843, conveyance records, WFP, LA. Lot one, square fourteen sold for three hundred dollars.

38. Manuscript census, 1850, WFP, LA, ancestry.com.

39. William Chew, act of emancipation, book AA, 317, July 25, 1827, conveyance records, WFP, LA.

40. William Chew, act of emancipation, book AA, 317, July 25, 1827, conveyance records, WFP, LA.

41. Manuscript census, 1850, WFP, LA, ancestry.com; Mary Constance Beauvais, succession, April 29, 1833, box 62, succession records, WFP, LA; Michael Ditto, succession, January 17, 1834, box 26, succession records, WFP, LA; William Marbury, succession, September 17,

1845, box 67, succession records, WFP, LA; WFP police jury minutes, June 1840–1855, 6, LLMVC, LSU.

42. Mary Shouler, sale to Billy Chew, book D, 266, March 8, 1831, conveyance records, WFP, LA; Moses Horn, sale to Billy Chew, book D, 204, March 15, 1831, conveyance records, WFP, LA. Lot six, square eleven sold for $120. Parish register A, 314, September 10, 1837, Grace Episcopal Church, St. Francisville, LA.

43. Cowles Mead, sale [of Harriet and May Lilly] to William Chew, bills of sale 1, 216, January 12, 1838, WFP, LA.

44. 1839 La. Acts, 78, §1.

45. Chew family, act of emancipation and bond, book G, 7, June 3, 7, 1839, conveyance records, WFP, LA.

46. Louisiana complied marriage index, 1718–1925, ancestry.com (2004); manuscript census, 1850, WFP, LA, ancestry.com; William Chew, sale, book M, 109–10, February 18, 1841, conveyance records, WFP, LA. This included lots four, five, and six in square six. Cyrus Ratliff, succession, sale to Grace Church, book N, 333, April 25, 1860, conveyance records, WFP, LA. Lot three, square six sold for $1,460.

47. Moses Esquire, sale to William Chew, book G, 212, April 13, 1841, conveyance records, WFP, LA. Lots five, seven, eight, nine, ten, and eleven in square eleven sold for $425.

48. William Chew, donation to George Chew, book G, 214, April 24, 1841, conveyance records, WFP, LA; Benjamin Lavergne and Eliza Winn, sale to William Chew, book H, 313, February 4, 1843, conveyance records, WFP, LA. Lot one, square fourteen sold for three hundred dollars.

49. Charles Smith, sale to William Chew, bills of sale 2, 254–55, April 4, 1845, WFP, LA; Wilson Chew, act of emancipation, book 1, 116, June 23, 1845, conveyance records, WFP, LA.

50. Manuscript census, 1850, WFP, LA, ancestry.com.

51. Sarah Jackson, record of free status, book K, 132, November 4, 1850, conveyance records, WFP, LA.

52. *Bayou Sara Ledger*, "Yellow Fever: Calm Reflection," February 18, 1854.

53. This quote was obtained via the author's visit to the cemetery, June 29, 2021.

54. Michelle Carter, Our Lady of Mount Carmel Catholic Church, St. Francisville, LA, email to author, June 14, 2021.

55. George Chew, Wilson Chew, Mary Chew, and Harriet Williams, amicable partition, book M, 336, May 18, 1857, conveyance records, WFP, LA; Wilson Chew and George Chew, sale to/exchange with rector, wardens, and vestrymen of Grace Church, book M, 109–10, March 14, 1856, conveyance records, WFP, LA. Wilson Chew sold lots four and five in square six for one hundred dollars.

56. Wilson Chew and Mary Chew, sale to Jane Muse, book M, 339, May 18, 1857, conveyance records, WFP, LA; Harriet Chew, sale to Margaret Ann Jordan, book N, 6, February 17, 1859, conveyance records, WFP, LA.

57. Manuscript census, 1860, Lorain County, OH, ancestry.com.

58. Martin C. Pannell, sale to Norman Davis, book G, 106, March 26, 1840, conveyance records, WFP, LA. Lot eighty-seven, square eight sold for one hundred dollars. James Washington Dudley, sale to Juliet Cornish, book G, 167, January 2, 1841, conveyance records, WFP, LA. Lot 262, square twenty-five sold for three hundred dollars. Zachariah Canfield, sold to Catherine Collins, book H, 84, November 8, 1841, conveyance records, WFP, LA. Lot ninety, square eight sold for $150. Zachariah Canfield, sale to Catherine Collins, book H, 171, March 11, 1842, conveyance records, WFP, LA. Lot eighty-nine, square eight sold for two hundred dollars.

James M. Baker, sale to Ellen Wooten, book G, 199, March 29, 1841, conveyance records, WFP, LA. Lots 331, 333, 335, square twenty-seven sold for three thousand dollars. James W. Dudley, sale to Mary Ann Cornish, book H, 186, April 23, 1842, conveyance records, WFP, LA. Lot 269, square twenty-five sold for seventy-five dollars. Pleasant H. Harbor, sale to Catherine Collins, book 1, 490, July 29, 1848, conveyance records, WFP, LA. Lot ninety-one, square four sold for $529.88. George Harrison, sale to Ellen Wooten, book K, 154, December 5, 1850, conveyance records, WFP, LA. Lot two, square one sold for fourteen hundred dollars.

59. Drury L. Mitchell, sale to Ann Maria Gray, book 1, 218, February 27, 1846, conveyance records, WFP, LA; West Feliciana Rail Road Company, sale to Josephine Gray, book 1, 589, May 12, 1849, conveyance records, WFP, LA; John C. Morris, sale to Ellen Wooten, book H, 191, March 9, 1842, conveyance records, WFP, LA.

60. West Feliciana Rail Road Company, sale to Henry Oconnor, book 1, 585–86; Henry Oconnor, sale to Angus McRay, book 1, 580; Angus McRay (lessor) and Henry Oconnor, (lessee), lease agreement, book 1, 581, May 12, 1849, conveyance records, WFP, LA.

61. Henry Oconnor, sale to Isaac N. Maynard and Mary E. Baines, book K, 374, January 20, 1852, conveyance records, WFP, LA.

62. Henry Oconnor, apprenticeship, book E, 361, March 14, 1835, conveyance records, WFP, LA.

63. Henry Oconnor and Ann Griggs were married by Grace Episcopal Church rector Rev. R. H. Ranney on May 12, 1838. Grace Episcopal Church, marriage record book, 274. Oconnor was sexton at Grace Episcopal Church in 1849. William Harriet Mathews, sale to Henry Oconnor, book 1, 373, June 3, 1847, conveyance records, WFP, LA. For one thousand dollars, Mathews sold to Oconnor "six negro slaves" identified as Ann, thirty-two, yellow; and children of Ann—John, nine, yellow; Henry, seven, yellow; Sarah, four, yellow; Mitchel, three, yellow; Emily, seven months.

64. Ann Oconnor and six children, act of emancipation, book K, 137, November 6, 1850, conveyance records, WFP, LA; manuscript census, 1850, WFP, LA, ancestry.com.

65. Manuscript census, 1850, WFP, LA, ancestry.com; manuscript census, 1860, WFP, LA, ancestry.com.

66. Henderson C. Hudson, sale to Ann Savage, book K, 301, September 23, 1851, conveyance records, WFP, LA; Anna E. Savage, sale to Maria Wicker, book M, 173, July 2, 1856, conveyance records, WFP, LA; Maria Wicker, sale to De La Fayette Stocking, book M, 239, January 13, 1857, conveyance records, WFP, LA.

67. Simon J. Robison, sale to Stanley Dickerson, book M, 231, December 23, 1856, conveyance records, WFP, LA; Stanley Dickerson, sale to Jean Jeantier, book M, 344, June 3, 1857, conveyance records, WFP, LA.

68. Antonio Nolasco and Gertrude Nolasco, sale to William B. Rucker, book L, 504, March 6, 1855, conveyance records, WFP, LA; Gertrude Nolasco, sale to Jesse Barkdall, book M, 280, March 13, 1857, conveyance records, WFP, LA; Gertrude Nolasco and Antonio Nolasco, sale to Conrad Bockel, book M, 485, March 17, 1858, conveyance records, WFP, LA. Lot eight, square one sold for nine hundred dollars.

69. George Chew, Wilson Chew, Mary Chew, and Harriet Williams, amicable partition, book M, 336, May 18, 1857, conveyance records, WFP, LA; Wilson Chew and George Chew, sale to/exchange with rector, wardens, and vestrymen of Grace Church, book M, 109–10, March 14, 1856, conveyance records, WFP, LA. Wilson Chew sold lots four and five in square six for one hundred dollars. William Chew and Mary Chew, sale to Jane Muse, book M, 339, May 18, 1857, conveyance records, WFP, LA. Mary Chew sold lot five, square eleven, and lots

Notes

six, seven, eight, three-quarters of nine, one half of lot ten, and lot eleven, square eleven for six hundred dollars. Harriet Chew Williams, sale to Margaret Ann Jordan, book N, 6, February 17, 1859, conveyance records, WFP, LA. Harriet Chew sold lot one, square fourteen sold for three hundred dollars.

70. Savannah Shields, sale to Betsy Morris, book M, 473, March 4, 1858, conveyance records, WFP, LA.

71. Mary Ann Gray, sale to Charles L. Mathews, book N, 257, February 16, 1869, conveyance records, WFP, LA; Margaret S. Hills, sale to Mary Ann Gray, book N, 258, February 16, 1869, conveyance records, WFP, LA.

Chapter 4. Earning a Living

1. Manuscript census, 1860, WFP, LA, ancestry.com. Many authors have written about free people of color as wealthy business owners and owners of plantations in and near New Orleans. See, for example, Dormon, *Creoles of Color*. For a study of plantation-owning free people of color in southwestern Louisiana, see Brasseaux, Fontenot, and Oubre, *Creoles of Color*.

2. La. Civ. Code, art. 158 and 159 (1825), (repealed and replaced April 1, 1826, with "An act for the regulation of the rights and duties of apprentices and indented servants, passed on May 21, 1806").

3. John Stirling, declaration [concerning Ann Eliza], book AA, 260–61, October 25, 1826, conveyance records, WFP, LA; manuscript census, 1830, WFP, LA, ancestry.com.

4. Aseriais C. Dunn, declaration [concerning Valcourt Vessin], book AA, 268, January 19, 1827, conveyance records, WFP, LA.

5. John Henry Vaughn, apprenticeship, book AA, 269, February 7, 1827, conveyance records, WFP, LA. The apprenticeship lasted until January 1, 1844.

6. Isaac and Ferdinand, apprenticeship, book C, 20–21, September 17, 1828, conveyance records, WFP, LA. For Isaac, the apprenticeship lasted until December 31, 1844; for Ferdinand, until May 15, 1849.

7. Charles and Margaret, apprenticeship, book D, 407, January 28, 1832, conveyance records, WFP, LA.

8. Milly Norrell and Robert Norrell, apprenticeship [to Peter Lebret], book E, 423, June 29, 1835, conveyance records, WFP, LA; Ben Norrell, apprenticeship [to Joseph Carmena], book E, 424, June 29, 1835, conveyance records, WFP, LA.

9. Lotan Gordon Watson, apprenticeship, book C, 31–32, January 15, 1829, conveyance records, WFP, LA.

10. Benjamin Lavergne, apprenticeship, book D, 200, March 13, 1834, conveyance records, WFP, LA.

11. Jacob Collins, apprenticeship, book AA, 319, August 1, 1827, conveyance records, WFP, LA; Jefferson Roberts, apprenticeship, book D, 356, August 10, 1833, conveyance records, WFP, LA; James Mitchell Jr., apprenticeship, book F, 321, June 25, 1836, conveyance records, WFP, LA; John McMin, apprenticeship, book F, 320, August 20, 1836, conveyance records, WFP, LA.

12. Samuel, apprenticeship, book C, 124, April 18, 1829, conveyance records, WFP, LA.

13. Charles McMicken, sale to Drury L. Mitchell, book E, 78, April 11, 1833, conveyance records, WFP, LA; Drury L. Mitchell, sale to John West, book F, 44–45, February 3, 1836,

conveyance records, WFP, LA; Charles McMicken, sale to Drury L. Mitchell, book F, 364, March 6, 1838, conveyance records, WFP, LA; Drury L. Mitchell, sale to West Feliciana Rail Road Banking Company, book G, 153, July 28, 1840, conveyance records, WFP, LA.

14. *Drury L. Mitchell v. John Swift*, civil suit, no. 1315, La. 3rd Jud. Dist. Ct. (May 6, 1833); *Swift and Cascaden v. Drury L. Mitchell*, civil suit, no. 1260, La. 3rd Jud. Dist. Ct. (May 11, 1837); *Drury L. Mitchell v. George Douse*, civil suit, no. 1455, La. 3rd Jud. Dist. Ct. (March 26, 1835).

15. *Drury L. Mitchell v. Charles McDermott*, civil suit, no. 2300, La. 3rd Jud. Dist. Ct. (April 23, 1840); *Drury L. Mitchell v. Charles McDermott*, civil suit, no. 2418, La. 3rd Jud. Dist. Ct. (November 24, 1840).

16. *Thomas Duval v. D. L. Mitchell*, civil suit, no. 534, La. 3rd Jud. Dist. Ct. (April 9, 1828); *John C. Morris v. D. L. Mitchell*, civil suit, no. 439, Parish Court, WFP, LA (April 5, 1831); *Collins Blackman v. Drury L. Mitchell*, civil suit, no. 440, Parish Court, WFP, LA (March 10, 1831); *David A. Barclay v. Drury L. Mitchell*, civil suit, no. 1386, La. 3rd Jud. Dist. Ct. (December 20, 1834); *John West v. Drury Mitchell*, civil suit, no. 2744, La. 3rd Jud. Dist. Ct. (May 7, 1842).

17. Ruffin Piper, act of emancipation and apprenticeship, book E, 403, May 26, 1835, conveyance records, WFP, LA; Henry Oconnor, apprenticeship, book E, 361, March 14, 1835, conveyance records, WFP, LA; John Chervis, apprenticeship, book E, 361, March 14, 1835, conveyance records, WFP, LA; West Feliciana Rail Road Company, sale to Henry Oconnor, book I, 585–86; William Harriet Mathews, sale to Henry Oconnor, book I, 373, June 3, 1847. This sale included Ann, thirty-two, yellow; and children of Ann—John, nine, yellow; Henry, seven, yellow; Sarah, four, yellow; Mitchel, three, yellow; Emily, seven months—for one thousand dollars. John Chervis, parish register, book A, 324, July 8, 1851, Grace Episcopal Church, St. Francisville, LA.

18. Hardesty Chervis, apprenticeship, book F, 379, January 23, 1838, conveyance records, WFP, LA.

19. Hardesty Chervis, succession, inventory, September 6, 1849, box 102, succession records, WFP, LA.

20. Moses Horn, will, July 1, 1841, box 43, succession records, WFP, LA.

21. Leucy Hutchinson, succession, inventory, January 29, 1838, box 42, succession records, WFP, LA.

22. Lewis C. Hutchinson, sale to Leucy Hutchinson, bills of sale I, 212, December 8, 1837, WFP, LA.

23. Lewis Hutchinson, acknowledgement of paternity, book F, 483, January 8, 1839, conveyance records, WFP, LA; Drury Mitchell, petition, August 13, 1839, succession of Leucy Hutchinson, box 42, succession records, WFP, LA.

24. Leucy Hutchinson, succession, inventory, December 4, 1841, box 42, succession records, WFP, LA.

25. D. L. Mitchell, sale to John C. Morris, book H, 397–99, May 1, 1843, conveyance records, WFP, LA; John C. Morris, sale to D. L. Mitchell, book H, 569, March 9, 1844, conveyance records, WFP, LA; D. L. Mitchell, sale to Maria Ann Gray, book I, 218, February 27, 1846, conveyance records, WFP, LA.

26. Manuscript census, 1850, 1860, WFP, LA, ancestry.com.

27. *D. L. Mitchell v. W. W. Leake*, agt. for H. Whitaker, civil suit, no. 1474, La. 7th Jud. Dist. Ct. (March 7, 1861); D. L. Mitchell, bill to Pierce Butler, November 7, 1860, box 5, folder 7, mss. 1026, Butler Family Papers, LLMVC, LSU; D. L. Mitchell, receipts, March 5, 1861, box 5, folders 13 and 16, mss. 1026, Butler Family Papers, LLMVC, LSU.

Notes

28. Drury Mitchell, succession, inventory, February 12, 1866, box 65, succession records, WFP, LA. In Mitchell's estate, a claim against A. Szabo for $1,562.71 was valued at twelve hundred dollars; a claim against the estate of Ann Swift for $350 was valued at three hundred dollars for a total of $1,550.

29. Aggy Waltz and [her children Malinda [thirteen], Frances [girl, eleven], Samuel [seven], Richard [six], Charles [four] and David [one] Waltz, apprenticeship, book H, 74, October 9, 1841, conveyance records, WFP, LA; Norrell children, apprenticeship, book N, 241, February 9, 1860, conveyance records, WFP, LA.

30. Thomas Purnell, agreement with Mary Doherty, book A, 294–95, book D, 64, February 10, 1827, conveyance records, WFP, LA.

31. Ann Maria Bouton, declaration of free status, book D, 267, March 16, 1830, conveyance records, WFP, LA; Ann Eliza Wilkins, declaration of free status, book D, 308, March 16, 1830, conveyance records, WFP, LA; manuscript census, 1860, WFP, LA, ancestry.com.

32. Albert Prince, declaration of free status, book C, 334, June 15, 1830, conveyance records, WFP, LA; George Murry, declaration of free status, book D, 337, January 31, 1831, conveyance records, WFP, LA; Norman Davis, declaration of free status, book D, 229, June 13, 1831, conveyance records, WFP, LA.

33. Thomas Phelps, declaration of free status, book H, 566, May 24, 1844, conveyance records, WFP, LA.

34. John Clay, declaration of free status, book D, 227, March 16, 1830, conveyance records, WFP, LA.

35. Manuscript census, 1850, WFP, LA, ancestry.com. Those men included Henry O'Connor, Andrew Jackson, John Shavers, Lewis Horn, John Walker, and John, Edward, and Alexander Purnell.

36. Hardy Perry, succession, December 10, 1850, box 80, succession records, WFP, LA.

37. Manuscript census, 1860, WFP, LA, ancestry.com.

38. Walter McClellan, curator's account of succession, November 28, 1817, box 71, succession records, WFP, LA; James Ficklin, curator's account of succession, April 15, 1818, and August 28, 1818, box 33, succession records, WFP, LA; John H. Johnson, sale to Judique Lacour, book A, 126, December 12, 18__, conveyance records, WFP, LA.

39. Robert H. Hewit, curator's account of succession, December 12, 1816, box 45, succession records, WFP, LA. While it is possible that Judique Lacour and Betsey Jackson were not the same people as Betsey Kemper and Julia Kemper Lacour, it is more probable that they are one and the same. Walter McClellan, curator's account of succession, November 28, 1817, box 71, succession records, WFP, LA; James Ficklin, curator's account of succession, April 15, 1818, and August 28, 1818, box 33, succession records, WFP, LA; Kesiah Middleton, succession, August 19, 1840, box 68, succession records, WFP, LA.

40. Manuscript census, 1860, WFP, LA, ancestry.com. The washerwomen listed included Fanny Hendrick, M. Coleman, B. Johnson, I. Johnson, M. Morris, Priscilla, and C. Brown. M. Coleman owned one thousand dollars in real estate and six hundred dollars in movables. Priscilla owned one thousand dollars in movables.

41. Manuscript census, 1850, WFP, LA, ancestry.com.

42. Free people of color were accepted as members of the Grace Episcopal Church. The rector (pastor) of the church conducted weddings and funerals for free people of color and offered church services to enslaved people on two plantations some distance from the church. Warren E. Milteer Jr. wrote that, before the 1850s, free people of color, enslaved people, and white people attended church together in Gates County, North Carolina.

Warren E. Milteer Jr., "Life in a Great Dismal Swamp Community: Free People of Color in Pre-Civil War Gates County, North Carolina," *North Carolina Historical Review* 91, no. 2 (April 2014): 156.

43. Manuscript census, 1850, 1860, WFP, LA, ancestry.com.

44. Betsy Archer, note to George Mathews, mss. 4358, Mathews-Ventress-Lawrason Papers, LLMVC, LSU.

45. A. P. Walsh, agreement with Aaron Griggs, February 3, 1823, folder 3b:18b and 3b:19c, mss. 887, 1820–1823, [A. P.] Walsh Papers, LLMVC, LSU.

46. Walsh, agreement with Griggs.

47. Manuscript census, 1860, WFP, LA, ancestry.com.

48. The 1850 census did not report the occupations of black or mulatto women living in households with white men and mulatto children. See family no. 11, Daniel Wicker, no. 56, Henry Robertson, no. 398, Hardy Perry, and no. 410, Thomas Purnell. Manuscript census, 1850, WFP, LA, ancestry.com.

49. John Rous, succession, lease agreement, April 18, 1818, box 89, succession records, WFP, LA; Ellen Wooten, sale to William H. Glass, book L, 122, June 28, 1853, conveyance records, WFP, LA. Nelly Wooten's name often appeared as Ellen Wooten in official documents.

50. Ellen Wooten, succession, inventory, September 1, 1853, box 111, succession records, WFP, LA.

51. Henry Stirling, sale to John Rous, 64, 1809, Vendor Index to Conveyances, Sm–Sz, WFP, LA.

52. John Rous, succession, December 19, 1817, box 89, succession records, WFP, LA.

53. John Rous, succession, December 19, 1817, box 89, succession records, WFP, LA. For comparison, a general store selling similar goods in 1817 had a merchandize value of $9,734. *McMicken v. Webb*, 36 US 25 (1837). The freight charge for shipping cotton was thirty dollars. Antonio Nolasco, October 15, 1815, mss. 1382, James Pirrie Papers, LLMVC, LSU.

54. Warren Stone, deed of sale, book N, 317, April 9, 1860, conveyance records, WFP, LA.

55. Brenda E. Stevenson, "What's Love Got to Do With It? Concubinage and Enslaved Women and Girls in the Antebellum South," in "Women, Slavery, and the Atlantic World," ed. V. P. Franklin, special issue, *Journal of African American History* 98, no. 1 (Winter 2013): 105. Enslaved men usually cost more than females unless those females were marketed as fancy girls or as good breeders.

56. In 1820, Henry Stirling held thirty-nine people in slavery. Thirty worked in agriculture. Five were females aged fourteen to twenty-five. Manuscript census, 1820, Feliciana Parish, LA, ancestry.com.

57. Clark, *The Strange History*, 61.

58. Clark, *The Strange History*, 65.

59. John Rous, succession, December 19, 1817, box 89, succession records, WFP, LA.

60. Matilda Stewart, sale to Antonio Nolasco, book A, 120, October 21, 1816, conveyance records, WFP, LA.

61. John Rous, succession, December 19, 1817, box 89, succession records, WFP, LA.

62. John Rous, succession, December 19, 1817, box 89, succession records, WFP, LA.

63. Sheriff's sale, book A, 196, April 4, 1818, conveyance records, WFP, LA.

64. John Rous, succession, lease agreement, April 18, 1818, box 89, succession records, WFP, LA.

65. John Rous, succession, act of t…orship, December 19, 1817, box 89, succession records, WFP, LA; manuscript census, 1820, F…ciana Parish, LA, ancestry.com.

66. Nelly Wooten, petition, Septe…er 6, 1823, succession of John Rous, box 89, succession records, WFP, LA.

67. *Ellen Wooten v. James Turner*, … Mart. (N.S.) 442, 5 La. Rpt. 151 (1828); civil suit, no. 194, La. 3rd Jud. Dist. Ct. (December …, 1824).

68. *Watts and Lobdell v. Hellen W…ten*, civil suit, no. 1276, La. 3rd Jud. Dist. Ct. (December 10, 1835).

69. Probate book 4 (1827–1829), 1… , June 6, 1828, WFP, LA.

70. John C. Morris, succession, in…ntory, February 6–19, 1850, box 65, succession records, WFP, LA; *Louisiana Journal*, July 28, …27 [advertisement]; Henry A. Lyons, invoice for purchases, January 3, 1839, box 1, fold… 17, mss. 1382, [Henry A.] Lyons Papers, LLMVC, LSU; John Holmes, letter to Thomas Butle… January 12, 1843, box 3c, folder 46, 48, mss. 1026, Butler Family Papers, LLMVC, LSU.

71. John C. Morris, sale to Ellen W…oten, book C, 236, December 1, 1829, and April 28, 1841, conveyance records, WFP, LA. T…is reads, "Having fully discharged and paid the debt of money and gratitude referred to on t… s sheet—I hereby declare this deed null and void now and forever. April 28, 1841."

72. John C. Morris, sale to Ellen W…oten, book C, 236, December 1, 1829, and April 28, 1841, conveyance records, WFP, LA.

73. *John C. Morris, Curator of Nol…co Estates v. James Turner, Former Curator*, successions of James and Antonio Nolasco, …robate Court (October 22, 1829).

74. Anne Royall, *Mrs. Royall's Sou…ern Tour, or Second Series of the Black Book* (Washington, DC: self-published, 1830), 3:8…3:87.

75. Bennet H. Barrow, diary, 48, M…y 19, 1838.

76. Royall, *Mrs. Royall's Southern …ur*, 3:89, 3:96; Frederick William Williamson and George T. Goodman, eds., *Eastern L…isiana: A History of the Watershed of the Ouachita River and the Florida Parishes* (Louis…lle, KY: Historical Record Association, 1939), 485.

77. David Dikson, sale to Ellen W…ten, bills of sale 1, 229–30, June 10, 1831, WFP, LA; David Dikson, sale to Ellen Wooten, …lls of sale 1, 230, December 20, 1831, WFP, LA.

78. Paul A. Kunkel commented o…he pervasive presence of slavery in Louisiana. See Paul A. Kunkel, "Modifications in Lo…siana Negro Legal Status under Louisiana Constitutions 1812–1957," *Journal of Negro His…ry* 44, no. 1 (January 1959): 7; Rev. H. Cowles Atwater commented that "familiarity with wr…g can paralyze the conscience to all sense of guilt." Atwater, *Incidents*, 65.

79. Heirs of John Ketchum, sale t… Nelly Wooten, book E, 224, March 18, 1834, conveyance records, WFP, LA; Ellen Wooten…succession, inventory, September 1, 1853, box 111, succession records, WFP, LA; John C. M…ris, sale to Ellen Wooten, book K, 50, August 1, 1834, conveyance records, WFP, LA.

80. John C. Morris, sale to Ellen W…oten, book F, 144, June 27, 1836, conveyance records, WFP, LA.

81. Harrison Jordan, sale to Nelly …ooten, bills of sale 1, 346, January 16, 1840, WFP, LA; Mary Stirling, sale to Nelly Wooten, b…ls of sale 1, 347, February 13, 1840, WFP, LA.

82. 1830 La. Acts, 90, §§10, 16.

83. James M. Baker, sale to Ellen W…oten, book G, 199, March 29, 1841, conveyance records, WFP, LA; John C. Morris, sal… to Ellen Wooten, book H, 191, March 9, 1842,

conveyance records, WFP, LA; Lemuel McCauley, sale to John Morris, book G, 174, January 18, 1841, conveyance records, WFP, LA.

84. [James] Rudman, account book, 1844–1848, mss. 881, LLMVC, LSU.

85. *Daniel Wicker v. Ellen Wooten*, civil suit, no. 167, La. 7th Jud. Dist. Ct. (October 23, 1848). This is the same Daniel Wicker who fathered children with Maria Wicker.

86. *Jean Gambo v. Nelly Wooten*, Parish Court, WFP, LA (June 1824).

87. John C. Morris, succession, inventory, February 6–19, 1850, box 65, succession records, WFP, LA; John C. Morris, will, probate record, book 1, 1811–1819, 136, May 8, 1815, WFP, LA.

88. George Harrison, sale to Ellen Wooten, book K, 154, December 5, 1850, conveyance records, WFP, LA.

89. Jacob Michael, sale to Ellen Wooten, book K, 466, March 19, 1852, conveyance records, WFP, LA.

90. Ellen Wooten, sale to William H. Glass, book L, 122, June 28, 1853, conveyance records, WFP, LA.

91. *Louisiana Chronicle*, "Planter's Exchange Restaurant Bayou Sara," December 20, 1854.

92. *Bayou Sara Ledger*, May 11, 1852 [advertisement]; *Bayou Sara Ledger*, August 20, 1853 [advertisement]; *Bayou Sara Ledger*, "Yellow Fever: Calm Reflection," February 18, 1854; sheriff's sale, book L, 391, August 26, 1854, conveyance records, WFP, LA.

93. US, Find a Grave Index, 1600s–Current, ancestry.com; *E. Wooten v. George Harrison*, 9 La. Ann. 234, 235 (1854).

94. La. Civ. Code, art. 1468 (1825, repealed 1987). This states, "Those who have lived together in open concubinage are respectively incapable of making to each other, whether inter vivos or mortis causa, any donation of immovables; and if they make a donation of movables, it can not exceed one-tenth part of the whole value of their estate." *E. Wooten v. George Harrison*, 9 La. Ann. 234, 235 (1854).

95. Royall, *Mrs. Royall's Southern Tour*, 3:90–92.

96. Ellen Wooten, succession, petitions, August 31, 1853, October 6, 1853, box 111, succession records, WFP, LA.

97. Ellen Wooten, succession, inventory, September 1, 1853, box 111, succession records, WFP, LA. For comparison, the governor of Louisiana received a salary of six thousand dollars in 1855. *Thibodaux Minerva*, "Salaries of Governors," July 28, 1855.

98. *Margaret Smith v. Estate of Ellen Wooten*, La. 7th Jud. Dist. Ct. (1853).

99. La. Civ. Code, art. 177 (1825). This states, "They can transmit nothing by succession or otherwise; but the succession of free persons related to them which they would have inherited had they been free, may pass through them to such of their descendants as may have acquired their liberty before the succession is opened."

100. Partition in kind, book L, 209, January 23, 1854, conveyance records, WFP, LA. Gertrude Nolasco and Antonio E. Nolasco each received seven slaves and two promissory notes of William Glass. Antonio received: Charles (thirty-three), valued at one thousand dollars; Lewis or Jim (twenty-five), valued at one thousand dollars; Big Henry (twenty-seven), valued at twelve hundred dollars; Little Henry (fifteen), valued at six hundred dollars; Melinda (thirty-five), valued at six hundred dollars; Natice or Rebecca (age?), valued at eight hundred dollars; and Azeline (seventeen), valued at eight hundred dollars. Gertrude received: Sam (twenty-two), valued at fifteen hundred dollars; Letitia (sixteen), valued at one thousand dollars; Lydia (thirty) and her two children, William (three) and infant Antoinette, valued at eleven hundred dollars; Easter (forty), valued at six hundred dollars; Willis (forty), valued at eight hundred dollars; David (fourteen), valued at six hundred dollars; Charlotte (thirty-five), valued at six hundred dollars. Gertrude Nolasco, sale to William Ball, book L, 251,

March 16, 1854, conveyance records, WFP, LA; Antonio Nolasco and Gertrude Nolasco, sale to William B. Rucker, book L, 504, M[arch] 6, 1855, conveyance records, WFP, LA; Gertrude Nolasco, sale to James Washington D[al]ley, book L, 514, March 29, 1855, conveyance records, WFP, LA; Gertrude Nolasco and Ant[on]io Nolasco, sale to Charles Stoer, book M, 19, August 22, 1855, conveyance records, WFP, L[A]; Gertrude Nolasco, sale to Jesse Barkdall, book M, 280, March 13, 1857, conveyance re[co]rds, WFP, LA; Antonio F. Nolasco and Gertrude Populus, sale to Charles Hofman and [I]saias Meyer, book M, 451, February 18, 1858, conveyance records, WFP, LA; Gertrude and [A]ntonio Nolasco, sale to Conrad Bockel, book M, 485, March 17, 1858, conveyance records, W[F]P, LA; Antonio Nolasco, sale to William Hearsey, book N, 174, December 1, 1859, conve[ya]nce records, WFP, LA; Gertrude Nolasco, sale to Isaac Freeland, book N, 387, August 16, 186[7,] conveyance records, WFP, LA; Gertrude Nolasco and Antonio Nolasco, sale to Edward [D]ouglass, book O, 639, October 8, 1867, conveyance records, WFP, LA; Gertrude and Ant[on]io Nolasco, sale to Conrad Bockel, book Q, 251, January 7, 1872, conveyance records, WFP, [L]A; Gertrude Nolasco and Antonio Nolasco, sale to Benjamin Blanton, book O, 376, Octo[be]r 19, 1872, conveyance records, WFP, LA.

101. George Douse, statement of a[cc]ount dated at Orange Hill, November 28, 1838, submitted in the succession of Robert H[ail]e, claim no. 56, January 30, 1844, box 43, succession records, WFP, LA.

102. George Douse, declaration of [fr]ee status, book D, 235, June 14, 1831, conveyance records, WFP, LA.

103. Henry Bains, sale to George [Do]use, book D, 233, May 25, 1831, conveyance records, WFP, LA; Elisabeth Kilbourne Dart, "[D]ouse, George, Planter, Taverner," in *A Dictionary of Louisiana Biography*, ed. Glenn R. [Co]nrad (Lafayette: Louisiana Historical Association, 1988), 1:254.

104. Anne M. Lobdell, letter to Le[wi]s Stirling Jr., February 1836, mss. 1866, [Lewis] Stirling and Family Papers, LLMVC, LSU.

105. Robert Haile, succession, clai[m] no. 56, January 30, 1844, box 43, succession records, WFP, LA.

106. Bennet H. Barrow, diary, 98, [Ap]ril 10, 1839.

107. Barrow, diary, 182, July 4, 1840.

108. Barrow, diary, 206, Decembe[r] 3, 1840.

109. Barrow, diary, 188, August 3, 1[84]0.

110. William Massingill, sale to G[eo]rge Douse, book D, 267, July 5, 1831, conveyance records, WFP, LA; Edward H. Barton, [sa]le to George Douse, book D, 374, March 6, 1832, conveyance records, WFP, LA.

111. Charles McMicken, sale to Ge[or]ge Douse, book E, 348, February 18, 1835, conveyance records, WFP, LA; Charles McMicke[n,] sale to George Douse, book F, 208, February 18, 1837, conveyance records, WFP, LA; *Willia[m] Cooke v. George Douse*, civil suit, no. 1707, La. 3rd Jud. Dist. Ct. (July 26, 1837). The note atta[ch]ed to the petition in the suit to collect a debt dated April 19, 1837, totaled $171.35. The suit [w]as dismissed at Cooke's request on December 25, 1837. *Barclay and Tenney v. George Douse*, [ci]vil suit, no. 1708, La. 3rd Jud. Dist. Ct. (July 26, 1837). The record of account, dated June 10[, 18]37, shows purchases from March 24 to May 23, 1837, totaling $411.55. The suit was dismiss[ed] at the request of Barclay and Tenney on December 25, 1837.

112. Henry Baines, letter to his wi[fe,] March 8, 1837, folder 1837, 1838, 1840, mss. 1209, Baines [Henry and Family] Papers, L[LM]VC, LSU.

113. A. M. Lobdell, letter to her bro[th]er, November 17, 1837, box 1, folder 9, mss. 1866, Stirling (Lewis and Family) Papers, L[LM]VC, LSU.

114. *William Cooke v. George Douse*, civil suit, no. 1707, La. 3rd Jud. Dist. Ct. (July 26, 1837); *Barclay & Tenney v. George Douse*, civil suit, no. 1708, La. 3rd Jud. Dist. Ct. (July 26, 1837).

115. *Charles McMicken v. George Douse*, civil suit, no. 1951, La. 3rd Jud. Dist. Ct. (May 31, 1839). The parish sheriff seized a tract of land on Woodville Road 34 93/100 arpents with improvements. See book H, 174, January 28, 1842, conveyance records, WFP, LA.

116. The original note is in Elisabeth Kilbourne Dart files, WFP Museum, St. Francisville, LA.

117. See, generally, vendor and vendee indexes to conveyances, H–O, from 1811 to June 30, 1974, conveyance records, WFP, LA. See, for example, book D, 142, October 4, 1830, and book E, 4, January 21, 1833.

118. Incorporation of Bayou Sarah Steam Boat Company, book D, 364, act of June 16, 1830, recorded April 5, 1832, conveyance records, WFP, LA. The steamboat *Brilliant* left New Orleans each Wednesday at 10 a.m. for Bayou Sara and left Bayou Sara for New Orleans each Saturday at 10 a.m., stopping in Baton Rouge and leaving there at 4 p.m. *Baton Rouge (LA) Gazette*, "New Orleans & Bayou Sara Packet," February 22, 1840.

119. 1830 La. Acts, 90; 1842 La. Acts, 123.

120. George Douse and family, affidavit of free status, book H, 244, September 1, 1842, conveyance records, WFP, LA.

121. George P. Douse died in New Orleans December 22, 1863. Orleans Deaths, 22:363, Vital Records Microfilm, LA State Archives.

122. Martha Morris, sale to Maria Battiste, book I, 183, December 31, 1845, conveyance records, WFP, LA.

123. Maria Battiste Wicker, Bettis Wicker, William Wicker, and John Wicker, act of emancipation, book H, 238, May 26, 1842, conveyance records, WFP, LA.

124. Manuscript census, 1850, Bayou Sara, WFP, LA, ancestry.com.

125. La. Civ. Code, art. 1468 (1825, repealed 1987).

126. Martha Morris, sale to Maria Battiste, book I, 183, December 31, 1845, conveyance records, WFP, LA. Lot seventeen, square ten sold for seven hundred dollars. *Bayou Sara Ledger*, "Yellow Fever: Calm Reflection," February 18, 1854; plantation diaries, September 15, 1853, mss. 1866, Sterling (Lewis and Family) Papers, LLMVC, LSU.

127. Appointment of agent and attorney in fact, book L, 544, June 11, 1855, conveyance records, WFP, LA; John F. Valentine, sale to John Holmes as agent for Maria Wicker, book L, 551, June 13, 1855, conveyance records, WFP, LA; John F. Valentine, sale to Maria Wicker, book L, 551, June 13, 1855, conveyance records, WFP, LA.

128. 1852 La. Acts, 214, §1; 1855 La. Acts, 377, §71.

129. Albert Wicker and Edward Wicker, permission to pass, book M, 416, December 29, 1857, conveyance records, WFP, LA.

130. Isaias Meyer and Phillip Adolphus, sale to Maria Wicker, book M, 70, January 19, 1856, conveyance records, WFP, LA. The sale included twenty-six feet and eleven inches fronting on Point Street, 119 feet back, adjoining a lot she already owned and that of Henrietta Coleman for $430.

131. Henderson C. Hudson, sale to Ann Savage, book K, 301, September 23, 1851, conveyance records, WFP, LA. The sale was for three hundred dollars. Anna E. Savage, sale to Maria Wicker, book M, 173, July 2, 1856, conveyance records, WFP, LA. The sale was for $1350. Maria Wicker, sale to De La Fayette Stocking, book M, 239, January 13, 1857, conveyance records, WFP, LA. The sale was for $1350.

132. Maria Battiste Wicker, acknowledgement of maternity, book M, 383, October 29, 1857, conveyance records, WFP, LA. All the children were of mulatto color.

133. Manuscript census, 1860, WFP, LA, ancestry.com; Greene family correspondence, October 14, 1866, Misc. G., mss. 4508, LLMVC, LSU.

134. Greene family correspondence, April 5, 1867, Misc. G., mss. 4508, LLMVC, LSU.

135. Maria Wicker, succession, inventory, May 12, 1868, box 115, succession records, WFP, LA.

136. Parish register A+, 220, September 29, 1858, Grace Episcopal Church, St. Francisville, LA.

137. Manuscript census, 1880, New Orleans, LA, ancestry.com.

138. Isaias Meyer and Phillip Adolphus, sale to Henrietta Coleman, book M, 68, January 17, 1856, conveyance records, WFP, LA. The sale was of a lot fronting forty-five feet on Point Street by 155 feet, with adjoining lots belonging to Maria Wicker, for three hundred dollars.

139. Henrietta Coleman, succession, inventory, April 10, 1867, box 20, succession records, WFP, LA.

140. Manuscript census, 1860, Bayou Sara, WFP, LA, ancestry.com.

141. Testimony in regard to alleged outrages in West Feliciana Parish, LA, June 21, 1876, 44th Cong., 1st sess., Bayou Sara, LA, 759–67, Special Collections, LLMVC, LSU.

142. Wilson P. Burton and Sarah Burton, sale to Hampton Whitaker, book M, 303, April 9, 1857, conveyance records, WFP, LA. Lot twenty-five in square three sold for $2,200, paid with four notes of five hundred dollars each. R. S. Spalding, sale to Hampton Whitaker, book M, 246, June 7, 1857, conveyance records, WFP, LA.

143. *False River (LA) Pointe Coupee Democrat*, "Notice," January 15, 1858, January 30, 1858, and February 6, 1858.

144. *Bayou Sara Phoenix Ledger*, "China Grove Hotel—Formerly Henshaw House," January 16, 1858.

145. Ann Reid, William W. Packie, and James Reid, sale to Hampton Whitaker, book N, 25, January 1, 1859, conveyance records, WFP, LA; Hampton Whitaker, lease to Jackson C. Banff, book N, 191, December 31, 1859, conveyance records, WFP, LA; Hampton Whitaker, sale to James R. Raby, book N, 210, January 3, 1860, conveyance records, WFP, LA; power of attorney, book N, 307, March 21, 1860, conveyance records, WFP, LA.

146. Hampton Whitaker, sale to John F. Irvine, book N, 327, March 31, 1860, conveyance records, WFP, LA.

147. Jordan Ritchie, succession, inventory, August 21, 1835, box 90, succession records, WFP, LA.

148. Antonio Piccaluga, succession, receipt, March 31, 1825, box 79, succession records, WFP, LA.

149. Antonio Piccaluga, succession, box 79, succession records, WFP, LA.

150. James Fair and Thomas Fair, statement, book D, 195, March 2, 1831, conveyance records, WFP, LA; manuscript census, 1820, Feliciana Parish, LA, ancestry.com.

151. Kesiah Middleton, act of emancipation, book D, 195, October 2, 1827, conveyance records, WFP, LA.

152. Antonio Piccaluga, succession, will, November 17, 1832, box 79, succession records, WFP, LA; book E, 136, conveyance records, WFP, LA.

153. Kesiah Middleton, acceptance of the succession of Antonio Piccaluga, book E, 136, January 22, 1833, conveyance records, WFP, LA; Antonio Piccaluga, succession, petition, January 22, 1833, probate record, book 6, 1832–1837, 243, WFP, LA.

154. *Kesiah Middleton v. Samuel Stevenson*, petition, civil suit, no. 1332, La. 3rd Jud. Dist. Ct. (July 30, 1833); Kesiah Middleton, sale to Cecilia A. Thompson, book E, 211, February 7, 1834, conveyance records, WFP, LA.

155. *Im La Keep v. Kesiah Middleton*, civil suit, no. 508, La. 7th Jud. Dist. Ct. (April 21, 1834). The petition was filed March 13, 1833, the answer on June 28, 1833, and the answers to interrogatories on July 10, 1833. See [Elisabeth K.] Dart Collection, folder 125, mss. 5023, LLMVC, LSU. Keep asked for ten dollars for the house call, $120 for twenty-seven days of lodging, thirty dollars for the firewood, seven dollars for the pantaloons, and twelve dollars for the handkerchief.

156. Jonathan Ellsworth, sale to Kesiah Middleton, book E, 247, May 12, 1834, conveyance records, WFP, LA. The sale was of Bayou Sara lot ninety-five, square eight for three hundred dollars. Jean Pierre Ledoux, sale to Jonathan Ellsworth and Kesiah Middleton, book F, 176, November 7, 1836, conveyance records, WFP, LA; release of mortgage, book F, 544, February 20, 1839, conveyance records, WFP, LA; Kesiah Middleton, sale to John Riley, book F, 227–28, March 6, 1837, conveyance records, WFP, LA.

157. Kesiah Middleton, succession, August 19, 1840, box 68, succession records, WFP, LA; Kesiah Middleton, sale to Marcia Carmouche, book F, 542, February 18, 1839, conveyance records, WFP, LA.

158. Kesiah Middleton, succession, inventory, April 3, 1840, box 68, succession records, WFP, LA.

159. Kesiah Middleton, succession, petition, May 16, 1840, Judgment, September 2, 1840, box 68, succession records, WFP, LA.

160. Kesiah Middleton, succession, testimony, April 25, 1840, box 68, succession records, WFP, LA.

161. Kesiah Middleton, succession, April 25, 1840, box 68, succession records, WFP, LA. The claims were from Dr. Samuel Jones for $276.25, from Dr. R. H. Horn for one hundred dollars for consulting with Jones; from Dr. William Lyle for $175, and from Dr. George W. Smith for $28.50.

162. Judith Kelleher Schafer pointed out that white people often used other legal disputes to raise the issue of the free status of litigants of color. Judith Kelleher Schafer, *Becoming Free, Remaining Free: Manumission and Enslavement in New Orleans, 1846–1862* (Baton Rouge: Louisiana State University Press, 2003), 101.

163. John Bettis, will, June 30, 1833, succession of Kesiah Middleton, box 68, succession records, WFP, LA.

164. Kesiah Middleton, succession, judgment, box 68, January 23, 1847, succession records, WFP, LA; *Hannah Bettis v. Samuel A. Jones, Curator*, civil suit, no. 246, La. 7th Jud. Dist. Ct. (January 23, 1847). Judge J. Weems recused himself in the probate court case no. 262 and appointed Thomas Butler as special judge to hear the case. Letter, July 13, 1843, box 3c, folder 49, mss. 1026, Butler Family Papers, LLMVC, LSU. Jones was entitled to a small commission for handling the succession.

165. Hannah Bettis, sale to Samuel Jones, book M, 104, March 3, 1856, conveyance records, WFP, LA.

166. Sales to Jesse Wilson, book AA, 53–55, December 1821 to January 1822, conveyance records, WFP, LA; Jesse Wilson, sale to Thomas N. Hosea, book AA, 53, January 8, 1824, conveyance records, WFP, LA; Hardy Perry, sale to Caroline Perry, book K, 152, December 10, 1850, conveyance records, WFP, LA; David Weeks, donation to Ann Maria Curtis, book A, 112, July 17, 1816, conveyance records, WFP, LA; Ann Maria Curtis, sale to Levi Sholar, book AA, 10, March 18, 1822, conveyance records, WFP, LA; John C. Morris, sale to Ellen Wooten, book H, 191, March 9, 1842, conveyance records, WFP, LA; James Haggerty, sale to Mary Ann Curtis, book A, 99, March 18, 1816, conveyance records, WFP, LA; Josias Gray, sale to Ann

Maria Gray, book AA, 329, June 23, 1830, conveyance records, WFP, LA; manuscript census, 1850, WFP, LA, ancestry.com.

167. Ira Berlin argued that entry into the slaveholding class demonstrated to white people the reliability of free people of color and allowed them to stake a claim to equality. Ira Berlin, *Generations of Captivity: A History of African American Slaves* (Cambridge, MA: Belknap Press, 2003), 139, 144.

168. Josias Gray, sale to Ann Maria Gray, book B, 307–8, July 11, 1839, conveyance records, WFP, LA; Henry Freeman Peterson, sale to Josephine Gray, book K, 540, April 3, 1845, conveyance records, WFP, LA; H. F. Peterson, sale to Maria Gray, book K, 41, June 15, 1848, conveyance records, WFP, LA; John F. Valentine, sale to Josephine Gray, book K, 42, February 19, 1850, conveyance records, WFP, LA.

169. Daniel Fields, sale to Norman Davis, bills of sale A, 239, July 8, 1833, WFP, LA; J. P. Boswell, sale to Norman Davis, bills of sale 1, 43–44, August 20, 1835, WFP, LA; Charles McMicken and James Turner, sale to Norman Davis, book F, 494–95, January 11, 1839, conveyance records, WFP, LA.

170. Elsey Scott, sale to Caroline M. V. Hall, bills of sale A, 233, April 5, 1833, WFP, LA; Elsey Scott, sale to Joseph Talary, bills of sale 1, 366, November 1, 1840, WFP, LA.

171. Lewis Stirling Jr., sale to Caroline Perry, bills of sale book 2, 213, May 27, 1844, WFP, LA; Caroline Perry, sale to Lewis Stirling Jr., bills of sale book 2, 214–15, May 27, 1844, WFP, LA; Philander C. Smith, sale to Caroline Perry, book I, 461, April 17, 1848, conveyance records, WFP, LA; Caroline Perry, sale to Obadiah Tate, book K, 262, May 20, 1851, conveyance records, WFP, LA; Caroline Perry, sale to Vincent D. Walsh, book N, 319, May 2, 1857, conveyance records, WFP, LA.

172. Hardy Perry, sale to Caroline Perry, book K, 152, December 10, 1850, conveyance records, WFP, LA.

173. Hardy Perry, donation to Caroline Perry, book K, 152, December 10, 1850, conveyance records, WFP, LA.

174. Lewis C. Hutchinson, sale to Lucy Hutchinson, bills of sale 1, 212, December 8, 1837, WFP, LA; George Brittion, sale to Mary Ann Brittion, bills of sale 1, 218, January 9, 1838, WFP, LA; Mary Ann Brittion and John Chefer [husband], sale to William M. Rankin, bills of sale 1, 337, February 13, 1840, WFP, LA; Pleasant H. Harbour, sale to Catherine Collins, book I, 490, July 29, 1848, conveyance records, WFP, LA.

175. Milteer, "Life," 156; Warren E. Milteer Jr., *North Carolina's Free People of Color 1715–1885* (Baton Rouge: Louisiana State University Press, 2020), 105.

Chapter 5. Black-White Personal Relationships

1. Welch, "Black Litigiousness," 378.

2. Julia Lacour, letter to A. P. Walsh, July 9, 1820, box 3a, folder 14a, mss. 887, [A. P.] Walsh Papers, LLMVC, LSU.

3. *James Calvin v. Jacob Potter and Amos Hoe*, judgment, civil suit, no. 67, La. 3rd Jud. Dist. Ct. (April 5, 1824).

4. George Pease, sale to Frank and Nancy, book F, 136, October 24, 1836, conveyance records, WFP, LA. Lot three, square six sold for $450. The record says square one, fronting on the courthouse. Square one is not near the courthouse.

5. David Bradford, statement, book G, 41, September 25, 1839, conveyance records, WFP, LA.

6. Frank Bradford, sale to Hannah Fouty, book K, 48, February 28, 1850, conveyance records, WFP, LA. Lot three, square six sold for one hundred dollars. The square numbers are different in the two acts of sale, but the 1850 act of sale specifically notes that this is the same lot bought from Maj. George Pease on October 24, 1846, and recorded in book F, 136 of the Parish conveyance records and states that the land was next to that of William Chew. Chew owned lots in square six. The one-hundred-dollar sale amount was the balance on the mortgage on the property Bradford owed to Daniel Turnbull, which Fouty agreed to pay.

7. David Bradford, release of rights of Hannah Fouty, book L, 373, July 25, 1854, conveyance records, WFP, LA; Hannah Fouty, sale to Cyrus Ratcliff, book L, 375, July 27, 1854, conveyance records, WFP, LA.

8. Probate record, book 1, 1811–1819, 203, June 29, 1816, WFP, LA.

9. Joseph Buatt, sale to Peggy Russell, book E, 461, September 11, 1835, conveyance records, WFP, LA; Joseph R. Thomas, sale to Peggy Russell, book F, 199, December 17, 1836, conveyance records, WFP, LA.

10. Peggy Russell, will, February 21, 1840, box 89, succession records, WFP, LA.

11. Peggy Russell, will, book G, 149, October 12, 1840, conveyance records, WFP, LA; probate record, book 8, 1840–1841, 43, November 25, 1840, Office of the Clerk of Court, WFP, LA.

12. Julia Gardner, will, book H, 442, March 7, 1842, conveyance records, WFP, LA; affidavit of free status, book H, 145, November 24, 1840, conveyance records, WFP, LA; Julia Gardner, succession, September 6, 1843, box 40, succession records, WFP, LA; will, probate record, book 9, 1841–1844, 416, March 7, 1842, WFP, LA.

13. Joseph R. Thomas, sale to Elsey Scott, book F, 195, January 31, 1837, conveyance records, WFP, LA. Lots two, three, and five, square two sold for $175. Elsey Scott, will, July 14, 1835, box 9999, unrecorded documents, conveyance records, WFP, LA; Elsey Scott, succession, 225, probate record, book 9, 1841–1844, March 15, 1842, WFP, LA.

14. Victor Dominique Vasse, sale to Betsey Givins, book F, 293–94, July 13, 1837, conveyance records, WFP, LA; Betsey Givens, sale to Simeon Chefer, book F, 456, November 12, 1838, conveyance records, WFP, LA. The sale was for $150. Simeon Chefer, sale to Betsey Givens, book F, 535, March 4, 1839, conveyance records, WFP, LA; Betsey Givens, donation to Mary Aronstien, book R, 310, March 13, 1876, conveyance records, WFP, LA; Mary Thornsberry [wife of Julius Aronstein], petition to accept a donation, book R, 309, March 14, 1876, conveyance records, WFP, LA.

15. Testimony in regard to alleged outrages in West Feliciana Parish, LA, June 21, 1876, 44th Cong., 1st sess., Bayou Sara, LA, 759–67, Special Collections, LLMVC, LSU.

16. Charles McMicken, sale to William and Ann Jones, book F, 407–8, March 8, 1838, conveyance records, WFP, LA; affidavit of free status, book G, 169, November 6, 1840, conveyance records, WFP, LA; act of emancipation, book F, 56, March 8, 1836, conveyance records, WFP, LA; La. Civ. Code, art. 193 (1825); act of emancipation, book G, 139, August 21, 1840, conveyance records, WFP, LA; William Jones and Ann Jones, sale to John Randall, book G, 213, February 20, 1841, conveyance records, WFP, LA.

17. *Phenix and St. Francisville and Bayou Sara (LA) Advertiser*, [advertisement] October 27, 1835; act of emancipation, book D, 83, February 16, 1830, conveyance records, WFP, LA; declaration of free status, book E, 278, September 12, 1834, conveyance records, WFP, LA; manuscript census, 1830, 1840, WFP, LA, ancestry.com.

18. Alexis de Tocqueville believed that, in the South, the legislation treated free people of color more harshly, but the habits of the white people were more tolerant and compassionate. De Tocqueville, *Democracy in America*, 461.

Notes

19. Stevenson, "What's Love Got to Do With It?," 100–101.
20. 1817 La. Acts, 18.
21. Stevenson, "What's Love Got to Do With It?," 108, 120.
22. Manuscript census, 1860, WFP, LA, ancestry.com.
23. Lucy, Sarah, and Charles, act of emancipation, book E, 149, February 1, 1832, conveyance records, WFP, LA.
24. Eighteen were freed during their father's lifetime; five were freed by his will.
25. Stevenson, "What's Love Got to Do With It?," 100.
26. Camille A. Nelson, "American Husbandry: Legal Norms Impacting the Production of (Re)Productivity," *Yale Journal of Law and Feminism* 19, no. 1 (2007): 9, 12–13.
27. Ann Maria, act of emancipation, book AA, 147, June 13, 1825, conveyance records, WFP, LA.
28. Ann Maria, act of emancipation.
29. William Hargis Gray, declaration of free birth, book AA, 187, May 2, 1826, conveyance records, WFP, LA.
30. Thomas Hardy Gray and Josephine Gray, act of emancipation, book AA, 234, July 4, 1826, conveyance records, WFP, LA.
31. La. Civ. Code, art. 913 (1825). This article reads, "The natural children of a father, if acknowledged, may inherit his estate if the father has no blood relatives and no wife at the time of his death."
32. William Draughan, sale to Josias Gray, book AA, 319, August 4, 1827, conveyance records, WFP, LA.
33. Josias Gray, sale to Ann Maria Gray, book AA, 329, November 23, 1827, conveyance records, WFP, LA.
34. Virginia Gray, declaration of free birth, book C, 242, September 24, 1828, conveyance records, WFP, LA.
35. Manuscript census, 1830, WFP, LA, ancestry.com.
36. Josias Gray, sale to Ann Maria Gray, book B, 307–8, July 11, 1839, conveyance records, WFP, LA. The fifteen persons transferred to Ann Maria included a husband and wife, both aged fifty years old, younger men and women, aged ten to twenty-two years old, and three children noted to be the children of a nineteen-year-old.
37. La. Civ. Code, art. 1468 (1825, repealed 1987).
38. Josephine Gray, William Hargis Gray, and Virginia Gray, declaration of free status, book G, 44, November 6, 1839, conveyance records, WFP, LA.
39. Manuscript census, 1840, WFP, LA, ancestry.com.
40. Josias Gray, succession, inventory, July 1, 1842, probate record, book 9, 1841–1844, 252, WFP, LA.
41. The creditors meeting, petition, probate record, book 9; Josias Gray, will, December 31, 1841, probate record, book 9, 1841–1844, 121, WFP, LA; bills of sale 2, 81–83, August 8, 1842, WFP, LA.
42. Emily Bridges, sale to Thomas R. P. Spence by Thomas R. Purnell [attorney in fact], book B, 557, November 13, 1822, conveyance records, WFP, LA. See, generally, conveyance records, WFP, LA, books B–N; probate sales, book E, 1848–1873, WFP, LA.
43. Manuscript census, 1850, WFP, LA, ancestry.com.
44. Manuscript census, 1820, WFP, LA, ancestry.com; Thomas Purnell, agreement with Mary Doherty, book A, 294–95, book D, 64, February 10, 1827, conveyance records, WFP, LA.
45. Anthony Doherty, affidavit, book D, 64, November 2, 1830, conveyance records, WFP, LA.

46. Mary Martin Purnell, Matilda Purnell, John Purnell, and Edward Purnell, act of emancipation , book H, 230, July 27, 1829, conveyance records, WFP, LA.

47. Manuscript census, 1830, WFP, LA, ancestry.com.

48. Manuscript census, 1850, WFP, LA, ancestry.com.

49. Robert Duer, succession, October 27, 1841, box 28, succession records, WFP, LA.

50. Albert G. Howell, sale to Thomas R. Purnell, book I, 81, March 22, 1845, conveyance records, WFP, LA.

51. Bennet H. Barrow, diary, 32, September 29, 1837.

52. Maria Clark, sale to Thomas R.P. Spence, book E, 35, February 2, 1833, conveyance records, WFP, LA; Thomas Spence, sale to Mary Martin, book H, 443, July 15, 1843, conveyance records, WFP, LA; Thomas Purnell, sale to Edward Purnell and John Purnell, book K, 279, June 14, 1851, conveyance records, WFP, LA; Edward Purnell and John Purnell, sale to Alexander Purnell, book L, 474, February 24, 1855, conveyance records, WFP, LA. John and Edward Purnell signed their names, but Alexander Purnell made a mark as his signature.

53. Mary Martin, acknowledgement of maternity, book M, 343, May 23, 1857, conveyance records, WFP, LA.

54. Mary Martin, sale to John J. Barrow, book N, 296, March 15, 1860, conveyance records, WFP, LA; Thomas Purnell and Mary Martin, sale to John J. Barrow, book N, 297, March 15, 1860, conveyance records, WFP, LA; Hezariah C. Moffitt, sale to Mary Martin, book S, folio 233, March 29, 1860, conveyance records, East Baton Rouge Parish, LA. The sale was of lot ten, square thirty-seven. Manuscript census, 1860, WFP, LA, ancestry.com; William Hargis Gray and Matilda Purnell, marriage, ancestry.com; confirmed in Diocese of Baton Rouge, *Catholic Church Records: 1858–1862* (Baton Rouge, LA: Diocese of Baton Rouge, 1989), 9:236, 9:237; John Douse and Mary Douse, petition, para. 7, July 29, 1922, succession of Richard Douse and Ann M. Douse, probate no. 3,364, 22nd Judicial District Court, East Baton Rouge Parish, LA.

55. Manuscript census, 1870, East Baton Rouge Parish, LA, ancestry.com; undated newspaper clipping found in Charles Hatfield's family Bible.

56. Brasseaux, Fontenot, and Oubre, writing about the southwestern Louisiana frontier, reported that emancipated concubines usually stayed with their former owner. Brasseaux, Fontenot, and Oubre, *Creoles of Color*, 8.

57. Clark, *The Strange History*, 44.

58. Manuscript census, 1840, WFP, LA, ancestry.com.

59. La. Civ. Code, art. 95 (1825). This article states, "Free persons and slaves are incapable of contracting marriage together; the celebration of such marriage is forbidden, and the marriage is void; there is the same incapacity and the same nullity with respect to marriages contracted by free white persons with free people of colour."

60. Bennet H. Barrow, diary, 133, November 6, 1839.

61. Barrow, diary, 188–89, August 3, 1840. Emphasis original.

62. Barrow, diary, 266, July 4, 1842.

63. Caroline Perry, declaration of intent to emancipate, book H, 231, July 18, 1842, conveyance records, WFP, LA. The declaration states the intent "to go to the City of Cincinnati in the State of Ohio, for the purpose of residing there + enjoying the benefit of the law of the said State of Ohio, which confers freedom on all slaves who are allowed by their owners to live in said State, and to return to the State of Louisiana after effecting her emancipation, if she thinks fit."

64. Caroline Perry, certificate of emancipation, book H, 247, September 3, 1842, conveyance records, WFP, LA; Negro Records, book 5, 763, August 5, 1842, Hamilton County, OH.

65. Manuscript census, 1850, WFP, LA, ancestry.com; Hardy Perry, sale to Caroline Perry, book K, 152, December 10, 1850, conveyance records, WFP, LA.

66. Hardy Perry, donation to Caroline Perry, book K, 152, December 10, 1850, conveyance records, WFP, LA.

67. Hardy Perry, sale to Caroline Perry, noted in Caroline Perry, sale to John Scott, book M, 593, September 4, 1858, conveyance records, WFP, LA; Lewis Stirling Jr., sale to Caroline Perry, bills of sale book 2, 213, May 27, 1844, WFP, LA; Caroline Perry, sale to Lewis Stirling Jr., bills of sale book 2, 214–15, May 27, 1844, WFP, LA; Philander C. Smith, sale to Caroline Perry, book I, 461, April 17, 1848, conveyance records, WFP, LA; Caroline Perry, sale to Obadiah Tate, book K, 262, May 20, 1851, conveyance records, WFP, LA; Caroline Perry, sale to Vincent D. Walsh, book N, 319, May 2, 1857, conveyance records, WFP, LA.

68. Caroline Perry, sale to John Scott, book M, 593, September 4, 1858, conveyance records, WFP, LA; Bridget Riley, sale to Caroline Perry, book N, 15, January 5, 1859, conveyance records, WFP, LA; confirmed by Bridget Riley and Henry H. Riley, children of Bridget Riley, book O, 114, February 12, 1866, conveyance records, WFP, LA.

69. Fanny, Cintheana, Samuel, and William Augustus, act of emancipation, book AA, 332–35, April 30, 1827, conveyance records, WFP, LA.

70. Samuel Hendrick, apprenticeship, book C, 124, April 18, 1829, conveyance records, WFP, LA.

71. Fanny Hendrick, affidavit of freedom, book D, 130, March 7, 1831, conveyance records, WFP, LA.

72. John Tillotson, donation to May Thomas, book F, 122, July 14, 1836, conveyance records, WFP, LA.

73. John Holmes, sale to Cynthia Ann Hendrick, book F, 377, February 27, 1838, conveyance records, WFP, LA. Lots 336 and 337 sold for nine hundred dollars. Cynthia Ann Hendrick, sale to Fanny Hendrick, book H, 276, November 25, 1842, conveyance records, WFP, LA. Lot 508 in square twenty-seven sold for $250, called lot 336 or 337 in Holmes deed. William Parker, sale to Fanny Hendrick, book H, 585, May 2, 1844, conveyance records, WFP, LA. Lot 415 in square thirty-seven sold for ninety dollars.

74. John Tillotson, sale to Fanny Hendrick, book I, 598, July 27, 1849, conveyance records, WFP, LA.

75. John Tillotson, donation to James E. Tillotson, book I, 623, November 15, 1849, conveyance records, WFP, LA.

76. Manuscript census, 1850, WFP, LA, ancestry.com.

77. Milteer, *North Carolina's Free People*, 140; Martha Hodes explained, "Those who held authority in antebellum Southern communities were likely to consider poorer white women to be the depraved agents of illicit liaisons." As initiators of these liaisons, white women bore the brunt of scorn. Martha Hodes, "The Sexualization of Reconstruction Politics: White Women and Black Men in the South after the Civil War," in "African American Culture and Sexuality," ed. John C. Fout, special issue, *Journal of the History of Sexuality* 3, no. 3 (January 1993): 402–17.

78. Milteer, *North Carolina's Free People*, 136, 140–41. Warren Milteer Jr. concluded that most free people of color in Gates County were descendants from white or American Indian women who married men of color rather than from white men who married women of color. Milteer, "Life," 146, 162–64.

79. Peter W. Bardaglio, "'Shameful Matches': The Regulation of Interracial Sex and Marriage in the South before 1900," in *Sex, Love, Race: Crossing Boundaries in North American History*, ed. Martha Hodes (New York: New York University Press, 1999), 113–14.

80. Winthrop D. Jordan, *White over Black: American Attitudes toward the Negro 1550–1812*, 2nd ed. (Chapel Hill: University of North Carolina Press, [1968] 2012), 171–72. John Hope Franklin cited a 1741 law requiring the mulatto children of white servant women to be bound as servants to their mother's masters until age thirty-one. Franklin, *The Free Negro*, 125. A law that regulated the offspring of relationships between black males and white females acknowledged that such relationships existed.

81. Brasseaux, Fontenot, and Oubre, *Creoles of Color*, 12.

82. Some historians have attributed the acceptance of relationships between black females and white males to a dearth of white women. See, for example, Brasseaux, Fontenot, and Oubre, *Creoles of Color*, 8. In 1830, in West Feliciana Parish, white men outnumbered white women 1265 to 860. Manuscript census, 1830, WFP, LA, ancestry.com.

Chapter 6. And Then the War Came

1. Clark, *The Strange History*, 49.

2. Curry, *The Free Black*, 9, 83–93, xvi–xviii.

3. 1850 La. Acts, 179.

4. 1852 La. Acts, 214–15; 1957 La. Acts, 55. According to Brasseaux, Fontenot, and Oubre, white hostility to free blacks crystallized in the 1850s. Many free people of color left south-central Louisiana under threats of violence. Brasseaux, Fontenot, and Oubre, *Creoles of Color*, 81.

5. Manuscript census, 1850, 1860, WFP, LA, ancestry.com.

6. Henry Oconnor, sale to Isaac N. Maynard and Mary E. Baines, book K, 374, January 20, 1852, conveyance records, WFP, LA; Anna E. Savage, sale to Maria Wicker, book M, 173, July 2, 1856, conveyance records, WFP, LA; Maria Wicker, sale to De La Fayette Stocking, book M, 239, January 13, 1857, conveyance records, WFP, LA; Stanley Dickerson, sale to Jean Jeantier, book M, 344, June 3, 1857, conveyance records, WFP, LA; Antonio Nolasco and Gertrude Nolasco, sale to William B. Rucker, book L, 504, March 6, 1855, conveyance records, WFP, LA; Gertrude Nolasco, sale to Jesse Barkdall, book M, 280, March 13, 1857, conveyance records, WFP, LA; Gertrude and Antonio Nolasco, sale to Conrad Bockel, book M, 485, March 17, 1858, conveyance records, WFP, LA; George Chew, Wilson Chew, Mary Chew, and Harriet Williams, amicable partition, book M, 336, May 18, 1857, conveyance records, WFP, LA; Wilson Chew and George Chew, sale to/exchange with rector, wardens, and vestrymen of Grace Church, book M, 109–10, March 14, 1856, conveyance records, WFP, LA; William Chew and Mary Chew, sale to Jane Muse, book M, 339, May 18, 1857, conveyance records, WFP, LA; Harriet Chew Williams, sale to Margaret Ann Jordan, book N, 6, February 17, 1859, conveyance records, WFP, LA.

7. Brasseaux, Fontenot, and Oubre, *Creoles of Color*, xiii, 7–8, 44, 49, 73, 74, 83, 119.

8. Sally McKee, *The Exile's Song: Edmond Dédé and the Unfinished Revolutions of the Atlantic World* (New Haven, CT: Yale University Press, 2017), 41.

9. Manuscript census, 1850, 1860, WFP, LA, ancestry.com.

10. Yellow fever struck Bayou Sara in February 1854. By September, 130 of the three hundred permanent inhabitants had died from the fever. *Bayou Sara Ledger*, "Yellow Fever: Calm Reflection," February 18, 1854, and September 10, 1854. Fourteen inches of rain measured in Baton Rouge caused the levee to break in Bayou Sara. *Bloomsburg (PA) Star of the North*, "The Storm in Louisiana: Terrible Loss of Life," August 20, 1856; Coates, "Some Notes," *Journal of Southern History* 9, no. 3 (August 1943): 385, table "Percentage of Heads of Families

Owning." In his study of West Feliciana planters in 1850 to 1860, Wattine Frazier noted that the planters enslaving fifty or more people controlled the agricultural, financial, and political life of the parish. They controlled from behind the scenes before 1850 but openly controlled political activity 1850 to 1860. Frazier, "The Great Planters," 173.

11. 1855 La. Acts, 377, §91.

12. *New Orleans Daily Crescent*, October 9, 1852. The entry reads, "Clarke & Co., publishers of London, have sold 150,000 copies of Uncle Tom's Cabin, and the demand is unabated." See also *Franklin (LA) Planter's Banner*, "Clippings from Our Exchanges," November 6, 1852, which says the book was translated into German; and *Baton Rouge (LA) Daily Comet*, December 22, 1852, which says the book was translated into Welsh.

13. Roger W. Shugg, *Origins of Class Struggle in Louisiana: A Social History of White Farmers and Laborers during Slavery and After* (Baton Rouge: Louisiana State University Press, 1966), 30–33, 161.

14. Berlin, *Slaves without Masters*, 198, 49, 185, 369, 351.

15. *Dred Scott v. Sandford*, 60 US 393 (1857). Chief Justice Roger Taney wrote that people of color were not citizens of the United States and added, gratuitously, that a black man had no rights that a white man must respect.

16. William Henry Chase, letter to George Mathews, February 8, 1836, box 3, folder 8, mss. 4358, Mathews-Ventress-Lawrason Papers, LLMVC, LSU.

17. 1837 La. Acts, 18.

18. La. Legis. Resolution (January 19, 1838).

19. 1844 La. Acts, 8.

20. 1850 La. Acts, 260.

21. In 1843, Wickliffe married Anna Dawson, daughter of Louisiana congressman John Bennett Dawson and the niece of Louisiana governor Isaac Johnson. John Dawson had been a judge in the parish before his election to Congress. Wickliffe and Anna Dawson moved to St. Francisville in 1846, after John Dawson's death. William H. Adams, "Governor Robert Wickliffe," Louisiana State Museum, accessed August 9, 2020, https://64parishes.org/entry/robert-charles-wickliffe.

22. Clayton E. Cramer argued that increasing numbers of free people of color in the slave states became an embarrassment to supporters of slavery who argued that people of color were naturally suited to slavery and not capable of managing as free people. Cramer, *Black Demographic Data*, 27. Edmund S. Morgan believed free people were more dangerous to society than enslaved people because they had rising expectations that, when frustrated, produced rebellion. Free men with disappointed hopes could make common cause with enslaved men. Morgan noted that the Virginia assembly deliberately fostered the contempt of white people for people of color and American Indians to avoid their combining forces to overturn the control wealthy people enjoyed. Morgan, *American Slavery*, 309, 328, 331.

23. 1857 La. Acts, 55; 1858 La. Acts, 214.

24. Manuscript census, 1850, 1860, WFP, LA, ancestry.com.

25. Robert C. Wickliffe, "Annual Message of Robert C. Wickliffe, Governor of the State of Louisiana, to the General Assembly," *Louisiana History: The Journal of the Louisiana Historical Association* 1, no. 4 (Autumn 1960): 373–74.

26. 1858 La. Acts, 169.

27. Southerners were willing to fight to protect their investments or, if not yet slaveholders, to protect their prospects in the slave-labor system. The chorus of the Confederate battle song, "Run, Yank, or Die" began, "Hurrah for slavery." Confederate Battle Song, folder 1861–1868, mss. 1209, Baines [Henry and Family] Papers, LLMVC, LSU.

28. Richard Douse, enlistment paper, service record, US Colored Troops, Seventy-Fourth Infantry, general records, Old Army, record group 94, National Archives, Washington, DC.

29. Company C, record of events for the Seventy-Fourth USCI 547; Richard Douse, pension file, surgeon's certificate, file no. C 2536643, Civil War and Later Pension Files, Records of the Veterans Administration, record group 15, National Archives; manuscript census, 1870, East Baton Rouge Parish, LA, 18, ancestry.com.

30. See, for example, *Wheeling (VA) Daily Intelligencer*, June 8, 1863; *Richmond (IN) Palladium*, June 19, 1863; *St. Cloud (MN) Democrat*, July 16, 1863.

31. US Civil War draft register records, Baton Rouge, LA, 4:37 (1864), National Park Service, Soldiers and Sailors Database.

32. Lawrence E. Estaville Jr., "A Small Contribution: Louisiana's Short Rural Railroads in the Civil War," *Louisiana History: The Journal of the Louisiana Historical Association* 18, no. 1 (Winter 1977): 99–100.

33. Butler and Williams, *Bayou Sara*, 91–93, 96; Coastal Environments, Inc., *Route 61 Revisited* (Baton Rouge: Louisiana Department of Transportation and Development Office of Highways, 2003), 34.

34. Estaville, "A Small Contribution," 101.

35. Cyrus Ratliff, succession, account of the administration, box 85, succession records, WFP, LA; Cyrus Ratcliff, succession, sale to Grace Episcopal Church, book N, 333, April 25, 1860, conveyance records, WFP, LA.

36. Robert Wickliffe, petition (1880), Succession of William Dalton, box 27, succession records, WFP, LA. Dr. William M. Dalton's November 26, 1859, will emancipated Susan Dalton and her children, James, Sarah, Thomas, and Samuel Dalton, and Susan's mother, Hannah. He left the remainder of his estate to Wickliffe after the people he freed were "comfortably provided for." In 1881, Susan Dalton sued Wickliffe to receive something from Dalton's estate. In 1878, Susan's son, Thomas Dalton, who had served as parish sheriff in 1876, was lynched.

37. Drury Mitchell, succession, box 65, succession records, WFP, LA; parish register A, 224, January 9, 1864, Grace Episcopal Church, St. Francisville, LA.

38. Manuscript census, 1860, WFP, LA, ancestry.com. George Chew, age fifty-three, worked as a drayman and lived with Sylvia, age fifty, and their child Mary Chew, age seventeen. Their real estate was valued at one thousand dollars and their movables were valued at six hundred dollars.

39. Fanny Hendrick, succession, testimony, box 48, succession records, WFP, LA.

40. *Fanny Hendrick v. Matthew Riley*, succession, administrator, civil suit, no. 538, La. 7th Jud. Dist. Ct. (March 27, 1868).

41. Fanny Hendrick, succession, box 48, succession records, WFP, LA.

42. Emily Baines, letter to Margaret Butler, January 11, 1865, box 1, folder 18, mss. 1068, [Margaret] Butler Correspondence, LLMVC, LSU.

43. Ann M. Lobdell, letter to Sarah Turnbull Stirling, July 9, 1865, box 2, folder 19, mss. 1866, [Lewis] Stirling and Family Papers, LLMVC, LSU.

44. John Lobdell, letter to his Aunt Nine, July 9, 1865, box 2, folder 19, mss. 1866, [Lewis] Stirling and Family Papers, LLMVC, LSU.

45. Scott McGehee, letter to J. Burrus McGehee, August 6, 1879, box 1, folder 5, mss, 1111, 1156, 1157, [J. Burras] McGehee Papers, LLMVC, LSU.

46. Philip B. Key, letter to P. Mathews, January 6, 1866, box 3, folder 4, mss. 4358, Mathews-Ventress-Lawrason Papers, LLMVC, LSU.

47. Philip B. Key, letter to P. Mathews, January 15, 1866, box 3, folder 5, mss. 4358, Mathews-Ventress-Lawrason Papers, LLMVC, LSU.

48. Emily B. Maynard, letter to Margaret Butler, December 15, 1869, box 1, folder 8, mss. 1068, [Margaret] Butler Correspondence, LLMVC, LSU.

49. Harriet Mathuro, letter to Margaret Butler, May 30, 1870, box 1, folder 9, mss. 1068, [Margaret] Butler Correspondence, LLMVC, LSU.

50. Martha Turnbull, diary, 1837–1895, not dated, TS, 30, Misc. T, LLMVC, LSU.

51. Ellen W. Chadwick, sale to Moses Lamb, book O, 130, February 26, 1866, conveyance records, WFP, LA.

52. Horace Mills, lease to William Brown and Bosen Green, book O, 398, January 1, 1867, conveyance records, WFP, LA.

53. Sylvia Chew, sale to Dempsey Turner and Ann Turner, book P, 73, March 4, 1868, conveyance records, WFP, LA. Before his death, George Chew had been sexton at the Grace Episcopal Church, as his father had been. Dempsey Turner now had that position. The lot Turner and his wife purchased was adjacent to the church property. Turner died April 11, 1877, when one of Turner's blood vessels broke while he was digging a grave.

54. Sylvia Chew, lease to Joseph W. Armstead, book Q, 297, March 15, 1872, conveyance records, WFP, LA. Cancelled May 6, 1872.

55. Ephemera I, People's and White Man's Reform Party, broadside circular, New Orleans, February 1870, mss. 3030, LLMVC, LSU. US district judge Edward Billings contended, "the hatred towards the former slave has not sprung from interest on the part of his former master but from self-reproach, the consciousness of having been in the wrong, from the rancor of seeing his former chattel emancipated and enfranchised." Edward C. Billings, *The Struggle between the Civilization of Slavery and That of Freedom, Recently and Now Going On in Louisiana: An Address Delivered by Edward C. Billings Esq., of New Orleans, at Hatfield, Mass.; Oct. 20, 1873* (Freeport, NY: Books for Libraries Press, 1971), 8.

56. An 1875 letter from J. R. Percy of Yazoo City, Mississippi, expressed the white-supremacist sentiment: "I hope Louisiana will fall in our wake at her next election. The people there must do as they do here . . . draw a good square color line, play bluff, talk big about Winchester rifles + etc. + let it appear to Mr. Darkey you don't care a straw for him." J. R. Percy, letter to "Old Friend," December 2, 1875, box 1, folder 13, mss. 4759, [J. H.] Percy Papers, LLMVC, LSU.

57. William Harriet Mathews, sale to Henry Oconnor, book I, 373, June 3, 1847, conveyance records, WFP, LA. Henry Oconnor was married to Ann Griggs on May 12, 1838, by the rector of Grace Episcopal Church. Grace Episcopal Church, marriage records, 274, St. Francisville, LA. Jones and Fair married January 5, 1837. Fair, emancipation, book G, 139, August 21, 1840, conveyance records, WFP, LA; Berlin, *Slaves without Masters*, 391. Berlin believed that most free people of color had ties by blood or marriage to people still enslaved.

58. Abraham Levy, lease to Albert Wicker, book O, 252, 446, July 16, 1866, conveyance records, WFP, LA; Robinson Mumford, sale to Albert Wicker, book O, 469, March 26, 1867, conveyance records, WFP, LA; Albert Wicker, sale to Thomas Butler, book O, 530, June 1, 1867, conveyance records, WFP, LA.

59. Manuscript census, 1880, New Orleans, LA, ancestry.com.

60. Testimony in regard to alleged outrages in West Feliciana Parish, LA, June 21, 1876, 44th Cong., 1st sess., Bayou Sara, LA, 759–67, Special Collections, LLMVC, LSU. White district attorney William W. Leake testified that he knew that a large body of white men had hung several black men, but he believed that these hangings did not provide "an occasion

for prosecution." He intended to make no effort to find out who killed them. Testimony, 732. Robert Hewlitt testified that he resigned from the police jury under threat of personal violence when "Young men from the country I did not know arrived with [a citizen's petition demanding his resignation] and carried pistols." Testimony, 770–72.

61. Henrietta Coleman, will, book O, 482, April 10, 1867, conveyance records, WFP, LA; Henrietta Coleman, succession, affidavit of death, April 10, 1867, box 20, succession records, WFP, LA.

62. Manuscript census, 1880, New Orleans, LA, ancestry.com.

63. Partition in kind, book L, 209, January 23, 1854, conveyance records, WFP, LA. Gertrude Nolasco and Antonio E. Nolasco each received seven slaves and two promissory notes of William Glass.

64. Manuscript census, 1860, WFP, LA, ancestry.com.

65. Manuscript census, 1870, WFP, LA, ancestry.com.

66. Heirs of De La Fayette Stocking, sale to Gertrude Nolasco, book Q, 347, August 12, 1872, conveyance records, WFP, LA; Maria Wicker, sale to De La Fayette Stocking, book M, 239, January 13, 1857, conveyance records, WFP, LA; Gertrude Nolasco, lease to Alfred F. Gastrill, book Q, 371, October 4, 1872, conveyance records, WFP, LA.

67. Manuscript census, 1900, East Baton Rouge Parish, LA, ancestry.com.

68. Judy Riffel, ed., *City Birth and Death Registers for the City of Baton Rouge, Louisiana, 1874–1918* (Baton Rouge, LA: La Comite' des Archives de la Louisiane, 2001), 149.

69. Jane Muse, sale to Sylvia Chew, book M, 428, January 27, 1858, conveyance records, WFP, LA. The sale was for the northwest quarter of lot nine, the north half of lot ten, and lot eleven in square eleven for $160.

70. Sylvia Chew, sale to Dempsey Turner and Ann Turner, book P, 73, March 4, 1868, conveyance records, WFP, LA.

71. Claim no. 4413, US Southern Claims Commission, July 22, 1871; 1997–2020 ancestry.com; Sylvia Chew, lease to Joseph W. Armstead, book Q, 297, March 15, 1872, conveyance records, WFP, LA; Sylvia Chew, sale to Alexander O. Bakewell, book Q, 356, August 31, 1872, conveyance records, WFP, LA.

72. Drury Mitchell, sale to Maria Ann Gray, book I, 218, February 27, 1846, conveyance records, WFP, LA; Maria Ann Gray, sale to Charles L. Mathews, book N, 257, February 16, 1860, conveyance records, WFP, LA; Margaret E. Browder, sale to Maria Ann Gray, book N, 258, February 16, 1860, conveyance records, WFP, LA.

73. Gray had crossed diarist's Bennet Barrow's property to visit Purnell. Gray and Purnell had two sons, William Alexander Gray, born January 8, 1855, and John Edward Gray, born January 3, 1857. Both children were baptized November 30, 1860. Diocese of Baton Rouge, *Catholic Church records: 1858–1862* (1989), 9:236, 9:237.

74. *P. G. A. Kaufman v. William H. Gray*, civil suit, no. 557, Parish Court, WFP, LA (March 22, 1872). Gray's interest was appraised at eight hundred dollars but was sold for $102; seizure of ten acres, book Q, 373, September 7, 1872, conveyance records, WFP, LA; manuscript census, 1880, WFP, LA, ancestry.com.

75. Peterson, sale to Josephine Gray, book K, 540, April 3, 1845, conveyance records, WFP, LA; John F. Valentine, sale to Josephine Gray, book K, 42, February 19, 1850, conveyance records, WFP, LA; Josephine Gray, sale to Felix McCarney and William Fitzpatrick, book K, 539, August 14, 1852, conveyance records, WFP, LA. The sale was for $350.

76. Manuscript census, 1860, WFP, LA, ancestry.com. The census taker listed M. Valentine (sixteen), J. Valentine (twelve), J. Valentine (ten), and J. Gray (four). Manuscript census, 1870,

WFP, LA, ancestry.com. The census taker listed Cora (nine) and James Gray (five). Miss Josephine Gray, sale to Newton Payne, book S, 249, February 14, 1880, conveyance records, WFP, LA; sheriff's sale, book T, 101, November 4, 1882, conveyance records, WFP, LA; manuscript census, 1880, WFP, LA, ancestry.com; Louie Torree, manuscript census, 1900, WFP, LA, ancestry.com.

77. Tax sale of lots eight and nine in square sixteen, book R, 87, and book R, 179, December 9, 1874, conveyance records, WFP, LA.

78. Tax collector, sale to Conrad Bockel, book R, 553, December 3, 1877, conveyance records, WFP, LA. The sale was for the Bayou Sara lots 414 and half of 413 for $11.90. Conrad Bockel, title confirmed, book S, 320, December 18, 1879, conveyance records, WFP, LA.

79. Tax collector, sale to Conrad Bockel [tax sale of lots 414 and half of lot 413], book S, 320, December 18, 1879, conveyance records, WFP, LA. Loren Schweninger concluded that, during the first fifteen years after the Civil War, free people of color lost most of the land they had owned in Louisiana. Only one in five property owners held onto their property after the war. Schweninger, "Antebellum Free Persons," 346, 356.

80. Historian Nell Irwin Painter wrote that, after the war, the role of people of color was to be only laborers, and the role of poor white people was to be enforcers. Blacks who wanted to own their own land and to be subsistence farmers were frustrated. Nell Irwin Painter, *Exodusters* (New York: W. W. Norton & Co., 1976), 67.

81. Manuscript census, 1860, WFP, LA, ancestry.com. During the period of 1868 to 1874, men of color from the parish served as members of both houses of the state legislature, on the parish police jury, as parish treasurer, as city councilmen, as mayor of St. Francisville, as parish judge, as a justice of the peace, as recorder, as sheriff, as a deputy sheriff, as constable in Bayou Sara, as constable in St. Francisville, as president of the school board, and on the Board of Visitors for Insane Asylum at Jackson. The following people of color were elected to the offices indicated: Hamilton, police jury, a justice of the peace; Robert Hewlett, mayor of St. Francisville, Board of Visitors for Insane Asylum at Jackson, police jury, parish treasurer, president of the school board; George Swayze, Board of Visitors for Insane Asylum at Jackson, constable in Bayou Sara, state senator, constable in St. Francisville, deputy sheriff; Robert Taylor, member of the legislature (1868–1870), sheriff (1872–1874); John S. Dula, recorder, justice of the peace, parish judge; J. W. Armstead, city councilman, justice of the peace, state representative (1872–1874). Testimony in regard to alleged outrages in West Feliciana Parish, LA, June 21, 1876, 44th Cong., 1st sess., Bayou Sara, LA, 759–67, Special Collections, LLMVC, LSU; Charles Vincent, *Black Legislators in Louisiana During Reconstruction* (Baton Rouge: Louisiana State University Press, 1976), 75, 147, 221, 227–34.

Epilogue

1. Charles H. Wesley, "The Negro Has Always Wanted the Four Freedoms," in *What the Negro Wants*, ed. Rayford W. Logan (Chapel Hill: University of North Carolina Press, 1944), 109.

2. Wesley, "The Negro," 110.

3. Leslie Pinckney Hill, "What the Negro Wants and How to Get it: The Inward Power of the Masses," in *What the Negro Wants*, ed. Rayford W. Logan (Chapel Hill: University of North Carolina Press, 1944), 71.

4. Sterling A. Brown, "Count Us In," in *What the Negro Wants*, ed. Rayford W. Logan (Chapel Hill: University of North Carolina Press, 1944), 331.

5. Old Dinah, act of emancipation, book AA, 403 July 2, 1824, conveyance records, WFP, LA.

6. Sandy, act of emancipation, book H, 464, February 20, 1839, conveyance records, WFP, LA.

7. Lucy, Sarah, and Charles, act of emancipation, book E, 149, February 1, 1832, conveyance records, WFP, LA.

8. 1804 Laws of the District of Louisiana, 107, §24.

9. It was not until 1859 that Louisiana used the law to limit the occupations available to free people of color. After 1859, free people of color could no longer get a license to "keep a coffee-house, billiard table, or retail store, where spiritous liquors are sold." 1859 La. Acts, 18.

10. George S. Schuyler, "The Caucasian Problem," in *What the Negro Wants*, ed. Rayford W. Logan (Chapel Hill: University of North Carolina Press, 1944), 289.

11. A. Philip Randolph, "March on Washington Movement Presents Program for the Negro," in *What the Negro Wants*, ed. Rayford W. Logan (Chapel Hill: University of North Carolina Press, 1944), 140.

12. Wesley, "The Negro," 105.

13. Wesley, "The Negro," 107.

BIBLIOGRAPHY

Primary Sources

Manuscript Collections

Amistad Research Center, Tulane University, New Orleans, LA
Tureaud Papers.

Charles Hatfield
Undated newspaper clipping found in family Bible.

Grace Episcopal Church, St. Francisville, LA
Grace Episcopal Church, marriage records.
Parish register A.
Parish register A+.

*Louisiana and Lower Mississippi Valley Collections,
Louisiana State University Libraries, Baton Rouge, LA*
Baines [Henry and Family] Papers, mss. 1209.
Bennet H. Barrow, diary, mss. 2978–2014.
[Margaret] Butler Correspondence, mss. 1068.
Butler Family Papers, mss. 1026.
[Elisabeth K.] Dart Collection, mss. 5023.
Ephemera I, People's and White Man's Reform Party, broadside circular, New Orleans, LA, February 1870, mss. 3030.
Greene Family Correspondence, mss. 4508.
James Pirrie Papers, mss. 1382.
[Henry A.] Lyons Papers, mss. 1382.
Martha Turnbull, diary, 1837–1895, not dated, TS, Misc. T.
Mathews-Ventress-Lawrason Papers, mss. 4358.

[J. Burras] McGehee Papers, mss. 1111, 1156, 1157.
[J. H.] Percy Papers, box 1, folder 13, mss. 4759.
[James] Rudman, account book, 1844–1848, mss. 881.
[Lewis] Stirling and Family Papers, mss. 1866.
Testimony in regard to alleged outrages in West Feliciana Parish, Louisiana, 44th Cong., 1st sess., Bayou Sara, LA, June 21, 1876, 759–67.
[A. P.] Walsh Papers, mss. 887.

Ohio History Connection, Columbus, OH

Ohio General Assembly House and Senate Resolutions.

Government Records, Archival

National Archives, Washington, DC

Orleans deaths indices, 1804–1885.
Undated letter of resignation to J. W. Douglass, commissioner, from B. T. Beauregard, record group 56, Treasury Department, Entry 258.
United States Colored Troops, Seventy-Fourth Infantry, general records, Old Army, record group 94.
Veterans Administration Records, Civil War and Later Pension Files, record group 15.

Office of the Clerk of Court, East Baton Rouge, LA

Succession records, 22nd Judicial District Court.

Office of the Clerk of Court, West Feliciana Parish, LA

Bills of sale books.
Civil suit records, La. 3rd Judicial District Court.
Civil suit records, La. 7th Judicial District Court.
Civil suit records, Parish Court.
Conveyance records.
Minute Record Book 1, 1824–1828. La. 3rd Jud. Dist. Ct.
Probate record books.
Probate sales books.
Succession records.
Unsorted records.
Vendor and vendee indexes to conveyances.

Office of the Secretary of State, State Archives, Baton Rouge, LA

Louisiana Death Records Index Database.

Louisiana newspapers

Bayou Sara Ledger, 1843–1854.
Bayou Sara Phoenix Ledger, 1858.
Louisiana Chronicle, 1854.
Phenix and St. Francisville and Bayou Sara (LA) Advertiser, 1835.

Bibliography

West Feliciana Historical Society Museum, St. Francisville, LA
Elizabeth Dart Files.

Federal Records, Published

An Act to Provide Internal Revenue to Support the Government, to Pay Interest on the Public Debt, and for Other Purposes. 38th Cong., ch. 173, §10 (June 30, 1864).
Clerk of the House of Representatives. *Abstract of the Returns of the Fifth Census.* Washington, DC: Duff Green, 1832.
DeBow, J. D. B. *The Seventh Census of the United States.* Washington, DC: Robert Armstrong, Public Printer, 1853.
Department of State. *Compendium of the United States Sixth Census.* Washington, DC: Thomas Allen, 1841.
Kennedy, Joseph C. G. *Population of the United States in 1860.* Washington, DC: Government Printing Office, 1864.
United States Census Bureau. *Seventh Census.* Washington, DC: Robert Armstrong, Public Printer, 1850.
United States Department of Commerce. *Historic Statistics of the United States, Colonial Times to 1970.* Bicentennial ed. Part 2. Washington, DC: Bureau of the Census, 1976.
US Civil War draft register records, Baton Rouge, LA, 4:37 (1864), National Park Service, Soldiers and Sailors Database.

Louisiana Acts of the Legislature and Statutes

1804 Laws of the District of Louisiana.
1806–1811 Acts of the Legis. Council, Territory of Orleans.
1812–1859 Louisiana Acts of the Legis.
Louisiana Civil Code (1825).

US Census Data, Ancestry.com, Online Database, Provo, UT (2004)

Claim no. 4413, US Southern Claims Commission, July 22, 1871.
Manuscript census, 1820–1900, Feliciana Parish, LA.
Manuscript census, 1860–1900, East Baton Rouge Parish, LA.
Manuscript census, 1860, Lorain County, OH.
Manuscript census, 1880, New Orleans, LA.
Louisiana complied marriage index, 1718–1925.
Louisiana. https://www.findagrave.com/memorial/87429324.
US, Find a Grave Index, 1600s–current.

Chronicling America: Historic American Newspapers, Library of Congress, Washington, DC

Alexandria (VA) Daily Advertiser, 1806.
Baton Rouge (LA) Daily Comet, 1852.
Baton Rouge (LA) Gazette, 1840.
Bloomsburg (PA) Star of the North, 1856.

False River (LA) Pointe Coupee Democrat, 1858.
Franklin (LA) Planter's Banner, 1852.
Louisiana Journal, 1827.
New Orleans Daily Crescent, 1852, 1860.
Richmond (IN) Palladium, 1863.
St. Cloud (MN) Democrat, 1863.
Thibodaux Minerva, 1854–1855.
Wheeling (VA) Daily Intelligencer, 1863.
Woodville Republican and Wilkinson County (MS) Advertiser, 1825.

Secondary Sources

Adams, William H. "Governor Robert Wickliffe." Louisiana State Museum. Accessed August 9, 2020. https://64parishes.org/entry/robert-charles-wickliffe.

Alexander, Adele Logan. *Ambiguous Lives: Free Women of Color in Rural Georgia, 1789–1879*. Fayetteville: University of Arkansas Press, 1991.

Atwater, H. Cowles. *Incidents of a Southern Tour: Or the South as Seen with Northern Eyes*. Boston, MA: J. P. Magee, 1857.

Bardaglio, Peter W. "'Shameful Matches': The Regulation of Interracial Sex and Marriage in the South before 1900." In *Sex, Love, Race: Crossing Boundaries in North American History*, edited by Martha Hodes. New York: New York University Press, 1999.

Berlin, Ira. *Generations of Captivity: A History of African American Slaves*. Cambridge, MA: Belknap Press, 2003.

Berlin, Ira. *Slaves without Masters: The Free Negro in the Antebellum South*. New York: Pantheon Books, 1974.

Berlin, Ira, and Philip D. Morgan, eds. *The Slaves' Economy: Independent Production by Slaves in the Americas*. London: Frank Cass, 1991.

Billings, Edward C. *The Struggle between the Civilization of Slavery and That of Freedom, Recently and Now Going On in Louisiana: An Address Delivered by Edward C. Billings Esq., of New Orleans, at Hatfield, Mass.; Oct. 20, 1873*. Freeport, NY: Books for Libraries Press, 1971.

Brasseaux, Carl A., Keith P. Fontenot, and Claude F. Oubre. *Creoles of Color in the Bayou Country*. Jackson: University Press of Mississippi, 1994.

Brown, Sterling A. "Count Us In." In *What the Negro Wants*, edited by Rayford W. Logan, 308–44. Chapel Hill: University of North Carolina Press, 1944.

Butler, Anne, and Helen Williams. *Bayou Sara: Used to Be*. Lafayette: University of Louisiana at Lafayette, 2017.

Clark, Emily. *The Strange History of the American Quadroon: Free Women of Color in the Revolutionary Atlantic World*. Chapel Hill: University of North Carolina Press, 2013.

Coastal Environments, Inc. *Route 61 Revisited*. Baton Rouge: Louisiana Department of Transportation and Development Office of Highways, 2003.

Coates, Harry L. "Some Notes on Slaveownership and Landownership in Louisiana." *Journal of Southern History* 9, no. 3 (August 1943): 381–94.

Cramer, Clayton E. *Black Demographic Data, 1790–1860: A Sourcebook*. Westport, CT: Greenwood Press, 1997.

Bibliography

Curry, Leonard P. *The Free Black in Urban America 1800–1850: The Shadow of the Dream.* Chicago: University of Chicago Press, 1981.

Dart, Elisabeth Kilbourne. "Douse, George, Planter, Taverner." In *A Dictionary of Louisiana Biography,* edited by Glenn R. Conrad, 254. Vol. 1. Lafayette: Louisiana Historical Association, 1988.

de Tocqueville, Alexis. *Democracy in America.* Translated by Henry Reeve. 4th ed. Cambridge, MA: Sever and Francis, 1864.

DeVille, Winston. *New Feliciana in the Province of Louisiana: A Guide to the Census of 1793.* Ville Platte: self-published, 1987.

Diocese of Baton Rouge. *Catholic Church Records: 1858–1862.* Vol. 9. (Baton Rouge, LA: Diocese of Baton Rouge, 1989).

Dorman, James H. *Creoles of Color of the Gulf South.* Knoxville: University of Tennessee Press, 1996.

Du Bois, W. E. B. *The Philadelphia Negro: A Social Study.* New York: Benjamin Blom, [1899] 1967.

Dunbar-Nelson, Alice. "People of Color in Louisiana: Part I." *Journal of Negro History* 1, no. 4 (October 1916): 361–76.

Dunbar-Nelson, Alice. "People of Color in Louisiana: Part II." *Journal of Negro History* 2, no. 1 (January 1917): 51–78.

Estaville, Lawrence E., Jr. "A Small Contribution: Louisiana's Short Rural Railroads in the Civil War." *Louisiana History: The Journal of the Louisiana Historical Association* 18, no. 1 (Winter 1977): 87–103.

Franklin, John Hope. *The Free Negro in North Carolina, 1790–1860.* Chapel Hill: University of North Carolina Press, 1943.

Frazier, Wattine. "The Great Planter in West Feliciana Parish, Louisiana, 1850–1860." MA thesis, Louisiana State University, 1969.

Hill, Leslie Pinckney. "What the Negro Wants and How to Get it: The Inward Power of the Masses." In *What the Negro Wants,* edited by Rayford W. Logan, 71–89. Chapel Hill: University of North Carolina Press, 1944.

Hodes, Martha. "The Sexualization of Reconstruction Politics: White Women and Black Men in the South after the Civil War." In "African American Culture and Sexuality," edited by John C. Fout, special issue, *Journal of the History of Sexuality* 3, no. 3 (January 1993): 402–17.

Johnson, Michael P., and James L. Roark. *Black Masters: A Free Family of Color in the Old South.* New York: W. W. Norton, 1984.

Jones, Martha S. *Birthright Citizens: A History of Race and Rights in Antebellum America.* New York: Cambridge University Press, 2018.

Jordan, Winthrop D. *White over Black: American Attitudes toward the Negro 1550–1812.* 2nd ed. Chapel Hill: University of North Carolina Press, [1968] 2012.

Kunkel, Paul A. "Modifications in Louisiana Negro Legal Status under Louisiana Constitutions 1812–1957." *Journal of Negro History* 44, no. 1 (January 1959): 1–25.

Logan, Rayford W., ed. *What the Negro Wants.* Chapel Hill: University of North Carolina Press, 1944.

Malone, Lee. *The Majesty of the Felicianas.* Gretna, LA: Pelican Publishing, 1989.

McKee, Sally. *The Exile's Song: Edmond Dédé and the Unfinished Revolutions of the Atlantic World.* New Haven, CT: Yale University Press, 2017.

Mills, Gary B. *The Forgotten People: Cane River's Creoles of Color*. Baton Rouge: Louisiana State University Press, 1977.

Milteer, Warren E., Jr. *Beyond Slavery's Shadow: Free People of Color in the South*. Chapel Hill: University of North Carolina Press, 2021.

Milteer, Warren E., Jr. "Life in a Great Dismal Swamp Community: Free People of Color in Pre-Civil War Gates County, North Carolina." *North Carolina Historical Review* 91, no. 2 (April 2014): 144–70.

Milteer, Warren E., Jr. *North Carolina's Free People of Color 1715–1885*. Baton Rouge: Louisiana State University Press, 2020.

Morgan, Edmund S. *American Slavery, American Freedom: The Ordeal of Colonial Virginia*. New York: W. W. Norton & Company, 1975.

Nelson, Camille A. "American Husbandry: Legal Norms Impacting the Production of (Re)Productivity." *Yale Journal of Law and Feminism* 19, no. 1 (2007): 1–48.

Painter, Nell Irwin. *Exodusters*. New York: W. W. Norton & Co., 1976.

Phillips, Ulrich B. "The Central Theme of Southern History." *American Historical Review* 34, no. 1 (October 1928): 30–43.

Randolph, A. Philip. "March on Washington Movement Presents Program for the Negro." In *What the Negro Wants*, edited by Rayford W. Logan, 133–62. Chapel Hill: University of North Carolina Press, 1944.

Rankin, David C. "The Forgotten People: Free People of Color in New Orleans, 1850–1870." PhD diss., John Hopkins University, 1976.

Reeves, Miriam. *The Felicianas of Louisiana*. Baton Rouge, LA: Claitor's Book Store, 1967.

Riffel, Judy, ed. *City Birth and Death Registers for the City of Baton Rouge, Louisiana, 1874–1918*. Baton Rouge, LA: La Comite' des Archives de la Louisiane, 2001.

Rowland, Dunbar, ed. *Official Letter Books of W. C. C. Claiborne, 1801–1816*. Vol. 4. Jackson, MS: State Department of Archives and History, 1917.

Royall, Anne. *Mrs. Royall's Southern Tour or Second Series of the Black Book*. 3 vols. Washington, DC: self-published, 1830.

Schafer, Judith Kelleher. *Becoming Free, Remaining Free: Manumission and Enslavement in New Orleans, 1846–1862*. Baton Rouge: Louisiana State University Press, 2003.

Schuyler, George S. "The Caucasian Problem." In *What the Negro Wants*, edited by Rayford W. Logan, 281–98. Chapel Hill: University of North Carolina Press, 1944.

Schweninger, Loren. "Antebellum Free Persons of Color in Postbellum Louisiana." *Louisiana History: Journal of the Louisiana Historical Association* 30, no. 4 (1989): 345–64.

Scott, Rebecca J. "Paper Thin: Freedom and Re-enslavement in the Diaspora of the Haitian Revolution." *Law and History Review* 29, no. 4 (2011): 1061–87.

Shugg, Roger W. *Origins of Class Struggle in Louisiana: A Social History of White Farmers and Laborers during Slavery and After*. Baton Rouge: Louisiana State University Press, 1966.

Sterkx, H. E. *The Free Negro in Ante-Bellum Louisiana*. Rutherford, NJ: Fairleigh Dickinson University Press, 1972.

Stevenson, Brenda E. "What's Love Got to Do With It? Concubinage and Enslaved Women and Girls in the Antebellum South." In "Women, Slavery, and the Atlantic World," edited by V. P. Franklin, special issue, *Journal of African American History* 98, no. 1 (Winter 2013): 99–125.

Stout, E. *Laws for the Government of the District of Louisiana, Vincennes, Indiana Territory*. New York: self-published, 1804.

Bibliography

Sundberg, Adam, and Sara Brooks Sundberg. "Happy Land: Women Landowners in Early West Feliciana Parish, Louisiana, 1813–1845." *Agricultural History* 90, no. 4 (Fall 2016): 484–510.

Tannenbaum, Frank. *Slave & Citizen: The Negro in the Americas*. New York: Vintage Books, 1946.

Thompson, V. Elaine. *Clinton, Louisiana: Society, Politics, and Race Relations in a Nineteenth Century Southern Small Town*. Lafayette: University of Louisiana at Lafayette, 2014.

Usner, Daniel H., Jr. "From African Captivity to American Slavery: The Introduction of Black Laborers to Colonial Louisiana." *Louisiana History: The Journal of the Louisiana Historical Association* 20, no. 1 (Winter 1979): 25–48.

Vincent, Charles. *Black Legislators in Louisiana during Reconstruction*. Baton Rouge: Louisiana State University Press, 1976.

Walker, David. *Walker's Appeal, in Four Articles; Together with a Preamble, to the Colored Citizens of the World, but In Particular, and Very Expressly, to Those of the United States of America*. Boston, MA: self-published, 1829.

Welch, Kimberly. "Black Litigiousness and White Accountability: Free Blacks and the Rhetoric of Reputation in the Antebellum Natchez District." *Journal of the Civil War Era* 5, no. 3 (September 2015): 372–98.

Welch, Kimberly M. *Black Litigants in the Antebellum American South*. Chapel Hill: University of North Carolina Press, 2018.

Wesley, Charles H. "The Negro Has Always Wanted the Four Freedoms." In *What the Negro Wants*, edited by Rayford W. Logan, 90–112. Chapel Hill: University of North Carolina Press, 1944.

West, Emily. *Family or Freedom: People of Color in the Antebellum South*. Lexington: University Press of Kentucky, 2012.

Wickliffe, Robert C. "Annual Message of Robert C. Wickliffe, Governor of the State of Louisiana, to the General Assembly." *Louisiana History: The Journal of the Louisiana Historical Association* 1, no. 4 (Autumn, 1960): 365–79.

Williamson, Frederick William, and George T. Goodman, eds. *Eastern Louisiana: A History of the Watershed of the Ouachita River and the Florida Parishes*. Louisville, KY: Historical Record Association, 1939.

Wilson, Evelyn L. *Laws, Customs and Rights: Charles Hatfield and His Family; A Louisiana History*. Westminster, MA: Willow Bend Books, 2004.

Woodson, Carter Goodwin. *The Mis-Education of the Negro*. Washington, DC: Associated Publishers, 1933.

INDEX

Abolition Society, 131
abolitionist literature, 22–24, 34, 35
Adelle v. Beauregard, 4, 7
Alabama, 13
Alexandria Daily Advertiser (Virginia), 29
Ambrose, Peter, 37; suit for freedom, 39
Annual Report of the Missionary to the Negroes, 24
antislavery movement, 6, 127, 129
apprenticeships, 69–72, 75–76; carpentry, 72
Arkansas, 13
Army Corps of Engineers, 130
Atwater, H. Cowles, 19, 25

Bacon's Rebellion, 17
Baines, Emily, 136
Bains, Henry, 71, 92
Banks, Thomas, 77
barbers, 76
Bardaglio, Peter, 124
Barker, Martin, 32–33
Baron, Robert, 33–34
Barrow, Bennet: attesting to free status, 34; challenging free status, 33; hunting runaways with Purnell, 117; objecting to free people of color, 25, 120–21; patronizing businesses of free people of color, 85, 91, 120

Bayou Sara Creek, 12, 80
Battiste, Maria. *See* Wicker, Maria
Beauvais, Constance, 30–40, 62
Berlin, Ira, 5, 8, 13
Bethune, Mary McLeod, 143
Bettis, Hannah, 41, 102
black veterans, 26, 132–33
Bouton, Ann Maria, 76
Boyd, Caroline, 36–37
Boyd, Jesse, 36
Bradford, Frank, 108
Brasseaux, Carl A., 9, 124–25
brickmakers, 76, 100, 103
Bridges, Emily, 56–57
Brittain, George, 34, 104
Brown, Sterling A., 143
Buatt, Joseph, 71, 108–9, 111
Butler, Ann, 75
Butler, Margaret, 137
Butler, Pierce, 74–75

Campbell, Ellen, 34
Cane River, 8, 16
carpenters, 76
Cat Island, 60, 100–101
Charleston, South Carolina, 27
Chase, William Henry, 130–31
Chew, Arie Ann, 37, 61–64

193

Chew, George, 37, 61–64, 76, 135, 140
Chew, Harriet, 37, 62–64
Chew, Mariah, 37, 60, 62
Chew, Mary, 37, 62–64
Chew, May Lilly, 37, 62–63
Chew, Susannah, 63
Chew, Sylvia, 63, 135, 137, 140–41
Chew, William, 60–64, 104; as drayman, 77; family, 37, 60–64; freedom for self and family, 36–37, 48; and sales, 67, 128
Chew, Wilson, 37, 61, 63–64, 76
Childress, Catherine, 42, 44
Civil War: black men in office after, 183n81; recovering from, 136–37
Claiborne, William, 20–21
Clark, Emily, 10, 81, 119
Clark, George, 56–57
class conflict, 130
Clay, John, 76
Coleman, Henrietta, 96–97, 135, 139, 142
Collins, Catherine, 104
colonization, 14, 49, 111
Committee of Vigilance (West Feliciana Parish), 24; thanking postmasters, 25
confederate guerillas, 133–34
Cornish, Julia Ann, 30, 32, 50
cotton and sugar cane production, 17
Coulter, James A., 30, 72, 122
Cramer, Clayton, 39
Cuba, 13, 19, 44
Curry, Leonard, 5–6, 127
Curtis, Ann Maria, 40–41, 53, 57, 70, 103

Davis, Abisha, 46
Davis, Cassy Ann, 37, 46
Davis, Daniel, 36
Davis, Norman, 42, 60, 76, 104
Davis, Priscilla, 37, 46
Davis, Rose Ann, 37, 46
de Tocqueville, Alexis, 14, 17
Dickerson, Stanley, 67, 128
Doherty, Mary, 75, 116
domestic slave trade, 44, 61, 76
Dorman, James H., 9
Douse, Amanda, 93
Douse, Daniel, 93
Douse, Elizabeth, 93

Douse, George, 31, 59, 91–94; son, 93, 133
Douse, John, 93, 133
Douse, Richard, 93, 132–33
draymen, 61–64, 77
Dred Scott v. Sandford, 130
Du Bois, W. E. B., 143; "little decencies of daily intercourse," 10
Dunbar-Nelson, Alice, 6–7

East Feliciana Parish, 11, 16
emancipation: in exchange for military service, 7; large scale/mass, 13, 38; laws governing, 43–50; during life of slaveholder, 43–50; as personal act, 13, 39, 47, 57; prohibited, 50; by travel out of state, 45–49; by will, 38–43
enslaved people: limited opportunities to earn money, 35–37, 128; mulattos, 48; prohibited from literacy, 5, 24; and sexual exploitation, 112
Estaville, Lawrence, 134

faithful service, 13, 38, 47–48
fancy girl, 80–81
farmers, 103
fear of insurrection, 17–18, 22, 45
fear that federal government would end slavery, 131
Feliciana Volunteers Fire Department, 91
Florida Militia, 130
Flowers, Sidney, 93
Fontenot, Keith P., 9, 124–25
Franklin, Benjamin, 146
Franklin, John Hope, 4–5, 27
Frazier, Wattine, 15
free people of color: born free, 50; employers of white men, 87, 99; entry into Louisiana prohibited, 19, 22, 32, 150n47; free status challenged, 32–33; free status in other litigation, 56, 102; identification in notarial acts, 21, 137; kidnapped, 23, 129; leaving the parish, 128; living throughout the United States, 12–13, 16; population in Louisiana and West Feliciana Parish, 15–16, 29; status registration requirement, 22, 69
free people of color owning enslaved people, 5, 9, 52–53, 55, 73, 101, 103–4. *See also* Gray,

Ann Maria; Gray, Josephine; Perry, Caroline; Whitaker, Hampton; Wooten, Nelly
freedom. *See* emancipation
French influence, 3–4, 7–13
French-speaking refugees, 19–21

Gambo, Jean, 87
Gardner, Julia, 34, 109–10
Givens, Betsey, 60, 110
Glass, William, 88
Gorham, Eliza, 45
Grace Episcopal Church: funerals for free people of color, 62, 93, 135, 139; land purchases from Chew family, 64, 66–67, 140; marriages of free people of color, 66–67, 139; sexton, 62, 64, 67, 77, 140
gradual emancipation statutes, 13–14
Gray, Ann Maria: land sales, 64, 67, 74, 115, 141; living with Josias Gray, 25, 44, 50, 114–16, 119; owning enslaved people, 103–4, 132
Gray, Josephine, 44, 60, 64, 114–15, 132, 141; owning enslaved people, 103–4
Gray, Josias, 25, 44, 114–16, 119, 123
Gray, Thomas Hardy, 44, 114–15
Gray, Virginia, 50, 114–15
Gray, William Hargis, 50, 77–78, 114–15, 118, 120–21, 141
Green, Sylvia. *See* Chew, Sylvia
Greene, George, 95–96
Greene, William, 95–96
growing class conflict, 130
Griggs, Aaron, 77
Griggs, Ann, 66, 139. *See also* Oconnor, Henry
Guibert, Celia, 37
Guibert, Louise, 37

Haiti. *See* Saint-Domingue
Haitian Revolution, 13, 19
Hatfield, Charles, 117
Hendrick, Cintheana, 45, 123
Hendrick, Fanny, 122–23, 135, 141
Hendrick, John, 135
Hendrick, William, 135–36
Higdon, Ann, 41
Hill, Leslie Pinckney, 143

Hoe, Amos, 36, 53–55, 57, 65, 107
Horn, Moses, 41, 73
horse stables, 86, 88
Houma, 11
housekeepers, 78
Hughes, Langston, 143
Hutchinson, Leucy, 73–74
Hutchinson, Lewis, 73–74; son, 73–74

indentured servants, 3, 6, 17, 34
Irvin, Frank, 46–47

Jackson, Sarah, 63
Jefferson, Thomas, 20
Johnson, Isaac, 42
Johnson, Joseph, 42
Johnson, Michael, 27
Jones, Samuel, 31, 101–2
Jones, William, 31, 110, 139
Jordyn, Winthrop, 124
Journal of Negro History, 6

Kemper, Betsey, 41, 52, 76–77
kidnappings, 23, 46, 129
Kirby, Jacob, 32
Kirkland, Moses, 39

Lacour, Judique, 52, 57, 76–77, 107
land sales, 51–68
large-scale emancipation, 13
legal system in Louisiana: courts offer equal treatment, 32, 55–57, 74, 99–100; laws impacting free people of color, 18–19, 144–45
LeJeune, Celia, 39–40
LeJeune, Joseph, 39–40
limited occupational expectations, 69
Lobdell, Ann, 92, 136
Lobdell, John, 92
Logan, Rayford W., 143
Louisiana Native Guards, 133

Malone, Lee, 12
maps, 58, 59, 61, 65, 79
Marbury, Willliam, 37, 57, 62
Marshall, Brisbane, 93
Martin, Mary. *See* Purnell, Mary

Mather, James, 20–21
McGee, Scott, 136
McMicken, Charles, 56, 82, 91–92, 110
Metoyer family, 8–9, 16
Middleton, Kesiah, 60, 98–103
midwives, 63, 74
Mills, Gary, 8–9
Mills, John, 12; son, 61–62
Milteer, Warren E., Jr., 6, 26, 104, 124
Mitchell, Drury, 72–75, 135; land sales, 51, 59–60, 64, 72, 141; litigant, 72–73; master of apprentices, 41, 48, 66, 72–73, 76; registration, 30; tutor, 74
Morgan, Edmund, 17
Morgan, Thomas Gibbs, 32, 47
Morris, John C., 54, 71, 83–90, 91
mosquito bars, 85
"mulatto" classification, 4, 78, 113
Murry, George, 76

Natchitoches Parish, 7–9, 16
Nelson, Camille, 113, 119
New Orleans: mayor reports on Cuban refugees, 20–21; miscegenation in early, 7; popular stories, 6; refuge for Cuban refugees, 19–21
Nolasco, Antonio, 80–82, 89; son, 82–83, 90, 139
Nolasco, Gertrude, 82–83, 89, 132, 139–41
Nolasco, James, 80–83
Nolasco, William, 82–83
Norrell, Milly, 71, 75
Norrell, William, 71
North Carolina, 4–5, 13, 21, 27, 124; shoulder patch, 22
notarial acts, 21, 137

occupations of free people of color, 69–105; chart, 78
Oconnor, Henry, 38, 65–67, 73, 77, 128, 139
O'Connor, Sally, 52
Ohio General Assembly, 14
opposition to slavery, 14
Orange Hill. *See* Douse, George
Orleans Parish, 7–9, 15–16
Oubre, Claude F., 9, 124–25
Our Lady of Mount Carmel Catholic Church, 63

People's and White Man's Reform Party, 137–38
Perry, Caroline, 46–47, 121–23, 104
Perry, Hardy, 35, 41, 46–47, 76, 104, 121–23
Phelps, Thomas, 34, 76
Phillips, Ulrich B., 19
Phoenix Ledger, 97
Piccaluga, Antonio, 98–100
Pointe Coupee Democrat, 97
Poydras, Julian, 20
promissory notes, 54, 64, 66, 87
Purnell, Alexander, 117–18, 133
Purnell, Ann Maria, 117–18
Purnell, Edward, 95, 117–18, 133
Purnell, Eugene, 117
Purnell, John, 76, 116–18, 133
Purnell, Mariah, 116–17
Purnell, Mary, 116–19
Purnell, Matilda, 116–18, 121, 141
Purnell, Sarah, 117–18
Purnell, Thomas, 46, 75, 116–19, 123
Purnell, William, 117–18

quasi-citizenship, 8

Randolph, A. Philip, 143, 145
Rankin, David C., 27
rape, 112–13
Rapides Parish, 15
Ratliff, Cyrus, 63, 101–2, 111–12, 134
records, government and public, 4
registration requirements (freedom status), 22, 69
Republic of West Florida, 12
restauranteurs, 80–98
Revolutionary War, 11
Rous, John, 80–81
Rous, John, Jr., 81–83
Rowland, Dunbar, 20
Royall, Anne, 85, 89
Russell, Peggy, 108–9, 111

saddlers, 71, 108
Saint-Domingue: refugees, 13, 19–21; revolution, 19
Savage, Ann, 66, 95, 128
Savage, Leah, 44, 50, 53, 63
Schuyler, George S., 145

Index

Schweninger, Loren, 5
Scott, Elsey, 31, 59–60, 64, 104, 110
Scott, Rebecca, 20
seamstresses, 76
segregation, 6, 10, 27, 51
self-enslavement, 50
sextons, 62, 64, 67, 76, 140
sexual exploitation of enslaved women, 112
Shelton, Jeremiah, 55–56
shoemaker, 34, 76
Shrim, John George, 42
Simms, Clara, 63, 74
Smith, Margarite, 82–83, 90
Spanish Capuchin monks, 11
Spanish influence, 3–4, 7–13, 35
St. Landry Parish, 7–9, 15–16
Sterkx, H. E., 8
Stevenson, Brenda, 112, 120
Stirling, Henry, 80–81, 85, 90
Stirling, John, 81
Stirling, Lewis, 91, 94
Stirling, Mary, 37, 86
Stirling, Sarah Turnbull, 92
Stowe, Harriet Beecher, 129

Tannenbaum, Frank, 7–8
taxes, land lost for unpaid, 141
Thompson, Elaine, 14
three-caste system (West Indies), 5, 9
Tillotson, James, 122–23, 135
Tillotson, John, 78, 122–23
Tocqueville, Alexis de. *See* de Tocqueville, Alexis
Treaty of Fontainebleau, 11
Treaty of Paris, 11
Turnbull, Martha, 137
Turner, Dempsey, 76, 137, 140
Turner, James, 82–85

Union Navy, 133–34

Vessin, Valcourt, 70

Walker, David, 22
Walker's Appeal, 22–24
Walsh, A. P., 34, 77, 107
washerwomen, 69, 76–77, 105
Welch, Kimberly, 107

Wesley, Charles H., 143, 146
West Baton Rouge Parish, 37, 63
West Feliciana Parish: Committee of Vigilance, 24; description, 11–12; history, 11–12; number of free people of color, 7; population loss 1850–1860, 128–29; slavery in, 14–15
West Feliciana Rail Road Banking Company, 51, 60, 64, 66, 72, 104, 133–34
West Feliciana railroad, 60
Whitaker, Hampton, 74, 97, 134
white friends, 144
white racial unity, 17–19, 137–38
white slaveholders freeing children, 113–23
white supremacy, 6, 17, 19, 29, 124, 130, 173n22
white veterans, 26
Wicker, Albert, 94–96
Wicker, Andrew, 95–96, 139
Wicker, Benjamin, 94–96, 139
Wicker, Bettis, 94–96
Wicker, Daniel, 38, 87, 94–96, 123
Wicker, Edward, 94–96
Wicker, John, 95–96, 139
Wicker, Maria, 38, 49, 66, 94–97, 139–40, 142
Wicker, Rachel Martha, 94–96
Wicker, William, 94–96
Wickliffe, Robert, 131–32, 134–35
Wilkins, Eliza, 37, 76
Wilkins, Lucinda, 34
Wilkins, Roy, 143
Williams, Grandison, 31–32
Wilson, Jesse, 30, 57, 103
Woodville Road, 58, 91
Wooten, Caroline, 80, 86
Wooten, Nelly, 80–91, 94; holding people enslaved, 84–86; land sales, 64, 67, 80, 85–88; litigation, 83, 87, 88–89; lived in Bayou Sara, 53, 57, 60; purchased granddaughter, 37, 86; sold hotel, 88; value of estate, 90

ABOUT THE AUTHOR

Evelyn L. Wilson has been fascinated with the history and culture of Louisiana since she moved there more than forty years ago. The state is known for its unique Spanish and French heritage and has provided a setting for romances, mysteries, and horror stories. After attending high school in New York and college in Ohio, Wilson felt she had stepped back in time when she moved to Louisiana. Intrigued by the *laissez les bons temps rouler* attitude of almost everyone, Wilson sought to understand the state and its population. This is Wilson's third book about Louisiana.

Wilson wrote *Laws, Customs and Rights: Charles Hatfield and His Family; A Louisiana History*, which describes the genesis of the state's second public law school organized to serve its black residents so that its older law school could remain segregated for white students only. Wilson's second book, *The Justices of the Supreme Court of Louisiana: 1865–1880*, provides biographical information about the eighteen men who served in that position during Reconstruction and includes contemporary events that explain the justices' high rate of turnover. Wilson also coauthored a legal textbook on Louisiana property law.

Wilson has her JD and PhD from Louisiana State University. Her undergraduate degree is from Oberlin College. She now lives in South Carolina and loves to travel. She has visited all fifty states and nearly fifty different countries. She believes the world is filled with interesting people and interesting things to learn.

Printed in the United States
by Baker & Taylor Publisher Services